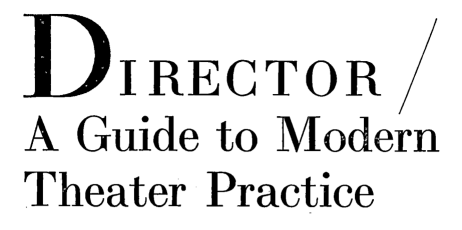

DIRECTOR
A Guide to Modern Theater Practice

W. A. GREGORY

FUNK & WAGNALLS   New York

Copyright © 1968 by W. A. Gregory
ALL RIGHTS RESERVED
Library of Congress Catalog Card Number: 68-15005
Published by Funk & Wagnalls, *A Division of* Reader's Digest Books, Inc.
Printed in the United States of America
by American Book–Stratford Press

The author is grateful to the following for permission to reprint brief passages in this volume:

CAMBRIDGE UNIVERSITY PRESS, for Brian W. Downs, *A Study of Six Plays by Ibsen,* Copyright 1948 by The Cambridge University Press.

THE CLARENDON PRESS, Oxford, for The Oxford translation of the *Works of Aristotle,* W. D. Ross, Ed.; E. K. Chambers, *The Medieval Stage;* and Arthur B. Keith, *The Sanskrit Drama.*

TOBY COLE, for Toby Cole and Helen K. Chinoy, Eds., *Directors on Directing,* Copyright © 1953, 1963 Toby Cole and Helen K. Chinoy.

COLLINS PUBLISHERS and STORM JAMESON, for Storm Jameson, *Modern Drama in Europe.*

COLLINS-KNOWLTON-WING, INC., for Elizabeth Sprigge, Trans., *Six Plays of Strindberg,* Copyright © 1955 by Elizabeth Sprigge.

THOMAS Y. CROWELL COMPANY and GEORGE G. HARRAP & COMPANY LTD., for Allardyce Nicoll, *The Theory of Drama.*

CROWN PUBLISHERS, INC., for Barrett H. Clark, *European Theories of Drama,* Copyright © 1965 by Crown Publishers, Inc.

J. M. DENT & SONS LTD. and THE TRUSTEES OF THE JOSEPH CONRAD ESTATE, for Joseph Conrad, *Lord Jim.*

HARCOURT, BRACE & WORLD, for T. S. Eliot, "Rhetoric," from T. S. Eliot, *Selected Essays,* Copyright 1932, 1936, 1950 by Harcourt, Brace & World, Inc., Copyright © 1960, 1964 by T. S. Eliot.

HILL & WANG, INC., for Stark Young, *The Theatre,* Copyright 1927, 1954 by Stark Young.

Contents

Part I
THE DIRECTOR

Introduction	3
His Evolution	7
His Responsibility	18
The Practical and Logical Artist	21
Interpretive or Creative?	25
The Artist	30

Part I I
THE DIRECTOR AND THE PLAY

Selection	37
Aristotle	40
Types of Plays	49
Rite-Role Analysis	54
Theater as Convention	57
Rites	60
Dramatic Actions	61
Roles	63
Types of Roles	64
Role-Rite Applied	72

The *Wild Duck* 76
    Synopsis 77
    The Wild Duck and Aristotle's *Theory of Criticism* 80
    Duck Classified 84
    Roles and Rites in *Duck* 86
    Rites and Dramatic Actions in *Duck* 89
    Roles in *Duck* 97
        RELLING 97
        OLD EKDAL 101
        HIALMAR 104
        GREGERS 111
        GINA 113
        HEDVIG 115
        WERLE 117
        MRS. SORBY 119
    Summary 119

Part I I I
THE DIRECTOR AND THE STAGE

Introduction 123
Blocking 127
Emphasis 130
    Methods of Achieving Emphasis (Pointing) 132
    Focus: Visual Line 133
    Focus: Actual Line 135
    Lines and Shapes 136
    Body Position 137
    Stage Area 138
Balance 145
Stability and Sequence 148
Stage Picturization 150
Movement 157
    General Rules for Movement 166
Blocking the Play 177

Part I V
THE DIRECTOR AND THE ACTOR

The Actor   185
   First Meeting   185
   The Actor—The Agent   187
   The Actor's Evolution   190
   Two Theories   198
   The Technical Actor   203
   The Method Actor   207
   Professionals and Amateurs   215
   Handling the Professional and the Amateur   220
   The Community Theater   225
Interpretation   229
   Psychic Communication   229
   Vocal Interpretation   231
   Actors and Interpretative Reading   234
The Working Rehearsal   253

Part V
THE DIRECTOR IN PRODUCTION

Casting   275
   Types of Auditions   286
   Casting in the Civic Theater   290
Rehearsals   292
   Prerehearsal Planning   292
   Experiment and Exploration   294
   Sample Rehearsal Schedule   298
   The Prompter   309
   The Curtain Call   309

The Musical 312
The Review 315
The Stage Manager 315
Performance 317
References 321
Appendix: Rite-Role Analysis of *The Wild Duck* 327
Rites 329
Roles 349
Bibliography 357
Index 361

Part I
THE DIRECTOR

Introduction

Whenever an actor, a stage manager, a light man meets a fellow theater worker, invariably the greeting will contain the all-important question, "Are you working?" If, as is too seldom the case, the answer is a smiling, "Yes, I'm doing blank down at blank," the second question, almost as important as the first, will be, "Who is the director?" Who is, or rather more to the point, *what* is the director in the theater of today? That is the question this book will attempt to answer.

Who is the director and what is his function? Obviously, some will say, a director is one who directs. Yes, but so is a traffic cop, and far too many directors in both the professional and the amateur theater see their function primarily as that of a traffic manager. Strangely enough, often those who see the director's role as that of a traffic expert understand neither the mechanics nor the theory behind this basic of play direction. Certainly the director must be equipped to handle stage traffic, must be able to keep his actors in view and prevent them from colliding center stage, but blocking involves much more than keeping an entrance clear or pointing an exit. Though this too, as any star will remind the director who momentarily has something else on his mind, is highly important.

Who and what is the director? He is the playwright's interpreter. He is the actor's friend, adviser, teacher, leader, and oftentimes, father; but always, and above all else, the director is the actor's inspiration. He is the final authority on all questions of staging, design, lighting, interpretation, etc. He is, in short, the final authority on all aspects of the theater other than the business end. And though he need not have anything to do with the box office, still he had better understand it, if, indeed, anyone can understand the fickle and unpredictable public.

In the professional theater the director is hired by and is directly responsible to the producer. On questions of staging the director is the recognized authority, but if his views should differ violently with those of the producer, he will be replaced by a director who is in closer agreement with that controller of the purse strings.

In the civic theater, the director is generally responsible to a board of directors, and in the college and university setup to the department head or at least to the administration of his division.

Even when the director is the owner of his theater he is, to a great degree, responsible to the public he seeks to move. Finally, he is responsible to his own standards, and he bears the responsibility of keeping those standards high.

There are those who will tell you that the director is God (provided, of course, he doesn't step on the toes of the Equity deputy), and some directors do often appear to confuse their powers with those of the Almighty. This is the kind of director who will brook no disagreement, will listen to no ideas, and will move not one iota from his view of the play and each character therein. Failure to test one's ideas against other ideas, and failure to attempt new and different ways of doing a particular thing is often the result of in-security within the director himself. The director who insists upon dictatorial authority often does not dare to have his ideas tested. Such a director is usually so insecure in his art and so fearful of losing his authority that he will permit no discussion. This kind of director seems to live in a deadly fear that some actor might take the play away from him. The attempt to place a personal stamp upon the drama often stamps the poet's concept out of the play.

While few will deny the director his right to all final authority, he is not omniscient, rather he is all too fallible. He can and often does become so involved in the play that he loses all perspective, and *any* outsider can be helpful by simply telling the director what he sees take place on the stage. The fact that the director is the final authority is not license to misuse that authority. The director must consider all suggestions, he must keep his mind open to change, for his is an awesome responsibility.

Who and what is the director? He is first and last an artist. His task is that of any artist: the creation of the beautiful. The director is an artist who borrows from the genius of Michelangelo, Van Gogh, Picasso, and Klee in order to give the poet's images dramatic, exciting line and color. He is the artist who borrows the movements of Noverre, Massine, Fokine and Martha Graham to bring the poet's suggested action to vivid dramatic life. The director is the artist who borrows from Beethoven, Mozart, Wagner, and Bartók to bring the playwright's emotions to life in vibrant dramatic sound. Finally, the director is that artist who borrows from the philosophies of Socrates, Christ, Nietzsche, Hegel, and Russell to give the poet's ideas an inspiring, hard-hitting dramatic meaning. The director is then that artist who uses the principles of all the arts as tools to help him bring the beauty, the meaning, the joy, and the despair of life to exciting dramatic life on the stage. "Why?" one might ask. In order that we as the audience might share the poet's insight into life and hence might live our own lives more fully, more deeply, and more dramatically.

To speak of living dramatically in a world pinned down by the threat of the superbomb may to some seem thoughtless and perhaps profane. But the fact that mankind may have found the "final solution" for mankind, and that we do live under the shadow of the bomb and total destruction, may well have taken the dramatic out of our lives. Perhaps the imagined glare of the bomb burst has turned this beautiful, exciting, and dramatic world into a mundane, gray, undramatic one. If the theater of today is holding the mirror up to nature, the lack of the dramatic and the exciting that is being reflected may be simply that a reflection cannot equal the horror of the original. Today's world of grays, where often the dramatic and the exciting seem more than a little fearful, where bored sophistication replaces a true response to life's drama, where anything that is different or stands out in any way is suspect, where we are afraid, deathly afraid, to go out on a limb or to take any sort of a position, is a difficult world for the theater. The artist, today as always, must dare. The director, as well as the playwright and the actor, must have the guts to be wrong. To fail gloriously. The director must learn to enjoy leaping to the end of the limb. He will be in for many painful falls, but he will also be in a position to climb out in the open where he can see the view. The director, or any artist, cannot "play it safe." If he is to be a truly creative artist, he must dare.

The director's job and the theater's task is to stir people

to life, through the presentation of various aspects of life. I am not arguing for a social theater. I am simply saying that men of the theater must be involved in life up to the hilt if the theater is to remain a bright spot in this "glareful" world. By dramatically exciting presentations the audience can become aware of the nobility and the beauty of life, and this is, as it has always been, the artist's responsibility.

Who and what is the director? He is that artist who believes that what the play is saying is worth saying, not necessarily from a philosophical viewpoint, but from a dramatic point of view. Whether or not the poet's views are founded in fact is immaterial to the director, provided that he believes them to be dramatically exciting, and artistically truthful. If the director is an artist who knows his craft, and if he is fortunate enough to have a cast of hard-working, talented actors, then he stands an excellent chance of making that play come to life on the stage and stirring the spark of life in his audience. He stands an excellent chance, under such circumstances, of moving people intellectually and emotionally, and when he can accomplish that he will have fulfilled the *raison d'être* of the theater and his role in it as a director. For the director's greatest responsibility is not to the actor, but to the audience, to move that audience by his staging of the poet's play.

His Evolution

The history of the director as we know him today is not a long one. As the final authority he is comparatively new on the theater scene and is still finding his way. As a director (in England, a producer) *per se*, it is only since the early

1900's that he has had a voice in the world of theater. Yet anyone who has had the experience of a rehearsal will agree that from the beginnings of play-acting to the present, someone must have been in charge. And in the beginning, that person was, in all probability, the author. The idea of acting out his words would have been his, and to him would have fallen the responsibility of taking charge of the proceedings.

In the Greek theater, the poets trained their own choruses and thus may be considered the first directors. During the Middle Ages, when the only theater outside the church was strictly an actors' theater of *jongleurs,* singer-reciters, and the strolling mimes, the forerunner of the actor-manager was probably born. In liturgical dramas the priests certainly handled the little staging required by such presentations as the *Quem quaeritis* and it is safe to assume they remained in control as long as the drama was played in the church. Even before the mystery cycle plays the author of the twelfth-century Anglo-Norman *Adam,* knew what he wanted from his actors and wrote his directions out in considerable detail:

Adam must be well trained when to reply and to be neither too quick nor too slow in his replies. And not only he, but all the personages, must be trained to speak composedly, and to fit convenient gesture to the matter of their speech. Nor must they foist in a syllable or clip one of the verses, but must enounce firmly and repeat what is set down for them in due order. Whoever names Paradise is to look and point towards it.[1]*

The playwrights, it would seem, were in charge.

In the seventeenth century, playwrights such as Molière were staging, acting, writing, and even booking the companies. The eighteenth century saw the development of the

* Numbered notes appear in References (pp. 351–359).

star, who became, in due time, the actor-manager of the following century. The actor-manager-director was responsible for the rehearsals, but for the most part he was concerned only with entrances and exits and how certain pet pieces of business were managed. Under such conditions as the eighteenth and nineteenth centuries afforded, the play was often sacrificed to the special talents of the crowd-drawing name. The dangers inherent in such a system are still to be viewed each season along the "Great White Way."

Though there is evidence that they were far from the first, still George, Duke of Saxe-Meiningen and his stage manager Ludvig Kronek in the 1880's were the principal influence in the development of the modern stage director. The influence of the Meiningen company on Europe and especially upon such giants as Constantin Stanislavski, André Antoine, and, through Otto Brahm, Max Reinhardt, was tremendous. The manipulation of crowds, so startling to the critics of that day, has become almost commonplace in the epic movies, yet the epics must acknowledge their debt to scenes such as this one described by Lee Simonson in *The Stage Is Set*:

Perhaps the most celebrated of the Meiningen mob scenes was the coronation procession of the dauphin in Schiller's *Maid of Orleans*. The crowd packed a shallow square under the portals of Rheims Cathedral. The stage was too small to hold them as they waited for the first sight of the cortége; they disappeared off stage, strained against soldiers trying to keep a lane free, climbed on each other's backs, stood on tiptoe, hopped up and down, packed every spare ledge on a fountain, jammed the stairways of near-by houses, leaned over window-sills on each other's shoulders. The mounting excitement was carefully timed as the royal procession crossed the stage into the cathedral and increasing bursts of cheers greeted each notable, such as

Dunois, when he was recognized. The crescendo of jubilation swelled at the sight of the dauphin under his canope. All the while trumpets repeated a single theme adopted from one of Brahms's chorals, with clarion insistence that mounted higher and higher until at the appearance of Joan it reached a climax of frenzy that usually incited an echoing ovation from the audience.[2]

As a young actor-manager, Stanislavski was tremendously impressed with the company and with the personality and work methods of Kronek:

Outside the theatre Kronek's relations even with the third-rate actors of his company were simple and friendly. He even seemed to flaunt this simplicity of conduct. But as soon as a rehearsal began and Kronek mounted his usual place, he would be reborn. He sat in complete silence and waited for the hands of the clock to reach the time allotted for the beginning of rehearsal. Then he would ring a large bell and declare in a quiet voice, "Anfangen." ["Let's begin."] Everything quieted down. The rehearsal would begin at once and continue until he rang the bell again. Then he would make his remarks in a dispassionate voice, ring the bell again, repeat the fatal "Anfangen" and the rehearsal would continue.

And now there was an unexpected stop and confusion on the stage. The actors whispered, the stage managers ran about. Something seemed to have happened. One of the leading actors was late, and it was necessary to leave his scene out. One of the stage managers tells this to Kronek and waits for his orders near the prompter's box. Everybody is quiet. Kronek tires them out with a long pause. This pause seems to be endless, threatening. Kronek pauses, decides, while everybody stands as if waiting sentence. At last he pronounces: "While we are in Moscow, the roles of the actor who is late will be played by actor Y, and as far as X is concerned, I will let him lead the mob actors in the rear. Anfangen!"[3]

The dangers of the dictatorial approach became apparent to the founder of the Moscow Art Theater only after he had been successful in imitating Kronek:

> The restraint and the cold-bloodedness of Kronek were to my taste and I wanted to imitate him. With time I also became a despotic stage director. Very soon the majority of Russian stage directors began to imitate me in my despotism as I imitated Kronek. There was a whole generation of despotic stage directors, who, alas, did not have the talents of Kronek or of the Duke of Meiningen. These directors of the new type became mere producers who made of the actor a stage property on the same level with stage furniture, a pawn that was moved about in their *mise-en-scènes*.[4]

Only later, after much more experience with his own company of actors, did Stanislavski come to respect the actor as a creative artist. Eventually, however, Stanislavski discovered that though the director could and must do a great deal, "He cannot do everything. The most important thing is in the hands of the actor, whom one must help, who must be guided in the proper direction."[5]

If the despotic director cannot claim Stanislavski as his spiritual father, he can make a much more convincing case for Gordon Craig. Certainly that *enfant terrible* of the first quarter of the twentieth century comes closer to demanding a dictator in the theater than most other theater theorists. Edward Gordon Craig, son of Ellen Terry, one of England's most famous actresses, has had a profound influence on the theater; yet his influence has been felt through his *avant-garde* theory rather than through his practical work. His many books and articles carry a solid impact and can still be read with profit. Craig, often damned for his Über-Marionette Theory, was one of the first to call for a single impression, a single interpretation to dominate a production. If, Craig argued, one central idea could so impregnate a production that the audience would be moved by a single unifying effect, then the theater would be able to take its place with the other arts.

Now, then, it is impossible for a work of art ever to be produced where more than one brain is permitted to direct; and if works of art are not seen in the Theatre this one reason is a sufficient one, though there are plenty more.

Do you wish to know why there are seven masters instead of one? It is because there is no one man in the theatre who is a master in himself, that is to say, there is no one man capable of inventing and rehearsing a play: capable of designing and superintending the construction of both scenery and costume: of writing any necessary music: of inventing such machinery as is needed and the lighting that is to be used.[6]

Or again:

The *régisseur*, or stage manager, is under the delusion that in truth he is the one who is the artist, the inventor, the master, but, poor fellow, he is nothing of the kind, for no one is the master: each throwing into the broth whatever ingredient he will. All are petty masters, each hindering the other.[7]

Craig was concerned, and rightly so, with the possibilities of more than one interpretation for the play. Indeed, this is one of the great problems in today's theater; either the director does not have the skill to convince the actor of the "rightness" of his view, or the actor (and, it must be admitted, often the director) is more concerned with his "creativity" than he is with the play itself. Craig, at that time a prophet crying in the wilderness, likened the theater to a ship without either a captain, or the means of finding one.

The theatre, unlike the ship, is not made for purposes of war, and so for some unaccountable reason discipline is not held to be of such vital importance, whereas it is of as much importance as in any branch of service. But what I wish to show you is that until discipline is understood in a theatre to be willing and reliant obedience to the manager or captain, no supreme achievement can be accomplished.[8]*

In today's theater, Craig's dreams of the director who could, and would, do and be all are clearly impossible. Time alone would prevent it, but above and beyond the time factor, in a one-man production the contributions of the actor, the scenic designer, the costumer, and the light-man would be missing. The result would, I believe, lack the interest and excitement possible when several creative artists pool their individual talents. I have too often seen a good actor take an idea of mine, add to it, change it, and reshape it until by reworking, the idea becomes far better than what was originally given to him.

Craig, it should be noticed, was well aware of the limiting time factor. And while Craig was speaking of the professional theater, the time factor in any theater situation—professional, civic, or collegiate—is such that unless the director is given every possible aid he will not have sufficient time for the job of staging the play, let alone designing, lighting, costuming, and composing music for it. Both in Craig's day and in this, much of the inartistic and the

* I was fascinated, when copying down the above quote from Mr. Craig, to read in the margin a note, obviously placed there by some young college student. (I had borrowed the book from the library of one of the better-known drama schools of the West Coast.) Beside Craig's comment on obedience in the theater, the student had written a large "FAH" and later on in the same section, in the same hand, appeared the learned comment, "Compare overdirection and commedia dell'arte!" I was especially taken with the exclamation point.

mediocre can be traced to the mad rush of production schedules.

Yet this hurrying and blundering is not so strange, after all, and anyone who has lived a year in a theatre can understand it. Day—afternoon—evening—night: these gentlemen of the theatre are continually on the rush. (I am speaking of the *modern* theatres; which are supposed to be in the advance.) Rehearsing in the morning, seeing people in the midday, studying parts, looking at scenery, play reading, attending receptions, an author to see, a critic to entertain, an artist to catch, incessant quarrels to smooth over, at least one new play to be brought out each month, capital to find, building to superintend, always one incessant hustle.

Where, then, is the time to stop and consider about the *art* of the thing? This may do very well for an oil business or a large grocery; these things *thrive* by hustling: not so an art. In this haste all thought of the principles or the beauty of the art is lost sight of and all desire to produce beauty departs.[9]

In the final analysis however, Stanislavski and Craig are not as far apart as some authorities have led us to believe. Books that have appeared since the publication of *An Actor Prepares* (1936) show that Stanislavski was often most explicit in what he demanded from an actor,[10] while Craig, in a preface to a later edition of *On the Art of the Theatre*, states unequivocally that his proposed Über-Marionette was a dream only: "I no more want to see the living actors replaced by things of wood than the great Italian actress* of our day wants all the actors to die."[11]

The end that both men sought was a unified production. The means were slightly different, but both recognized the director as the final authority and both strove to realize the poet's intent.

The director, as he has evolved in today's theater, is a

* Eleanora Duse.

known, off-Broadway producer who was attempting to learn the art of direction at the expense of a friend's summer stock audience. "He let me do anything I wanted, and he liked everything I did." Having worked with the actor for a few weeks, I was acquainted with the kind of thing he liked to do. He was a big man, and he moved very gracefully. Now here was an attribute that could be used, yet the actor was generally more interested in demonstrating his balletic prowess than in getting to the heart of the play. Shortly after that conversation, I had the opportunity of talking with the stage manager and several actors who had been involved in the aforementioned summer production. To a man they backed up the assertion that my actor had been allowed to do anything and had indeed been praised for anything he did. The "give 'em confidence" treatment had not only helped to instill bad habits in the actor, it had created chaos on stage and almost closed the theater.

On the other hand, during the same season I had an opportunity to observe a young director who had for several years been the "bright young man" of the Broadway theater. As the producer, and not knowing firsthand the work of this young director, I was rather startled to hear him tell the cast at the first reading that he was not going to block the play, that he did not know what it meant to block a play, and, in any case, it was impossible to block a play. The actors, it seemed, had to find out what would and what would not work for them. They were to move around until they found, apparently by accident, "the way." Part of my feeling of uneasiness left me when, after a few days of rehearsal, and after the director had begun to see what his cast could do, he began to suggest a few definite moves. My original uneasiness changed to wonderment when, after the "just wander around" beginning, I observed in the final few days of rehearsal that the director who did not believe in blocking a play was insisting upon exact conformity for each small gesture. The director, by his insistence on first letting the cast find their way, then increasing his own authority, and finally becoming completely dictatorial, did not stamp out the spontaneity; rather, the final result was a spirited opening that fooled half the critics and most of the audience. By taking so much time in the early stages of rehearsal to let the actors experiment with movement, the director had lost his opportunity to explore the author's intent with his actors. I came to the conclusion that too much time had been spent "finding the way" and not nearly enough finding the play. The business was clever, the production slick from every aspect, but the heart of the play, the all-important poet's intent, was not evident.

The point in the two incidents chronicled above is that in neither case did the director actually know his business. The bright young Broadway director arrived at an acceptable external product because he had excellent, if slightly self-conscious, taste. He knew the principles of direction, though he could not have spelled them out. He could select in accordance with the theory of stage movement, and he could build upon what he saw the actors invent.

The producer attempting to direct had no feeling for the "right" move, no understanding of the theory of direction. His taste as a producer is unexcelled on the off-Broadway scene, but he lacked the ability to select the wheat from the chaff in the variety of movement offered by his actors.

His Responsibility

Who is the director? The director is the final authority and must take full responsibility for any deficiencies in the finished product. He is the person responsible for what the audience sees, hears, and feels. He cannot excuse himself, as we are all wont to do, by sobbing that his actors were not capable, though this may well have been the case. His task, his commission, is to make them capable or to replace them. This, I would maintain, is just as true in a high school production as it is in the professional theater for, though most educators would not agree, where a public performance is given, the actor is expendable. He must be if the theater is not to become a psychodrama ward. The director's responsibility is not, in any case, to the actor, rather it is to the audience via the playwright's intent. The director must do all within his power to present to every audience a finished product that is beautiful, meaningful, artistically truthful and dramatically exciting. To achieve this end, he must use the best actors available to him, and wring from them the best performance of which they are capable.

This heavy responsibility does not lessen with the price of the ticket; the director must bear it even if the audience is paying only with their time. In order to fulfill his responsibility, the director must be willing to use every method, every technique that will help to achieve an artistically truthful and dramatically exciting performance from his actors. He must not be satisfied until he achieves a performance that goes directly and easily to the heart of the poet's intent. The lack of time (and what director does not cry in vain for that extra week), the ambiguities and faults of the script, the stubbornness of the producer, the lack of imagination displayed by his scene designer, the ineptitude of his casts, or the naggings of his wife will not excuse him from, or even lessen, his load. In spite of all, the director remains the same person, the final authority, the final arbiter of taste and meaning. He either achieves the performance he seeks or he does not; he succeeds or he fails. Even in the verdict of success or failure he alone is the judge, even in this he must be the final assessor.

Obviously I do not mean to imply that each performance is either a complete success or a complete failure, yet in each production the director must answer for himself whether or not he has met and fulfilled his responsibilities. No director can always answer, "Yes, this is the best I could have done with the material I had at hand." No director can be right all the time, nor can he always "make it." The director cannot, nor can any artist, always turn out a masterpiece or even a good piece of work, but he can, as can any artist, know how close he came to his original concept. The morning-after reviews, the number of curtain calls, the ebullient back-stage celebration, and even the lines at the ticket office must not mislead the director in his personal evaluation of his work. Most directors can look back to plays that were artistic failures, shows they could not bring themselves to watch, that were resounding box-office hits. The reverse situation is probably even more in evidence, for all directors have had plays that failed to catch the attention of the public or the mind of the reviewer, but are nonetheless among their most cherished memories.

How, the reader may well be asking, is it possible to

speak of the responsibility to the audience in one breath, and in the next to maintain that box office is not a criterion of success? Such a stand is possible, for the director's responsibility to the audience is not necessarily to please, not simply to amuse, but rather to move that audience emotionally and intellectually within the context of the play. Perhaps one of the greatest temptations the director faces is to forget the play and "play to the house"—certainly this is one of the recurring traps for the actor. The clever, slick director, the young Broadway "bright boy" mentioned earlier, can often fool an audience into thinking they have seen a play, when in reality all they have been watching is a series of brilliant tricks set up and executed by the director at the expense of the play.

Few experienced directors have not succumbed to the temptation at one time or another to use direction savvy to cover what they have interpreted as slow spots in the writing, or as is perhaps more often the case, to cover the defects or failings of an actor. There are even times when the director must resort to such tricks, if the alternative is to lose the audience, but when the director resorts to such a technique in order to demonstrate his own virtuosity, then that director is prostituting his art.[12]

This book takes the view that while the director cannot always be successful and while techniques can be misused, or worse, become an end in themselves, still a knowledge of the principles of stage direction will ease the way toward the accomplishment of the director's task. Contrary to the bright young director mentioned above, there *are* ways to block a play, there are methods of analysis, of working with the actor, and of reaching the heart of the play; and a knowledge of these methods combined with sensitivity, insight, enthusiasm, and a love of the theater will increase the director's chances of delivering an artistically truthful and dramatically exciting production built around the author's intent and thus help him to fulfill his responsibility to his audience.

The Practical and Logical Artist

No doubt there are a few who will maintain that whenever the word "practical" is used to modify the word "artist" the result is a modified artist, but such does not have to be the case. It may well be that if one is "practical" he would have nothing to do with the theater; likewise, if one is completely the artist, he will not concern himself with the practical. But in today's theater, the director, above all others, must keep his feet on the ground. At the same time the director must let his mind and imagination soar with the author's. There exists a popular belief, especially in the world of "practical business," that all artists are impractical dreamers whom one humors when it will not hurt the bank account too much. The fact of the matter is, I believe, that artists are concerned with things other than the financial, and while a life built solely around the creative arts, with no thought of paying the rent or having food on the table, is hardly practical in today's world, the rate of death by heart attacks in the realm of the young executives does not seem to indicate a very "practical" adjustment to the existing world either. It is impossible for man to live a full life without the arts, and

it is likewise impossible for him to live any sort of a full life
without a place to live and food to eat. The theater director
is always concerned with the practical side of the production
for the artistic side cannot exist without it. His scheduling
alone can make or break a play. If, as is so often the case in
the amateur theater, he also controls the purse strings, the
existence of the theater will depend upon his practical sense.
The director in today's theater is, through necessity, a
strange mixture of the creative artist, the practical businessman, the logician, and the scholar. The actor can, and some
will claim he must, work on emotion and leave intellectual
content alone. The director cannot and must not. His is the
conscious application of artistic principles to achieve a
predetermined effect. The playwright may, and often does,
write better than he knows; he may not, and often does not,
know his own creation; but the director, in order to direct,
must *know*. Furthermore, his knowing cannot be a vague
feeling; he must be able to verbalize his feelings.

The playwright deals with ideas. True, he may be dealing
with particular ideas in order to achieve an emotional
response, but it is the idea that will arouse the emotion. One
might generalize to the extent of saying that theater is an
attempt to make the audience think in order that they might
feel, in order that they might think about what they felt.

The poet writing the single poem can say, "the poem does
not mean, it is," and if we do not have to read the poem
aloud to an audience we can accept this meaningless phrase.
But the director cannot say, "the line doesn't mean, it
simply is; just read the line, don't worry about where you
go or what the character means, just read the line." If the
playwright is not using ideas expressed in words to make
the audience feel, then he must be using nonverbal symbols

for that purpose. In any case, the director must be able to explain to the actors what symbols are being used and why they are so used. Always the pattern is there and the director must be enough of a logician to find it, even if the playwright did not consciously think of creating such a pattern. The director must be enough of a logical thinker to follow the playwright's method of arriving at the final curtain. If, taking an example from the theater of the absurd, the poet is attempting to show that there is no rhyme or reason to life, no sense, no logic, the director must be able to see the pattern the playwright chose, or he will not have any audience left when Act Three opens. Always the director must think practically enough to explain to the actor *what to do* in the scene in order to make a particular point.

Though mankind has striven unsuccessfully for centuries to prove to himself that he is a logical animal and that he lives in a logical world, though he may believe that the wellsprings of art are deep in the nonlogical soul, and that the best art is pure emotion without logical meaning, still it is impossible for the director to think of a play without a logical meaning. For even if such a play did, or does, exist, the director would still have to decide logically what conventions he would use to get across to the audience the message of "no meaning." The actor may not, as some famous actors claim, have to know; he may only feel that he is right, but the director who cannot verbalize his feelings about a play will have to be a great pantomime artist or cease to be a director.

Unless one is lost, he cannot start anywhere without knowing either where he is going, or at least the direction in which he is headed. The director must always know where he is going, and how he expects to get there. In other words, if the director is going to direct, then he must have a direction in mind. The audience need not necessarily know where they are going every minute, but they must, like the well-known politician who always rode backward on a train, know where they have been when the journey ends and the curtain falls.

In the excitement of directing, it is all too possible to start without knowing where one is going. Even if this hurdle is avoided, the danger still remains of becoming so involved in what one is doing with, or to, the play that one forgets why he is doing whatever it is that he is involved in trying to do. This is not, I hasten to add, unlikely; rather, it is probable.* The director must fight the tendency to become so involved in the small problems of getting the scene blocked, interpreted, paced, propped, or what have you, that he forgets what he was attempting to do with it in the first place. This sort of problem is always present in any kind of production, but is perhaps more evident in television where the director is so burdened with technical details and difficulties that the actors, as long as they don't forget their lines or blocking, are ignored.

The director who is not practical and logical, no matter how sensitive he may be, will often miss the author's intent. He cannot be all emotion and feeling, and he can never be stupid. A stupid, unintelligent director can only direct stupid, unintelligent performances. To play upon, and often with, the emotions of the audience (and of the actor) takes more than sensitivity of feeling. It takes sensitivity and intellect, for the director must be able to translate both ways. He must be prepared to intellectualize the emotional, and emotionalize the intellectual, since they are of equal importance.

* See preceding sentence.

Very well then, the director must be practical and logical, but why does he have to be an artist? And as far as that goes, just what is an artist?

Interpretive or Creative?

Even before one attempts to discuss the question of the artist, the question of the creative or the interpretive artist is bound to arise. Is the director, whom we have discussed as needing logic and practicality, a creative artist, or is he simply an interpretive artist? The question always seems to delight theater theorists, though it is of small concern to the producing artist. Strangely enough, the theater worker or student who delights in the question seldom challenges the word "artist"—that he is an artist is assumed. The *kind* of artist is the important question.

To the producing artist, the creative-interpretive argument is what one actor I recall refers to disdainfully as "actor talk," and as he points out, actors *do*, they don't just talk. Still, though it may be a hypothetical question, it is one which will affect the would-be director's attitude toward his chosen field. Though I may be accused of avoiding the question, I would maintain that all artists are creative and all are interpretive. Does the actor or the director simply interpret the playwright? Does the painter simply interpret the landscape, the poet, love? Few would disagree that one production of a play is separate and distinct from every other production. This is demonstrated when even a small cast change is necessitated, and every attempt is made to maintain a particular interpretation. Certainly, when one sees the original New York production and then later sees the national company on tour, he will have seen two quite different shows. It is virtually impossible to reproduce a play. Even the same cast will, after a time, change the play. Some will say that only the interpretation has been changed; I would maintain that the *play* differs. The values differ because additions have been made to the author's original intent. For though the goal is to realize on the stage the author's intent, this can only be done if the intent of each of the artists working on the play corresponds to that of the author. This fact is both the principal weakness and the main strength of the producing theater. It is a weakness because far too many directors are neither creative, nor any other kind of artist; they are instead actors who have decided that directing is a step up toward greater security, or, as is often the case in television, they are technicians who have never been concerned with the art of direction. It is a weakness because a creative artist can ruin a great play if he insists upon adding to the author's work. Finally, it is a weakness because too many theater artists are not willing to subordinate themselves to the play. The fact that each artist brings his own intent to the play is the strength of the theater because a fair play can become a very good one when the right director gets hold of it. It is a strength when the artist adds to the author's intent through his own experiences. And finally, it is a strength when the creative artist interprets a great play in the light of his day and age.

A play, much as a musical composition, has more than its original form. Two distinct forms must be considered; that which the playwright saw in his mind's eye and tried to capture on paper, and that which is conjured up in the director's, the actor's, the designer's eye when he reads and discusses the play. Otto Baensch has come up with a definition of form that holds promise for the director. Baensch equates form and rhythm:

If, therefore, we want to define rhythm in general, we have to say: rhythm is the alternation between heavy (stressed) and light (unstressed or less stressed) parts, insofar as it follows certain rules.

But these rules operate by combining heavy and light parts to make rhythmic sensuous unities of lower and higher order in the form of various kinds of alternation of heavy and light stresses. In the construction of such rhythmic sensuous unities, next to each other, in each other, and one above another, the form of the work originates: it is nothing else but its total rhythm. Only inasmuch as a work has form, i.e. rhythm, is it a work of art.

In relation to the total content of a work of art, the form is something abstract, schematic. All its particulars take part in it only because, as heavier or lighter members and groups, they have their meaning in it . . . The pure tonal qualities of sounds and harmonies are material; the pure tonal qualities of syllables and words are material; the objective meanings of words and sentences are material. So are the expression-values of colors and forms *per se,* the character of the substances used, the objects reproduced, etc. All of this has its effect and lives in the work of art only insofar as it is carried by its rhythmic groundswell, incorporated in the proportional relation of its rhythmic structure. So the relation of the rhythm of a work of art to the material through which it appears is like that of a category of perception to the sensuous contents it governs, that of the logical form of a treatise to the specific thoughts connected by it.[13]

The playwright has taken care of the literary form of the dramatic work of art, but he has not, and cannot, take care of the theatrical form. It is the director's task to discover and shape the best form for the staging of the work. For, when the play is to be transferred from the page to the stage, both the form and the content of the play, as conceived by the poet, must find a suitable stage form. If the director is successful in his search for the correct stage form for his particular cast and situation, he will find that in staging the work of art within that particular form he has created a new work of art. It is in this aspect of his work that the director becomes a creative artist in his own right. This is not adapting, not merely interpreting, it is rather the process of creating a play from a piece of dramatic literature.

The chosen form must reveal the play both as literature and as theater. The critics of our day, at least the vast majority of them, do not seem to grasp this point. But any director whose inspiration has failed him at a crucial moment and who has failed to create the right physical action pattern, the right tempo, the right rhythm, the right sound pattern, even the right piece of business—and thus has failed to create the right form—knows the vital importance of finding the best form for the play, the cast, the time, and the place. He has seen the play damned by the critics and the public as an unworthy piece of dramaturgy, when it is his chosen theatrical form that is at fault. But when he is completely successful in finding the right form for the script, and in the final production, "form and content harmonize completely, then it [the work of art] has universal validity for all contemplating subjects. It is 'eternal.' "[14]

The playwright must trust the director to find the right form just as he must trust the actor, the costumer, and the scene designer for their contribution. The good playwright takes this multiple artistry into consideration in his writing and uses it to the play's advantage. Thornton Wilder, for example, has pointed out that the playwright, through his work in the theater, learns to use the talents of his fellow artists to the play's benefit. Wilder suggests that the playwright is primarily interested in the story movement and that he leaves to the actor the details of characterization. Both Wilder and G. B. Shaw have stated that a good actor can, and will, add much to the author's characterization. Almost any director who has had the experience of rehearsing a new play with the author present has heard him mumble to himself or exclaim openly, "That's what I meant," or, "I never thought of that!"[15]

For the imaginative person, it would be impossible to work for weeks with good lines and not add one's creative thought to that of the playwright. By so doing a new play is created.

In a larger sense, however, few would deny that the interpretive realm is the principal concern of the playwright's coworkers. Even here, in the realm of interpretation, the director, working with the actor, must be highly creative if he is to interpret successfully. It is interesting that Augusto Centeno, in his introduction to four essays, *The Intent of The Artist,* makes no distinction between the words interpreter and creator: "The four American artists" —Sherwood Anderson, Thornton Wilder, Roger Sessions, and William Lescaze—"who speak to us in these pages are four authentic interpreters (and creators) of the realness of our times and lives."[16]

These four artists use their creative powers to interpret the life they see around them. The theater artist uses his interpretive powers to create a living play that will reveal the playwright's drama. The director then is an artist, he does interpret and he creates. But, and we are back where we started, what is an artist?

The Artist

The real problem is to define or explain the term "artist." It is not enough to say that an artist is one who creates. Such a definition would of necessity include the inventor who may or may not be an artist. The inventor is not included in the select group for the very reason discussed above. He may create but he does not interpret. The inventor uses the materials at hand for a practical purpose. The artist uses the materials and techniques of his particular art to interpret, reveal, explain, via the beautiful, some aspect of life. By his process of isolating the beautiful for lesser mortals to see, the artist helps to interpret life. As Shaw pointed out, he teaches us to see, to hear, and to feel. The artist helps man in his attempt to find and understand his place in the universe by making him more aware of the universe through his senses. The artist discovers beauty in life, then lifts it from life, by means of the tools and skills of his art, until it stands revealed for all who will look. Whoever isolates, through selection, a bit of beauty, an artistic truth, whoever lifts that beauty or that truth out of the disorder of living into the orderliness of art, that person is an artist.

Centeno speaks of the necessity for the artist to take possession of the truth because to become significant, truth must be "liberated" by the act of "possessiveness."

Scientific truth has its opposite in the falsehood, moral truth in the lie; but art has for its two poles the significant and the nonsignificant or insignificant. And this significance is always a reference to possessiveness. A truth—moral, social, etc.—does not become artistically significant until it has been possessed in feeling, in motion, in tone; until it has been liberated from its close context into a larger sense of human livingness. . . . *Macbeth* and *Crime and Punishment* are something more than simplifications of the commandment "Thou shalt not kill!" *King Lear* does something more than prove filial ingratitude to be wrong. Here the meanings are issues of livingness, which elude any form of expression except the poetic. The drawings in the Cave of Altamira are something more than a pattern for efficient prehistoric hunting. Man, surrounded by mortality, craves more than one life, hence art, as a symbolic possession of all life. Religion, philosophy, and science also originate in this same human anguish. But they must insist on finding the absolute and permanent, and in doing so disturb the livingness itself, as art does not. They command, propose or state, but do not possess. The work of art is not a commandment, a proposition, or statement. The work of art is a single act of possession.[17]

It is the director's responsibility to use his talent and his skill until the words of the play, hopefully already firmly set in the "larger sense of human livingness," are *literally* brought to life within that livingness.

The desire, the necessity, to give some concrete form to certain subjective feelings is what makes a man an artist. "Not knowledge or morality," argues Centeno, compel men to become artists, "for art, per se, is neither of these. Not even beauty, for natural beauty exists independent of any artistic realization. Art is a symbolic possession of life—and a possession so complete, yet so undisturbing to life's rhythm, continuity and flux, that it is glorious for man to know that he can do it and that he must do it in order to live in all fullness."[18] The artist must be a dedicated person if he is to be a true artist, the director must be a dedicated artist if he is to make the theater his life's work. The level of theater, amateur or professional, matters not at all; if the director is not dedicated to the theater he will have little success.

When one speaks of the professional theater one assumes that a dedication exists or at least did exist before success or the lack of it jaded the outlook. Obviously, all professionals are not dedicated to their work, but a surprising number are. This is not always true in the amateur theater. Especially in the educational field, the director needs truly to "have the call." He is not, and no slur is intended, just another teacher. He must count on putting in many, many extra hours, and his responsibility is not lessened by the fact that he is playing to a high school audience. The high school director, or the director in the children's theater, must be so drawn to the theater that he cannot leave it alone.

Far too many audiences in this country have had their taste for live drama lowered and destroyed because some misguided high school principal turned the class play over to a coach or history teacher that the class elected so that the children would have a chance to act or, worse still, so that the class could make some money. Far better that the students' time be spent on something in which competent leadership is available. For if there is no artistry, no artistic integrity, on the part of the director, the rehearsal periods will be drudgery for him, a harmful waste of time for the students, and disappointing, boring, and taste-destroying for the audience. Play direction is an art and must be treated as such. Certain techniques can, as in all arts, be taught, but only the artist will know when and how to use what. The young director starting to learn the art of the theater and particularly the art of direction should, I believe, ask himself, Can I do otherwise? If he can, then the theater—college, civic, or professional—is not for him.

Centeno suggests that the artistic activity is a love activity; that the artist takes possession of, or surrenders to, his object as a lover takes possession of, or surrenders to, his loved one. It is this possession which is to Centeno the "livingness" of art. Whether or not one agrees with this position, none can deny that the involvement of the artist with his art is greater than his involvement in any other aspect of life.

The burden of the artist, in this case the burden of the director, is not lightly to be assumed. His work will permeate his life. To the working director all aspects of life suddenly become related to the play then in rehearsal. The problems of the play are continually arising in the most casual conversation and in the most unexpected places. The director is everywhere confronted with the play until it seems to him that life is about the play, rather than the play about life.

No pseudo-approach to directing can take the place of talent and know-how, no affectation will accomplish his task. The director is an artist. He cannot dodge the fact. He cannot hide his lack.

Who is the director? He is a sensitive artist, and proud of his artistry; he has an above average intelligence and is not ashamed of his intellect; he is a psychologist, and he had better be quiet about that.

The director's art is evidenced in his choice of form and his use of direction techniques. His intellect is evidenced in his understanding of the author's play. His grasp of psychology is evidenced in his effectiveness with his actors. All three attributes must be present if he is to achieve artistically truthful and dramatically exciting renditions of the author's intent.

Part II
THE DIRECTOR
AND
THE PLAY

Selection

"The play's the thing"—not the director's ego nor the actor's psyche, not the designer's brilliance nor the light-man's ingenuity. "The play's the thing" that must catch not only the conscience, but the very being of those working with it. The play is the source of all the frustration, all the pain and anger, but it is at the same time the source of the excitement, the joy, and the beauty that go to make up the theater. The play is the source of all the director's problems, whether of interpretation or personality, but the director must always remember that the source of the problems contains all his answers.

The director must live closely, intimately, with the script twenty-four hours a day for a number of weeks, and for this reason it behooves him to (1) make sure he has a voice in the matter of play selection, (2) make sure he knows what he is talking about in play selection, and (3) make himself heard. The chosen script must, unless the director is deliberately seeking a mental breakdown, hold his interest for the rehearsal time, be worthy of the actors' time, and promise to be interesting and exciting to the audience.

The problems of selection are usually outside the realm of the professional director. He may take the job or he may not, but when he works he will be working as part of the producer's staff, not as the prime mover as he so often is in the amateur theater. Though the director in the amateur theater does not take the risks of the professional producer, he still finds that choosing the "right" play for any group can be a real bugbear.

Play selection is difficult not only for the obvious problems of casting and financing, but because when all else fails, the "harping critic" can always attack the choice of plays: "What we need is more serious drama." "Well, I sorta enjoyed it, but is it really a play?" "I come to the theater to get away from my worries. I don't want to be involved in someone else's!" "Nothing like a good musical to pep you up!" "My god, have you ever seen such trivia? It's disgusting!" "Why can't we do more plays like *Getting Gertie's Garter?* That's what any audience really wants." "Now, I have this friend, and he just finished a play that's just what you want. Can't miss. Bound to pack the house every night." And so on, *ad nauseam.*

The director who attempts to please every member of the audience with his selections is doomed to failure, for one of the great difficulties in the theater is, as has been said, "Everybody has two businesses—his own and show business." And if that statement was true before the advent of television, it is gospel in this day and age. Any passerby can and will give a running critique of the faults of the last four choices. Unfortunately, play selection is the easiest job in the world, as long as one is not in a position where it is a part of the job.

It might seem, then, that the best policy would be to ignore the advice just given about the director letting his voice be heard in play selection. Let someone else choose and take the blame. This may appear to be the easy way out, but as many high school teachers and civic theater directors have learned, it is simply the shortest route to the booby hatch. You, as the director, are going to live with the play more intimately than the proverbial newlyweds, and try as you may you won't be able to leave your mistress for long. She will turn up in every conversation, every story you read, and every movie you see. Duck around the corner for a quick drink and the bartender will start telling you a story that is a strange parallel, or strange contradiction, to the problems the author has set forth in his play.

Since you are going to wrap the next four to eight weeks of your life around this new mistress, make sure that you can stand to know her that well. Choose carefully and choose with your own interest foremost. If you move into a school or a situation where a committee has in the past chosen the plays, make every effort to change that precedent. Have an advisory committee by all means, but take the final responsibility on your own shoulders and suffer the slings and arrows of the outraged public with a bloody but unbowed head.

In passing, just a word about the matter of breaking, or, if you prefer, setting precedents. I grew up in the home of a Methodist minister. We moved on the average of once every two or three years, and one of the important lessons I learned about moving into a new position was to make the changes needed, or desired, quickly. Ask for improvements and changes as soon as the need is seen. Don't wait until you feel you are established; by then it may be too late.

If, in the amateur theater, the director is, as I suggest, to be the final authority in the selection of the play just as he is the final authority in all other aspects of the production, then he must make sure that his standards for play selection are high. What is a play? The question has been discussed and debated since Aristotle, and, in all probability, long before his *Poetics* was conceived.

Aristotle

Defining a play is not an easy task. It is interesting that while you will seldom hear the question, Is it literature? you will often hear, Yes, but is it really a play? Such a question has always left me cold; it generally means that the play under discussion does not fit a ready-made formula, or that the speaker could not follow the action of the play. Drama theory has attracted the critics since Aristotle, and, as Allardyce Nicoll points out in *The Theory of Drama*, it is not difficult to see why.

The drama is at once the most peculiar, the most elusive, and the most enthralling of all types of literature. It is so deeply associated with and dependent upon the whole material world of the theater, with its thronging crowds and its universal appeal; it lies so near to the deeper consciousness of the nation in which it takes its rise; it is capable of addressing itself so widely and so diversely to peoples of far distant ages and of varying climes; it is so social in its aims and in its appreciation; it is so prone to descend to the uttermost depths of buffoonery and farce, and yet ascends so easily and so gloriously to the most magnificent heights of poetic inspiration, that it stands undoubtedly as the most interesting of all the literary products of the human intelligence.[19]

All drama criticism stems from Aristotle (384–322 B.C.). This remarkable man of antiquity, who wrote profusely on a great range of subjects, stands not only as the symbol of the inquiring spirit of mankind but still, after more than two thousand years, as *the* authority for drama criticism.

Aristotle lived at the end of the golden age of Greek drama, long before the romantic drama was conceived, and it is therefore absurd to attempt to apply his dictums to drama that reflects a way of life completely unknown in his day. Yet, in spite of the fact that no one now suggests strict adherence to Aristotle's rules, he provided in his *Poetics* a basis for drama criticism and theory that has influenced the Western world since his time. The director, no matter what his experience, will be a better director if he is familiar with the *Poetics*.

Aristotle describes the parts of the tragedy as follows:

PLOT: The most important of the six [parts of tragedy] is the combination of the incidents of the story. Tragedy is essentially an imitation not of persons but of action and life, of happiness and misery. All human happiness or misery takes the form of action; the end for which we live is a certain kind of activity, not a quality. Character gives us qualities, but it is in our actions—what we do—that we are happy or the reverse. In a play accordingly they do not act in order to portray the Characters; they include the characters for the sake of the action. So that it is the action in it, i.e. its Fable or Plot, that is the end and purpose of the tragedy; and the end is everywhere the chief thing. . . . We maintain, therefore, that the first essential, the life and soul, so to speak, of Tragedy is the Plot.

CHARACTER: Character in a play is that which reveals the moral purpose of the agents, i.e. the sort of thing they seek or avoid, where that is not obvious—hence there is no room for Character in a speech on a purely indifferent subject.

THOUGHT: Thought is shown in all they say when providing a particular point or, it may be, enunciating a general truth

. . . the power of saying whatever can be said, or what is appropriate to the occasion. [Thought would be replaced by theme in modern criticism.]

DICTION: The expression of their thoughts in words, which is practically the same thing with verse as with prose. [Diction then is the dialogue of the drama.]

MELODY: . . . the greatest of the pleasurable accessories of Tragedy. [In so far as we know, song or melody played an important part in the drama of early Greece. It is probable, though by no means certain, that the drama of which Aristotle wrote was closer to our opera than to the modern form of drama.]

SPECTACLE: . . . though an attraction, is the least artistic of all the parts, and has least to do with the art of poetry. The tragic effect is quite possible without a public performance and actors; and besides, the getting-up of the Spectacle is more a matter for the costumier than the poet. [The spectacle, according to Aristotle, was not just the scenery, as it is often interpreted, but rather the production *as a whole*. It is that element of the theater with which the director is most concerned.]

On the construction of the tragedy, Aristotle wrote:

Having thus distinguished the parts, let us now consider the proper construction of the Fable or Plot, as that is at once the first and the most important thing in Tragedy. We have laid down that a tragedy is an imitation of an action that is complete in itself, as a whole of some magnitude; for a whole may be of no magnitude to speak of. Now a whole is that which has a beginning, middle, and end.

A beginning is that which is not itself necessarily after anything else and which has naturally something else after it; an end is that which is naturally after something itself, either as its necessary or usual consequence, and with nothing else after it; and a middle, that which is by nature after one thing and has also another after it. A well constructed Plot, therefore, cannot either begin or end at any point one likes; beginning and end in it must be of the forms just described.[20]

Many plays fail because the author did not follow Aristotle's advice and pay particular attention to this beginning, middle, and end. The director must often fill in the beginning for his actors, and must very often watch the middle and ending, making sure that where the playwright has failed in making his connections clear-cut, the stage action clarifies rather than further muddles the plot line.

In order to be a good tragedy the play must contain, according to Aristotle, either Peripety, that is, a reversal, or Discovery, or both.

A Peripety is the change of the kind described from one state of things within the play to its opposite, and that too in the way we are saying, in the probable or necessary sequence of events; as it is for instance in Oedipus: here the opposite state of things is produced by the Messenger, who, coming to gladden Oedipus and to remove his fears as to his mother, reveals the secret of his birth.

A Discovery is, as the very word implies, a change from ignorance to knowledge, and thus to either love or hate, in the personage marked for good or evil fortune. The finest form of Discovery is one attended by Peripeties, like that which goes with the Discovery in Oedipus.

A third part is Suffering, which we may define as an action of a destructive or painful nature, such as murders on the stage, tortures, woundings, and the like.[21]

Aristotle's classic definition of the tragedy is as follows (italics supplied):

A tragedy, then, is the imitation of an action that is serious and also, as having magnitude, complete in itself; in language with pleasurable accessories, each kind brought in separately in the parts of the work; in a dramatic, not a narrative form; with incidents arousing pity and fear, wherewith to accomplish its catharsis of such emotions. Here by "language with pleasurable accessories" I mean that with rhythm and harmony or song superadded and by "the kinds separately" I mean that some portions are worked out with verse only, and others in turn with song.[22]

The reader is advised to study all of the *Poetics* for himself, and to judge Aristotle's dictums with care and flexibility. Perhaps the point of greatest disagreement between Aristotle and the modern critic is the order of importance of the elements of the tragedy. Character, in the opinion of many, outweighs plot. I am in agreement with Stark Young who argues that since the characters of a play express themselves in actions and those actions make up the plot, ". . . it follows that the plot includes, or can at least include, them both, and can be therefore of all the elements in the play the most inclusive, and therefore most largely and completely expressive of the play's essential idea or quality."[23]

What difference, the young director may well ask, does it make to me? Let Aristotle rest in peace and let the critics of today be damned. The difference it makes to the director is evident first of all when he considers play selection. It becomes more evident when he begins to discover the strengths and weaknesses of the script. The debate between plot and character begins to affect the director when he finds he has chosen a particular play because he liked one character, or the basic idea of the drama, but that plot line is weak or, even as it happens in a few dramas, almost nonexistent. He will be wise to remember that if on the morning following a performance the audience cannot remember what the play "was about," attendance will drop off very rapidly. It is not enough for the critic—professional or amateur—to say, "It is about this man and his ideas about life." If this is the reaction, then the play should have been written as a novel.[24]

A knowledge of Aristotle will give the director a foundation on which to build his standards for play selection. He needs to be able to define a play, and he won't do much better than to familiarize himself with Stark Young's definition :"A play is a piece of literature about a section of life written in such a way that it will go over the footlights, in such a way that what it has to say it can say in the theater. That is the sole test. If it can do this it is a play, good or bad."[25] A good play is one that will go over the footlights in such a way that it will move the audience in the way the author intended it be moved. A good play must have that quality which is best described as "good theater." Good theater neither demands nor rejects what might be called literary values. It does demand that these literary values— poetry, style, individuality, and theme—fall within the boundaries of the theatrically effective. Further, to be a good play, the piece must have truth within the form the dramatist has selected, that is to say, it must have theatrical truth. The probability of the situations found in Daly's *Under The Gas Light* or in King's *See How They Run* being duplicated in real life is as remote as one can imagine. Yet in both cases, within the form the author has chosen, they are theatrically true. Not only are they theatrically true, they have the dramatic reversal, the dramatic surprises that are necessary in any drama. The same can be said for the dialogue, for the characters, improbable as they may be, in a situation as improbable as it may be, do speak words that make sense for those characters in that situation. The playwright, to create theatrically acceptable dialogue, must be able to improvise for each actor words that are true as well as actable. Allardyce Nicoll has described Shakespeare's genius for dialogue by comparing Hamlet, as written, with a Hamlet scenario that might have been used by the Italian *commedia dell'arte*:

What Shakespeare has done is to put himself, as it were, in the place of the finest, most gifted, and most inspired actor of this kind [*commedia dell'arte*] and to write down for him the most delicate and subtle dialogue he could possibly have imagined. This, we may say, is what is meant by perfect dramatic poetry; it is simply inspired improvisation captured by the artist as it is extemporized and made permanent. When an actor speaks of a "good" part he does not always mean merely a "fat" part; more often he means a part with such dialogue that every line, every word, rings true. Similarly "good dialogue" does not by any means invariably signify poetic dialogue; it is dramatic language subordinated to character and eminently suitable for histrionic enunciation. The perfect dramatist is he who is able to put himself in the place, not of a series of living characters, but of a company of actors each of whom is taking a certain part in his play and who at the same time has the ability to prevent his own personality from intruding into what should be the dialogue of another's. There may be as much poetry, as much sheer lyricism as you like in a drama; only that poetry must not seem the poetic speech of one man, and it must be subordinate to the essential requirements of the stage performance.[26]

It is, as someone has said, the intensity of vision that makes the poet. In the theater the poet's vision, whether he writes in prose or verse, takes the form of men playing roles in established ceremonies or rites.

If we assume then that the director is going to choose the drama, and that he has standards which will result in his choice being good theater, the most important question he can ask himself is: Does this play excite me, does it challenge me, will it hold my interest throughout the rehearsal period? If the director cannot, regardless of any other values he may find in the play, answer Yes to the excitement, the challenge, and the interest, then the play is the wrong one.

There are, it seems to me, three basic questions that the selector of the drama to be produced answers in most amateur situations. The first and the most important is the question Do I like it? Secondly, Can the group afford to produce this play? And finally, What chance do I have of casting it reasonably well?

If the answer to the first question is a strong enough Yes, if it is a driving, compelling Yes, then the second and third questions can be ignored for "love will find a way." I would warn the director in such a situation, however, that his love for the play will be severely tested during the rehearsal period, and possibly destroyed if the play runs for very many performances.

Of course, no matter how strongly the director desires to produce a particular play, certain limitations do exist and must be considered. One does not, for example, choose *Mr. Roberts* if one is directing a production for a Catholic girls' school, nor does one do *Little Women* for the state reformatory for boys, nor *King Lear* with junior high school students. Recognition of such "natural" limits, which requires only a modicum of common sense, need not be discussed.

The point, excluding such limits, is that almost no play need be discarded because of costs beyond royalty. There is always a way to do it inexpensively and imaginatively. *Peer Gynt,* done with two stepladders, two planks, and imaginative lighting, makes for exciting theater.

Casting will be discussed later, but I may say here that I

don't believe it is wise to wait for the perfect cast. Too many plays never see production when the perfect man or woman for the role is demanded. On the other hand, I would not advise a production of *King Lear* without a Lear in mind. Nor would I attempt *Peter Pan* without a method of flying Peter. Often the director is forced to go outside of his group to cast, and such a procedure is usually possible when the situation demands it. In any case, it is the audience, not the feelings of the group, that should be considered. It is the audience who, because of its suffering, will force all live theater to suffer if its tastes are lowered or destroyed. The director will quickly learn that it is neither wise or expedient to attempt a well-loved play in impossible producing conditions.

The above is no reason to decide on the clap-trap, however, as there are many great plays and many new plays waiting to see the light of production; moreover, life is much too short to waste directing plays that lack the excitement necessary for a true, creative experience. Even the very young director should have a host of plays with small, large, or medium casts, whichever best fits his needs. It is most inadvisable, I believe, to choose a play with seventeen roles because there happen to be seventeen members in the drama club. Better in such a situation to look over the list of "must do sometime" plays beginning with four characters and if necessary keep looking through the eight character dramas. If the director has any voice at all in choosing his plays, he has a definite responsibility to expose his audience to good dramas. He must look further than the Broadway box-office record when choosing his play.

As to the type of play being selected, comedy, tragedy, melodrama, or farce—and I shall discuss each shortly—the rule of thumb should be: the less experienced the cast, the more basic the drama. As a matter of fact, if the group is allowed a free hand in choosing, the reverse will be true, and the more inexperienced they are, the lighter the comedy they will decide to do. There is a feeling among amateurs that the lighter the play the easier it is to do well. Again, the reverse is actually the case. The lighter the comedy the greater must be the technique of the actors involved. Hence it is that the more real feeling the cast can get hold of, the easier time they will have being truthful in their acting. Good comedy technique is extremely difficult, and few amateurs can handle it well. All plays are difficult to do well. I have not yet found the easy play to direct, but the more feeling and emotion within the play, the easier it is to get a portion of it across to the actors, and, in turn, the easier it is for them to get part of what they understand and feel across to the audience. Young directors and young actors will do better to cut their teeth on basic emotional reactions, rather than intellectual Shavian or drawing-room Cowardish comedy.

Types of Plays

The director needs to be able to think in terms of types of plays. Both the form he gives the final product and the style with which he treats it will depend largely upon the kind of play he is directing. It will not serve simply for the director to say, "If the protagonist is successful, it is comedy, if he is not, then it is tragedy." The ending alone will not suffice to classify the drama. The fact that the happy ending served its purpose in 1318 for Dante—and he had no hesitance in labeling his work a comedy since, "in its beginning it is horrible and foul, because it is Hell; in its ending, fortunate, desirable, and joyful, because it is Paradise"[27]—will not aid the director in his attempts to classify modern plays.

While most critics would maintain, along with Aristotle, that the highest form of drama is the tragedy, such a belief need not negate comedy, farce, or melodrama. Involved in a life we know must end in death, we cannot help being moved more profoundly by the defeat of life than by a momentary triumph over a particular facet of that life. It is as Stark Young writes: "All things pushed to their bounds are tragic, for despite the wills and passionate desires that we exert upon them, they have an end at last, and at last are taken from us."[28]

The distinction between comedy and tragedy can only be made by a thorough examination of the author's treatment, since "tragedy and comedy are to be defined according to the impression which the dramatist wishes each to have on the assembled audience in the theatre."[29] The hero's defeat is tragic only when we agree that his struggle is edifying and when we want him to conquer. No matter what the theme of the play, the author can give it a comic or a tragic treatment. The director must follow suit. If the author wants murder and sudden death accomplished lightheartedly, if he wants, then, a light tone to his play, he will have written a comedy. A few years ago there appeared a Broadway hit called *Kiss and Tell*. The play concerned the seeming pregnancy of a happy-go-lucky teen-age girl as a result of an alleged affair with her gawky freckle-faced next-door boyfriend. The play was highly successful and extremely funny, yet the basis of the plot was the supposed ruination of a lovely young girl. The author was successful in writing a family comedy around a situation which in many families would be tragic. His treatment from beginning to end was light and fun-filled. To make a distinction between comedy and tragedy we turn once again to Nicoll: "Comedy assumes that life is eternal and death a dream; tragedy assumes that death is inevitable and that its time of coming is of no importance compared with what a man does before his death."[30] In tragedy, we feel ennobled by witnessing the struggle of a good man against odds he cannot overcome; in comedy we laugh at the animalness of man, or his incredible attempts to hide his origins.

Farce originally comes from the Latin *farcire*, meaning "to stuff"; hence in the theater farce means a drama "stuffed with low humor and extravagant wit."[31] Farce in the late seventeenth century came to mean the short funny play. As most plays were then five acts long, the farce was generally three, hence less time was available to the dramatist to develop his characters. He started dealing with exaggerated incidents, these incidents often ended up as simple slapstick. Thus farce came to mean a short comic play. In our day and age farce deals with exaggerated situations which generally border on the impossible. The characters are "flat" and we learn about them only as they react to the impossible situation within which they are embroiled.

Melodrama was at first a serious drama with a great dependency on songs. Originally closely allied to tragedy, melodrama moved away from the nobility of character and the inevitability of plot and concentrated on situation and the spectacle. Characters tended to become stereotypes and the mechanical effects—i.e., floods, fires, etc.—became as important as the drama. "Song, show, and incident became the prevailing characteristics in it, as buffoonery and extravagant development of plot did in farce."[32]

The director need not concern himself overly much with which genre of the drama is the greatest and which is the least. His concern must be that each play is "good theater" within its classification. A good farce is downright fun to stage occasionally, just as it is fun for the actors to play. A melodrama done within the style of its day is charming and even exciting to watch. The melodrama presents a challenge in style for the director, the actor, and the scenic designer. The director can safely leave the discussion of which form is the greater to the literary critic; his concern should be with finding good theater within each form and then transferring the play from the page to the stage.

If we assume that the play has been chosen, that it is a play the director is anxious to do, that it will fit within the budget limitations, that apparent casting problems can be overcome, that the director has classified it and knows whether he is dealing with comedy, tragedy, farce or melodrama, then finally, he must be ready for auditions. But though he may have applied Aristotle's standards in his selection, he has not yet studied the play. He has not yet gotten under the skin of the drama. He does not yet know what he is about to cast, or what he is to stage.

Though it is the play itself that is the final source of all interpretation problems, several sources outside the play should be researched before the director's actual analysis is begun.

Ignoring the script itself for the moment, the most important source, I believe, is the author himself. When the play under consideration is a contemporary piece, the author is often available for consultation. If the budget allows transportation from his home to the place of rehearsal, the money is generally well spent. When the author is not available, his other published works are and should be studied closely. Everything the particular playwright has written is a help in understanding anything he has written.

A knowledge of his life, when available, can be illuminating though too great a stress on this one aspect can be dangerous. If a knowledge of the author's private life is necessary to understanding the play then choose another play, but if being thoroughly familiar with his life, his times, and his philosophy of life helps give the actors a better idea of what they are doing then any amount of research is worthwhile.

A history of the play can at times be helpful, though the fact that a particular audience or critic reacted in a particular manner to a particular production may be meaningless in the existing situation. On the other hand, knowledge of how the play has been produced and received may suggest what to avoid.

Critical opinion, other than the morning-after reviews, can give a considerable amount of insight into the play. The first reviews to hit the street are highly important to the original production but seldom have much connection with the drama itself. Unless one holds the critic in great regard, and I know of few writing for the dailies who merit this regard, the daily reviews are interesting but seldom helpful in understanding any play. Hopefully the critics in this country will take stock of themselves and decide to raise their standards. The exceptions to the above may be found in the second piece that often appears in the New York Sunday papers, as well as the articles in certain current magazines and newspapers. The criticism appearing in the weekly and the monthly is often of a higher standard than that written in a rush to make an early morning deadline.

For his working analysis however, the director must return to the script itself.

Rite-Role Analysis

The problem of play analysis can be approached from many and varied angles. Some favor the "motivational-unit"[33] approach. Dean speaks of titling the scenes for purposes of picturization; Stanislavski prefers the unit and objective approach; while the literary approaches are almost as numerous as the number of writers from Aristotle's time to the present. The rite-role approach adds one more possible aid to the director in his search for the author's intent.

The rite-role method of play analysis provides the director, it seems to me, with the specific kind of analysis needed for play direction. The director needs to know considerably more than does the actor who may be following some variation of the Stanislavski system. The objectives (or goals or actions) of the scene (or unit or beat) are helpful, very helpful, to the actor who plays a single character, but in such a case it is purposely a one-sided view, the view of the character. The director needs a system that will allow him to work with the actor within his, the director's, framework. The director needs a system that deals with his problems of staging in terms of that staging. In other words, the director needs a system that will dissect the play into theatrical segments. While the actor is rightly concerned with the specific action, the director must know each line from at least three separate and distinct viewpoints. First, he must be able to help the actor to the correct action for each line, that is, he must know the line from the character's point of view. Secondly, he must know the meaning of the line in terms of the particular plot, and thirdly, he must know the larger, more generalized meaning which ties the line to the author's overall intent, that is, the connection of the line to the basic theme of the drama.

A system which does, in my opinion, fulfill these requirements has been developed from an idea originated by Professor David Thompson of the University of Minnesota. It is this rite-role analysis that is the basis of this chapter.

As stated in the opening words of this chapter, "The play's the thing." But the play that is performed, the play that the audience sees, or, as is all too often the case, the play the audience never sees, is a direct result of the director's analysis. He cannot help making some sort of analysis, even though he may not do so consciously, for unless he is completely unable to reason, he will make connections between lines and character. Rather than depend upon the spur of the moment interpretation, he will be wise to have as complete a breakdown as is possible. Every facet of play direction—casting, blocking, set designing, costuming, interpretation, tempo, and rhythm—will depend upon his analysis.

The rite-role method of analysis is, I believe, the most workable system for the director as it does succeed in breaking down the play in staging terms. Such an analysis uncovers the staging problems as well as the emotional and intellectual problems of the drama. The completed analysis will reveal relationships, similarities, and differences that can be staged and played. The unit and objective, the motivational unit, and Dean's scene titling are all included. Finally, the rite-role approach discovers the author's intent in dramatic terms and suggests how that intent can be conveyed to the actor in acting, rather than academic, terms.

Though similar ideas have been suggested in the past,[34] in most cases the concept has been applied to poetic or romantic drama only. However, the rite-role approach to analysis will work on any drama. Francis Fergusson, in his provocative book *The Idea of a Theater*, does hint at such an application in his discussion of "Hamlet as Ritual and Improvisation." "Both the ritual and the improvisational elements in Hamlet," says Fergusson, "are essential—as essential as the stories in the structure of the whole. The Elizabethan theater, at once as frankly 'theatrical' as vaudeville, and as central to the life of its time as an ancient rite, offered Shakespeare two resources, two theatrical 'dimensions' which the modern naturalistic tradition of serious drama must try, or pretend, to do without."[35]

The rite-role method of analysis assumes that, as Fergusson suggests, the modern playwright is only pretending to do without the "ritual and the improvisational elements"; that both the rites and the improvisational (role) elements are still an integral part of the drama; and further, that once the director has uncovered these rites and roles, he will have uncovered both the plot and character skeleton of the drama as well as the author's intent.

The rites and roles in modern drama are not as obvious as in the drama of Shakespeare or of the Greeks, because they are not as obvious in life today as they were then. This approach to analysis assumes that as life, or at least the

living of life, has become more informal so have the rites in
the theater. The action on stage is now, as it was in Aristotle's time, the "imitation of an action." Stage action is
always a representation of particular "real" actions in life.
All stage action is selected and designed to solicit a particular response from the audience, just as the rites of primitive
man were designed to solicit a particular response from
nature and later, as man became more sophisticated, to
solicit a particular response from the performers and/or the
onlookers. The rites in life today, that is, the set forms of
conducting any ceremony, blend into one another, almost
without notice. The rites of daily living are certainly considerably less formal than in ancient times when life itself
seemed to depend upon fulfilling the proper rituals. One
might almost say that we, in our informal age, have made a
rite out of informality. But when any action is selected for
the stage it undergoes a heightening and is metamorphosed
via the stage conventions of the time into a recognizable
rite.

Theater as Convention

The first difficulty the young director is apt to find here is
remembering to think of the theater as a collection of conventions. Yet, as many writers have pointed out, and as
becomes apparent to the theater student once he gives it a
little thought, the theater is nothing but a collection of
conventions that have meaning for a particular audience.
The Hindu theater, where the fingers alone can convey
almost any possible combination of meanings to the person
who knows the conventions of that theater, would be interesting but not meaningful to the readers of this book. Just as

the stage manager in black is ignored by the audience in the Oriental theater, because the convention is accepted that black is invisible on the stage, so the convention of the actor waiting for the laugh or doing a take while still ignoring the audience adds to, rather than detracts from, our enjoyment when watching a comedy.

Perhaps a better example is the shift of the conventions over the years in the idea of "realistic acting." Since Stanislavski became the actors' "Bible," directors and actors have spoken long and loud about being "real," being "believable," on the stage. Actually, being believable on the stage is the process of making your audience feel with your character, understand your character, and believe in the possibilities of your character. This, in turn, is the process of making the audience accept the conventions of the particular production. Most of us have difficulty in accepting the conventions of any age other than our own. We do not think of the acting of Garrick's day as being "real." Some schools speak of it being presentational rather than representational, yet in its own day, this style of acting was accepted as holding the mirror up to nature. Look for a moment at Henry Fielding's comment concerning the acting of Garrick as described in his great novel *Tom Jones:*

When the scene was over Jones said, "Why, Partridge, you exceed my expectations. You enjoy the play more than I conceived possible." "Nay, sir," answered Partridge, "if you are not afraid of the devil, I can't help it; but, to be sure, it is natural to be surprised at such things, though I know there is nothing in them; not that it was the ghost that surprised me, neither; for I should have known that to have been only a man in a strange dress; but when I saw the little man [Garrick] so frightened himself, it was that which took hold of me."———

"And dost thou imagine, then, Partridge," cries Jones, "that he was really frightened?"———"Nay, sir," said Partridge, "did not you yourself observe afterwards, when he found it was his own father's spirit, and how he was murdered in the garden, how his fear forsook him by degrees, and he was struck dumb with sorrow, as it were, just as I should have been, had it been my own case."[36]

To perform the conventions demanded by the style of the play well and truthfully is, in each age, to act believably. The melodramatic style of the writing in Daly's *Under The Gaslight* demands a like style in the playing; nonetheless the production, well staged and well performed, will bring the tears very close to the surface even as we smile at the quaintness of the style.

Once the director can think of the theater as a collection of conventions, he will be ready to see the connection between the rites of living and those of the stage. As the theater is always holding the mirror up to nature there is a close connection between the degree of formality one finds in life and that which one finds on the stage. Remember that the theater mirror is also a magnifying glass, hence the subject the mirror reflects is always larger than life. The word "theater" implies, just as does the word "acting," a degree of exaggeration. Thus, when in the Restoration age, for example, the ceremonies, or rites, of living were more formal than ours of today, so the rites enacted upon the stage were more formal than those in present-day life. And so it is in the modern drama. By the selection of the action, the playwright has formalized that action to a greater degree than would be found in life. He has then, by his selection, either made a ritual of informality[37] or formalized the informal rite.

Rites

"Rites," says Thompson, "in literature are the most obvious and basic elements—so obvious, in fact, that readers tend to ignore them by not sustaining their implications throughout a reading. They are the different scenes which, taken together, make up the plot. They may be as public as a coronation or as private as a soliloquy."[38] For purposes of the director's analysis, a rite is any situation or ceremony enacted by a character or a group of characters that has a recognizable pattern. For example, a man eating his lunch alone will quickly set up a recognizable pattern; he will start with his sandwich and end with his fruit. If he lunches in the same place every day he will make a regular rite of eating, even down to the detail of which object occupies what space on the table. Indeed, in a very short time he will feel a bit uneasy if for some reason he is forced to change some order of his rite of Lunch. In much the same manner, an individual alone on stage (or in life) often will make a rite out of Taking a Drink; he lifts the bottle to the light, sees that it is half full, pours out a small amount in a glass, checks the color by holding the glass to the light, downs the liquid, gazes a few seconds at the empty glass, utters a satisfied "Ahhhhh—," returns the glass to the table, and the rite of Taking a Drink is completed.[39]

The above example of taking a drink might be a complete rite in itself or a single *dramatic action* going to make up a rite. The physical actions of having a drink, if performed by a single character, would probably constitute a complete rite, but if several characters are on stage, the action, "having a drink," would probably be one of many dramatic actions going to make up the rite of The After-Dinner Drink or the rite of The Cocktail Party.

Dramatic Actions

Dramatic actions correspond with Dietrich's motivational unit and the smallest units that Stanislavski discusses. They are the main lines of actions within the scene, and change as the dialogue or the physical actions implied in that dialogue change direction. For example, in the opening scene of Act II of Ibsen's *Ghosts,* the rite in progress might well be labeled The Policy Conference, and within this rite some twenty-four separate dramatic actions can be found.

(MANDERS *and* MRS. ALVING *come in from the dining room*)
MRS. ALVING: (*calls into the dining room from the doorway*) Aren't you coming in here, Oswald?
OSWALD: No, thanks. I think I will go out for a bit.
MRS. ALVING: Yes, do. The weather is clearing a little. (*she shuts the dining room door, then goes to the hall door and calls*) Regina!
REGINA: Yes, ma'am.

These four opening speeches of Act II are together a dramatic action and might be labeled "keeping track of the children." The rite of The Policy Conference continues:

"seeking a solution"
MANDERS: I suppose he can't hear us?
MRS. A.: Not when the door is shut. Besides, he is going out.
MANDERS: I am still quite bewildered. I don't know how I managed to swallow a mouthful of your excellent dinner.
MRS. A.: (*walking up and down, and trying to control her agitation*) Nor I. But what are we to do?

MANDERS: Yes, what are we to do? Upon my word I don't know; I am so completely unaccustomed to things of this kind.

MRS. A.: I am convinced that nothing serious has happened yet.

MANDERS: Heaven forbid! But it is most unseemly behavior, for all that.

MRS. A.: It is nothing more than a foolish jest of Oswald's, you may be sure.

MANDERS: Well, of course, as I said, I am quite inexperienced in such matters; but it certainly seems to me——

Here Manders is interrupted by Mrs. Alving, thus the dramatic action of "seeking a solution" comes to an end, but the rite of The Policy Conference continues:

"making the decision"

MRS. A.: Out of the house she shall go——and at once. That part of it is as clear as daylight.

MANDERS: Yes, that is quite clear.

These two speeches go to make up the dramatic action of "making the decision."

"examining the decision"

MRS. A.: But where is she to go? We should not be justified in——

MANDERS: Where to? Home to her father, of course.

MRS. A.: To whom, did you say?

MANDERS: To her—— No, of course Engstrand isn't——

The fourth dramatic action of the rite of The Policy Conference ends abruptly in the middle of Manders' speech, as he changes the subject and goes into the new dramatic action, "doubting the facts."

MANDERS: But, great heavens, Mrs. Alving, how is such a thing possible? You surely may have been mistaken, in spite of everything.

In her reply to the doubting Manders, Mrs. Alving moves into the sixth dramatic action, "convincing the doubter."

MRS. A.: There was no chance of mistake, more's the pity. Joanna was obliged to confess it to me——and my husband couldn't deny it. So there was nothing else to do but to hush it up.

As these examples demonstrate, a dramatic action continues as long as the subject of the dialogue or the physical action of the scene remains constant. Breaking a play down first of all into the rites, then into the dramatic actions within the rite, allows a director to follow every twist and turn of the plot as well as to have the central theme of the segment constantly before him in the rite. When the director has conditioned himself to look for and find, beneath the contrived informality and the conventions of modern drama, the rite upon which the scene is based, he will find that he is automatically thinking in theatrical terms. The very word "rite" implies and demands some sort of staging and once the rite is discovered and named it becomes impossible to think of it without thinking in terms of the staging it will take.

Roles

The concept of a character within a play acting a role is found from Shakespeare to the present. T. S. Eliot has referred to Cyrano as a man who is watching himself act and points to the parallel found in Shakespeare:

The really fine rhetoric of Shakespeare occurs in situations where a character in the play *sees himself* in a dramatic light . . . Is not Cyrano exactly in this position of contemplating himself as a romantic, a dramatic figure? This dramatic sense on the part of the characters themselves is rare in modern drama . . . in plays of realism we often find parts which are never allowed to be consciously dramatic for fear, perhaps, of their appearing less real. But in actual life, in many of those situations in actual life which we enjoy consciously and keenly, we are at times aware of ourselves in this way, and these moments are of very great usefulness to dramatic verse. A very small part of acting is that which takes place on the stage. Rostand had—whether he had anything else or not—this dramatic sense, and it is what gives life to Cyrano. It is sense which is almost a sense of humor (for when anyone is conscious of himself as acting, something like a sense of humor is present). It gives Rostand's characters, Cyrano at least, a gusto which is uncommon on the modern stage.[40]

Eric Bentley also chooses Cyrano as the character who sees himself acting. "He lives for beauty as an idea. As to the actual possession of it, he will realize that Christian has a prior claim. Yet he assigns to himself a role of more intelligence, talent, and heroism. And he plays it—plays it *as a role* to the very end."[41]

If we assume that the sense of a character seeing himself in a dramatic light is not as rare in the modern drama as Eliot would have us believe, but that the roles are, as are the rites, simply more informal than those assumed by Cyrano's flamboyant Cadets of Gascoyne, then we will have the basis for the rite-role analysis.

Types of Roles

But one does not have to be conscious of his role in order to play it. In life we are continually meeting the person who is so lost within his role that he, in effect, is that role and none other: the businessman to whom life has become simply a business; the school teacher who is always in front of her third-grade class; the minister who makes a point out of ministering; the beautiful girl, or more pathetic, the faded beauty who still plays "beautiful girl." The unconscious role-player in the theater is that character who is so lost within his role that he becomes either a comic or a pathetic character. He often bears the brunt of the playwright's humor simply because he does not know he is play-acting.

Pastor Manders in Ibsen's *Ghosts* does not realize that he is pushing his role of minister into the absurd when he states that, "It is no longer your businessman and adviser, no longer your old friend and your dead husband's old friend, that stands before you now. It is your priest that stands before you just as he did once at the most critical moment of your life." He has been the priest from beginning to end and he can act no other role. Even as businessman, he played the priest by recommending no insurance on the home.

Staying with Ibsen, George Tesman, the husband in *Hedda Gabler,* is quite another kind of unconscious role-player. Here there is a pathetic quality about the unimaginative bookworm married to the equally unimaginative, beautiful, sophisticated decadent. Gregers Werls in *The Wild Duck* and Malvolio in *Twelfth Night* are two other examples of the unconscious role-player. Whether we snicker, laugh aloud, or smile sadly at the unconscious role-player will be dependent upon the type of rite in which the playwright has placed him.

It is not, however, the inability to change his role that is the deciding factor in labeling an unconscious role-player, rather it is his inability to see himself in a dramatic light.

The unconscious role-player is incapable of seeing life as a drama, hence he is incapable of seeing himself acting, and thus is always without that quality which Eliot likened to a sense of humor. Willy Loman, in Miller's *Death of a Salesman*, never sees himself as an actor playing salesman. His failure to see what the role is—the "man way out there in the blue, riding on a smile and a shoeshine," as Charlie puts it—is a great part of his tragedy. A sense of seeing himself in a dramatic light would have made Willy a much more successful salesman and, in passing, destroyed the play.

Many characters found in the modern drama appear to have flashes of seeing themselves as actors acting. Just as Eliot points out, "in many of those situations in actual life which we enjoy consciously and keenly, we are at times aware of ourselves in this way."[42] Generally, such characters will have an undercurrent throughout the drama in which we sense that just below the surface they are aware of what they are doing, that is, they are aware that they are acting. These semi-conscious role-players lack the theatrical possibilities that the fully conscious role-player possesses, but they carry within themselves a greater spark than is often realized in performance. Such a character, because he does not have the insight into his own life to see clearly that he is role-playing, is apt to take himself and his role a little too seriously. In life we meet the bright young executive or the agency man on his way up, or very often the young actor or theater major who pushes his role until he becomes obnoxious. "Hap," in Miller's *Death of a Salesman*, is such a character. He plays the role of playboy, but it is hard work, and though just below the surface he knows it, still, he cannot admit that his role is an unreal one.[43] Nora, in Ibsen's *Doll's House*, is another excellent example of playing but not quite admitting to herself that she is role-playing. The Captain in Strindberg's *The Father* is another interesting example of this type of character. He drops into the role of officer and husband, almost without knowing it, but has flashes of himself as an actor. Some of his greatest lines come as, for an instant, he sees himself acting and paraphrases the "hath not a Jew eyes" speech, or, in the final scene, as he lies helpless in the straight jacket:

Take away this cat that's lying on me. Take it away! (NURSE *removes the shawl and puts the pillow under his head*) Bring my uniform. Put my tunic over me. (*The* NURSE *takes the tunic from a peg and spreads it over him. To* LAURA) Ah, my tough lion's-skin that you would take from me! Omphale! Omphale! You cunning woman, lover of peace and contriver of disarmament. Wake, Hercules, before they take away your club! You would trick us out of our armour, calling it tinsel. It was iron, I tell you, before it became tinsel. In the old days the smith forged the soldier's coat, now it is made by the needlewoman. Omphale! Omphale! Rude strength has fallen before treacherous weakness. Shame on you, woman of Satan, and a curse on all your sex! . . .[44]

It is the conscious role-player, however, that usurps most of the great roles in dramatic literature. The character who knows what he is doing all the time, who seems to stand outside himself and watch himself act a series of roles, usually, as Eliot suggested, with the ability to laugh at his own role-playing but playing with a relish nonetheless: Hamlet playing his madness, Cyrano playing the romantic hero to the hilt, yet watching another climb the balcony to collect the reward; Cleopatra setting the scene and costuming herself for her last performance; Shakespeare's fools, standing within and without the situation at the same time, but always playing the fool. Tennessee Williams shows us the conscious role-player in his aging beauties and his hard-working degenerates. Strindberg almost always has a character in his dramas who is born, even as Strindberg said of himself, "without a film over the eyes" and who, in his most lucid moments, compares himself to an actor on the stage. The French theater abounds in such characters as does the work of George Bernard Shaw. Christy, in *Playboy of the Western World,* is a great role because he is playing for his onstage audience.

In life or on stage, a character who knows he is playing, a person who does not take himself in dead seriousness all the time, gains our respect. On the other hand, he receives our laughter or our pity—in many cases a little of both—when he does not "see himself in a dramatic light." Biff sums up Willy in the final scene of *Salesman:* "The man didn't know who he was." Morell, in Shaw's *Candida,* is not the distasteful character he might well be because, to a degree, he sees himself as the poet sees him and recognizes his role as such. Doolittle, in *Pygmalion* or in *My Fair Lady,* is such a delightful character because he so enjoys his role and plays it with such relish. Engstrand in *Ghosts,* the fantastic Ulric Brendel in *Rosmersholm,* and many of the characters in *Peer Gynt* are such "plums" because they see and enjoy their own acting. A character, then, becomes a conscious role-player in direct proportion to the degree that he sees himself as acting for his onstage audience.

The unconscious role-player is nearly always defeated, tricked, fooled, and often humiliated by the conscious role-player. Engstrand is able to wrap Manders around his finger, without Manders being in the least aware of what is happening, primarily because Engstrand knows he is acting

while Manders is lost in his role of "helpful priest." The
women in Shaw's plays often are able to befuddle the men
because the women know they are playing the pursuer
rather than the pursued.

The fourth and last classification of role-players is the
single role-player, that character who is seen only in the
pursuit of his work: the servant, the cook, or the characters
in the background scenes. While it is doubtlessly true that
these characters live a full life within the confines of their
homes, we, as a result of the playwright's decision, are
interested in them only in the single roles their jobs assign
them. It is as Strindberg says in his foreword to *Miss Julie:*
"If these minor characters seem abstract to some people,
this is due to the fact that ordinary people are to a certain
extent without individuality, showing, while working, only
one side of themselves. And as long as the spectator does not
feel a need to see them from other sides, there is nothing
wrong with my abstract presentation."[45] The Flabby Gentleman and The Thin Gentleman in *The Wild Duck* are
single role-players, as are such characters as The Old
Gentleman and the Logician in Ionesco's *Rhinoceros.*

Viewing a character as a single role-player can often
simplify things for the director and the actor, for while deep
character studies and detailed psychological motivations for
actions are fine in their place, the maid's real task is to get
the tea things off in order that the table can be used to
spread out the stolen plans later in the scene.

These then are the types of role-players one will meet in
the drama: the *single role-player,* that person who, via the
playwright's intent, exhibits only one facet of his personality; the *unconscious role-player,* that character who cannot
see himself in a dramatic light and hence can never realize

that he is playing a role in the comedy of life; the *semi-conscious role-player*, that character who has flashes of himself playing, but cannot for any length of time see himself in a dramatic light; the *conscious role-player*, that character who knows he is playing, who sees life as a drama, and usually takes great pride in his own performance.

Just as the length of the overall rite and the dramatic action within that rite will vary, so may the period of time a role is maintained by a character vary. The role may change consciously or completely unconsciously; just as in life we change our roles to fit the rite in progress, so on the stage the character may make a conscious shift in his thinking and playing, or he may fall automatically into the new role demanded by the shifting conditions. A character may drop into and out of a role in a few seconds, or may maintain a basic role throughout the drama. Often a character is required to change into a new role almost before the audience has recognized the old. Labeling the changes will be a great help to the actor in such sudden transitions.

An interesting example of such a quick shift of roles is found in the final speech of Madam Helseth, the housekeeper, in Ibsen's *Rosmersholm*. Madam Helseth enters expecting to find Rebecca prepared to leave. She is, at the entrance, in her familiar role of "servant," yet this is not the simple single role-player who will announce: "The carriage awaits, M'lady." The "servant" is the head housekeeper, and she believes that she is about to bid her last farewell to Rebecca. But Rebecca's position in the house is not an easy one to define, especially from Madam Helseth's viewpoint, since Rebecca West came as a sort of lower-class companion to the ill Beata. Rebecca speaks of the friendship between herself and the housekeeper, and certainly Madam Helseth

is more than a simple servant taking orders from Miss West.
The housekeeper enters in the role of servant, but the
servant who will bid her final farewell to a friend who is
only half a step above her. From a moral viewpoint, Madam
Helseth cannot help putting herself above Rebecca, for she
believes her to be carrying Rosmer's child. Yet Rebecca is
not, the housekeeper feels, really to blame, for she says, "I
don't see that there is much to be said against you. It's not
easy for a lone woman to be always on her guard, that's
certain.——We're all of us human, Miss West." The "servant and friend" has determined to be as helpful as possible
to the fallen woman while registering at least mild disap-
proval of the master's supposed actions. The moment
Madam Helseth notices the room to be empty she drops her
role of "servant and friend" and becomes "righteous
woman" while she attempts to spy upon her employer. When
she sees "that white thing there" (the white horses, or the
white shawl Ibsen has been so careful to plant), she becomes "frightened woman."

"servant"

MADAM HELSETH: Miss West——the carriage is——(*Looks
around*)
"righteous woman"
Not here? Out together at this time of
night? Well——I must say——! H'm!
(*Goes to hall, looks around, and comes in
again*)
Ah, well well. (*Goes to window and looks
out*)
"frightened woman"
Oh good God! That white thing there——!
My soul! They're both of them out on the
bridge! God forgive the sinful creatures

————if they're not in each other's arms!
(*Shrieks aloud*) Oh—down—both of
them! Into the mill race! Help! Help! (*Her
knees tremble; she holds on to the chair
back, shaking all over; she can scarcely
get the words out*) No. No help here——
the dead wife has taken them.

In Madam Helseth's short appearance on the stage, she
must wind up one of the greatest of the modern tragedies.
Within a very short space of time, the actress must play
three fairly complicated roles, the first conscious, the last
two unconscious, and each role must be clear-cut if the
audience is to follow the playwright's intent and catch,
through the eyes of the frightened woman, the chill of the
supernatural.

When the director knows what type of role-player he is
dealing with, he will have the key to his approach to the
actor playing the role. To be able to talk with an actor about
the character in acting terms, rather than in psychological
or literary terms, is to meet him on his ground. Inability to
identify the type of role-player often makes for dull, plod-
ding performances that fail to catch the imagination of
either actor or audience. Seeing the characters as role-
players, in well defined rites, gives a dramatic flair to the
scene. With our modern "realistic" drama, and our "realistic" acting methods, we are often unable to see the dramatic
in the theater, let alone in life.

Rite-Role Applied

By breaking a play down into well-defined rites, the
director knows precisely what it is he is attempting to stage.
When the rites are broken down into the dramatic actions,

each nuance of the plot and line can be seen in its proper perspective, that is, as a part of some ceremony in progress at a particular time. Finally, when a role is assigned first of all to each rite and then, if necessary, to each dramatic action, the play is laid open for inspection. When the interaction between the rite and the role is examined in detail, the director has a key to the structure and the meaning intended by the playwright, as well as to his basic approach to the actors. Such a breakdown brings to the eye contrasts and parallels that may well escape the harried director until too late in the rehearsal period.

The director who can master the rite-role technique of play analysis will find that rather than becoming tied up in useless terminology, he is thinking in terms of what staging the play will take. The great advantage to such an approach is that it allows the director to think as a director. He is never faced with the problem so often met after an exhaustive literary analysis: "Fine, that's great, but how do you go about staging it?" A rite is a staged ceremony, a role is that which is acted, and with such an analysis the director is off and running instead of being bogged down with interesting but unstageable symbols.

A second advantage of such a method is that the director can think, as he must, in very general terms about the drama but at the same time this method presents him with a detailed, line by line breakdown. He can think, for example, of *Ghosts* as a play in which the central character is attempting to escape from a role, but which demonstrates at the final curtain that the escape is impossible. He may classify a particular play as an attempt to maintain a role, an attempt to bring oneself into harmony with a role or the existing rites. He will, once he becomes familiar with the technique, classify the play under some such heading, and by his heading know which aspects of the play will need pointing and which will stand alone.

A quick look at *A Doll's House* will reveal that one of the most difficult aspects of the play is the lack of variety in the role-playing of Nora. The fact is that Nora stays remarkably close to the role of doll-child throughout the drama. The actress who does not understand the difficulty inherent in this role is bound to become tiring before the evening is over. Only in the final scene, the rite of Family Conference, often referred to as the "settling of accounts scene," does Nora leave her almost too cute role of doll-child. Then suddenly, much too suddenly for many contemporary actresses who have attempted her, she becomes the "emancipated woman."

A rite-role analysis of *A Doll's House* suggests that the role of Nora is going to have to find its variety within the doll-child realm. The variations between doll-child, doll-wife, doll-mother, and doll-flirt must be marked. The analysis also suggests that the final scene must be played as a struggle within Nora herself, a struggle to give up the warm and comfortable role of doll-wife, rather than a struggle between a suddenly liberated woman and a dull, stodgy husband. Certainly, a rite-role breakdown of *A Doll's House* will convince any but the most stubborn that Nora is far from the "little innocent" she plays. Seen as a semiconscious role-player who suddenly sees herself and her playing, not in a dramatic, but in a cold, hard light of reality, this old-fashioned drama takes on new meaning and new life. The director will begin to see the connection between the role and rite when he notices that all the rites, except those with Krogstad, are controlled by Nora's role. She dominates the rites by making them conform to her role.

Rather than a timid little squirrel, Nora becomes a strong role-player. A rite-role analysis of *A Doll's House* may well add another play to the "must do sometime" list. Especially if it has never been seriously considered "because after all, women have their rights now."

Having discussed the difficulties of play selection and play analysis, let us try a practical application of the methods and techniques discussed above.

We are going to find, study, and analyze a play for a group of college students primarily at the junior and senior level. Most of the people we will be using have had a fair amount of college experience, and we are familiar with what they can and cannot do. Our budget is in fair shape so number of settings, costumes, and the like will not be a problem as long as some caution and common sense are used. As the director, I have chosen my playwright, but not yet my play. I have decided that this is the year for an Ibsen drama. Now, which one will best suit our needs?

When one thinks of Ibsen one thinks of either *Ghosts* or *A Doll's House*. These two plays are most apt to be found in the anthologies, and both are landmarks in theatrical history. *Ghosts* is a five-character tragedy built around a middle-aged woman. Supposing that we choose *Ghosts*, Mrs. Alving will be the big casting problem although Manders will not be simple. But a five-character drama for the major production? We should be able to do better than that. Let's save *Ghosts* for a studio production. *A Doll's House?* The cast list calls for eleven; Helmer, Nora, Doctor Rank, Mrs. Linde, Nils Krogstad, Helmer's three young children, Anne, the nurse, a housemaid, and a porter. The three children might be a problem, though one can always come up with

three children if necessary. No, an examination of the play
will demonstrate that again we are speaking of five main
characters, the same as with *Ghosts,* three men, and two
women. Nora will be easier to cast for age than will Mrs.
Alving but the difficulties of the role are certainly not
smaller. We will throw out *A Doll's House* on the same
grounds as *Ghosts;* we should be able to do better in number
of characters. *Rosmersholm?* Once again, a small cast and
again a big problem of age. Believable middle age is often
most difficult for college actors, though certainly here are
some of Ibsen's greatest creations. *The League of Youth?*
No small-cast problem here and lots of different types. Yet
The League has never struck me as a very good Ibsen play.
The dialogue, even allowing for the awkwardness of the
Archer translation, seems forced. *The League* lacks diction;
Ibsen here was struggling for a nonpoetic form. I can't feel
that he found it. Then too, *The League* seems more "foreign" and more "dated" than do most of Ibsen's social or
psychological dramas. No, the director is not happy with
The League; he doesn't feel the urge to direct it, so out it
goes.

The Wild Duck

What about *The Wild Duck?* Here is a play that has always
had a great appeal. Cast? Eight principals, seven minor
roles, and as many extras or as few as we want in the first
act. Budget? The show calls for two sets. Costumes will help
the show and should be used. The budget can take it and

now that the director has thought of *Wild Duck*, he begins
to get a little excited about doing it. It is a good play . . .
a great play . . . it is certainly challenging and exciting.
Casting Hialmar will be the problem. Hialmar must be a
talented actor and he must be intelligent enough to see what
Ibsen is doing with this character. He will be tough to cast,
but I think we can find him. Hedvid, a girl of fourteen
. . . yes, we can find a college girl to play the role. In fact,
we will need a girl older than fourteen, one who can already
understand what Hedvid is, in truth, reaching for. Yes, we
can cast it reasonably well. We can afford it and the director
wants to direct the play. Now before we rush off half-cocked
over the idea of producing *The Wild Duck*, let's check our
own feeling of excitement against Aristotle's calmer judgment. A synopsis will give us a place to begin. We will then
take a brief look at the plot, character, thought, diction,
melody, and spectacle, as well as the beginning, middle, and
end.

Synopsis

The play is centered around the Ekdal family. Prior to
the opening curtain the grandfather, Old Ekdal, has run
afoul of the law. Knowingly or unknowingly (the point is
never clarified), Old Ekdal used fraudulent, or at least inac-
curate, maps and as a result headed an operation that cut
government timber illegally. The ensuing trial found Lieutenant Ekdal guilty but Werle, his partner, innocent. Ekdal
went to prison and Werle went on to become a most successful "merchant, manufacturer, etc." Either as the result of a
guilty conscience, as his son believes, or from simple Christian charity, as Hialmar seems to believe, Werle has been a

generous benefactor to his ex-partner's family. It is Werle who has suggested a business to Hialmar, has advanced the money to set him up in business, and has even introduced Hialmar to Gina and made it possible for them to marry. During the action we learn that Werle has "had his way" with Gina before Hialmar married her. Whether or not he was circumventing a paternity charge by making the marriage possible is never settled. Gregers, Werle's son, obviously believes Hedvid, the baby born within a year of the marriage, to be his half-sister. The weakness of Hedvig's eyes, coupled with the coming blindness of old Werle, is, to say the least, rather damning circumstantial evidence.

The play opens as the guests are leaving the well-spread table of the elder Werle, who is giving a dinner party in honor of Gregers' return from the seventeen-year stay at "the works." Gregers, who, as a result of his mother's influence, has always distrusted his father, becomes suspicious of Werle's many kindnesses to the Ekdal family and resolves to find out whether or not his suspicions are founded in fact. After a perfunctory investigation, Gregers satisfies himself that his suspicions are correct and immediately casts himself as the savior, or as he phrases it, "an amazingly clever dog; one that goes to the bottom after wild ducks when they dive and bite themselves fast in the tangle and seaweed, down among the ooze." Gregers now sees his mission in life: to make a true marriage out of the ill-fated union of his boyhood friend, Hialmar Ekdal. Much to his amazement and his disgust, Gregers finds that the Ekdals are quite happy in their degraded life. They have completely adjusted to their circumstances. With the help of an old garret, which houses poultry, rabbits, discarded Christmas trees, and one wild duck, Old Ekdal has managed to forget the "cool sweeping breezes, the free life in the woods out on the uplands, among beasts and birds." Hialmar, a shining light in his college days, has found refuge in the dreams of a wonderful invention that will revolutionize the art of photography. Hedvig, the daughter, who has never known any other life, is quite happy dreaming in the garret and helping her mother around the house. Gina, the wife and mother, is much too busy to dream, as the responsibilities of both the household work and the business fall on her.

It is the down-at-the-heels Doctor Relling who has inspired the "life illusion" for Hialmar. He has done the same for his own roommate, Molvik, a defrocked priest. Relling attempts to head off the light-bringing, illusion-shattering efforts of Gregers, but in spite of his protests, Gregers blunders ahead with his plan and informs Hialmar of his wife's former relationship with Werle. When Werle unfortunately chooses this particular moment to send Hedvig a birthday gift of a handsome settlement, Hialmar sees the possibilities of Hedvig's illegitimacy and disowns his sensitive daughter. The fact that Hialmar uses the knowledge as an excuse for a magnificent melodramatic scene is lost on the child and she is badly shaken. We have been forewarned by Relling that Hedvig is passing through a difficult physical stage—"Her constitution's changing, sir."—and that she must be treated "cautiously." Notwithstanding the warning, Gregers suggests that the child prove her love for her father with a blood sacrifice: she must kill the wild duck. When her father again disowns her, she takes his pistol and slips into the garret. As Hialmar is enjoying a melodramatic scene explaining how foolish he has been to ever imagine that Hedvig loved him, a shot is heard from the garret.

Hedvig has placed the muzzle of the gun to her own breast, thus making the blood sacrifice Gregers had suggested to her. The reformer is terrified, but attempts to seek some self-comfort by noting that Hedvig's death has ennobled Hialmar. Relling shatters this ray of hope with his cynical remark that "Most people are ennobled by the actual presence of death," and his all too accurate prophecy: "Before a year is over, little Hedvig will be nothing to him but a pretty theme for declamation."

The Wild Duck and Aristotle's *Theory of Criticism*

So much for the synopsis. Now to see if *The Wild Duck* will hold up when it is measured against Aristotle's standards. The purpose of using Aristotle is only to check our own enthusiasm for the play, it is not to find out what the play is about or how we will go about staging it.

First is the Plot, Aristotle's "soul" of the tragedy, centered in the Ekdal family. The conflict that gives rise to the action is Gregers' attempt to rectify what he believes is an untruthful marriage. The basic plot itself, then, is one of a do-gooder who brings disaster to those he is attempting to aid. The Peripety is, as Aristotle recommended, tied closely to the Discovery, or in this case the alleged discovery, as we are never positive where the truth lies. Gregers informs Hialmar of Gina's former connections with his father, old Werle, but instead of using the knowledge to establish a "true marriage" and "a communion founded on truth, and free from all taint of deception," as Gregers naïvely believes he will, Hialmar denies his child, thus setting the stage for the tragedy to follow. While it may seem at the first reading to be submerged in symbolism, the plot is actually clear-cut, strong, and easy to follow.

Second on Aristotle's list is Character: "that which reveals the moral purpose of the agents." All the characters are drawn with a bold hand, but notice that Ibsen has reversed the usual character traits in the mind of the audience. The truth-teller, assuming that Gregers is correct in his assumptions, is responsible for the tragedy, while the illusion-maker—the lie-teller—is the only sensible and admirable male in the cast. Though the characters' lines are strong and difficult to miss, it is remarkable how often they are misinterpreted, probably because of the Ibsen image that often goes with his plays. All too often Hialmar has been played as if Gregers' view of him is the correct view, rather than Relling's view. The moral purpose is revealed through the characters themselves. We are still on firm ground with *The Wild Duck*.

Third on Aristotle's list is Thought. Ibsen uses his "power of saying whatever can be said or what is appropriate to the occasion" most directly with Relling; it is he who makes the specific application of the thought of the play, and it is he who generalizes from that specific. Always the thought is one of the most interesting elements in an Ibsen drama. In *The Wild Duck* it might be stated thus: "Is the truth, or the supposed truth, helpful, or does mankind need the lie in order to live?" In *The Wild Duck* the answer is fairly obvious: mankind needs the lie if he is to find any happiness in life.

Diction is number four on our list: "the expression of their thought in words." The diction in *The Wild Duck* is excellent. The actability may range from fair to excellent depending on the translation the director chooses, but even in a stilted translation the diction is precise and revealing. Everything comes to the audience via the diction and the added action. But more important, everything comes to the director and the actor via the diction. All the characters speak always in character; there is no possibility of confusing one of Gregers' speeches with one of Hialmar's; even when Hialmar is quoting Gregers, the flavor is all Hialmar's. Each character bares his soul, or in Hialmar's case, his lack of one, in his diction. Hialmar is revealed for what he is even in these simple lines: "Well, stout is scarcely the word; but I daresay I look a little more of a man than I used to"; "I should not call them curls exactly; I should rather say locks." Perhaps it is with Hedvig that Ibsen demonstrates his genius for character and diction. Her line, after Gregers has first introduced the symbolism of the dog diving down into the weeds and ooze for the wild duck, "Do you know, Mother—I think he meant something quite different by that," is beautifully contrasted with her father's reaction to the departing guest, "Ah, now one can get a mouthful of food at last."

Number five, Melody, we can pass over quickly, though music does appear in the play, and Ibsen's directions concerning Hialmar's rendition of his flute solo are important: *"pipes up vigorously and plays a Bohemian peasant dance, but in a slow plaintive tempo, and with sentimental expression."*

The final element on Aristotle's list, Spectacle, becomes very important in *The Wild Duck*. Even if spectacle is limited to scenery rather than, as suggested earlier, encompassing the entire visual aspect of the play, it occupies an important place in the production of *The Wild Duck*. The impression of the family that the audience carries from the theater will, in some respects, be dependent upon their impression of the garret. Certainly the moonlight lighting, as opposed to the hard light of day, will demand two different reactions to this odd extension of an upper apartment.

A cursory examination of the elements necessary to a good play would seem to bear out the decision to do *The Wild Duck*. At least all the elements are there and all are handled well by the playwright. What about the construction? Probably no writer since Aristotle has understood play construction as well as Henrik Ibsen. Out of the past come the catalysts that throw the family into tragedy. The beginning brings the two together, the revelation by Gregers is made in the middle, and that revelation brings about the end. The play moves always forward, and at the moment when Hialmar is willing to forgive and forget, the shot announces that the sacrifice has been made. Such a brief examination is enough to demonstrate that Aristotle can be useful and a closer examination will demonstrate even to the most sceptical that *The Wild Duck* is an extremely well-written, well-constructed play.

We can go ahead and take the next step, that of classification. Is *The Wild Duck* melodrama, comedy, tragedy, or farce? Classifying this Ibsen drama becomes a bit of a problem. Ibsen calls it a tragicomedy[46] and once wrote an actor,[47] after watching his interpretation, that the word "tragi" was as important as the word "comedy." Certainly the two intermingle and become almost inseparable. Moreover, as if this intermingling were not sufficient in itself, one soon finds that the entire play has been sprinkled liberally with elements of both farce and melodrama. Perhaps a look at the play's history and the critical opinion of a few "Ibsen experts" will aid in classifying this play which Ibsen himself describes as occupying "a position by itself among my dramatic works; in its method it differs in several respects from my former ones."[48]

The Wild Duck Classified

The play appeared in 1884 following *An Enemy of the People,* as *Enemy* had followed *Ghosts,* which in turn had followed *A Doll's House.* It is not necessary to be an authority on Ibsen to direct one of his plays, but the director who is tackling an Ibsen production will be a better director if he is familiar with the plays immediately preceding the one about to be directed. Ibsen himself is often quoted as saying, "All of my plays are a part of only one work." *The Wild Duck* is related to *Ghosts* in the interest in physical defects that plague the children, but it is much more closely related to *An Enemy of the People.* In *Enemy,* Stockman, the tubby, beef-eating, toddy-drinking reformer is the comic hero of the drama. The reformer who is stoned for his complete lack of political skill, who cannot make the public listen to the truth, is still the most admirable and lovable character in the drama. There can be little doubt that it is with Stockman that Ibsen wants us to identify, even if he does want us to laugh at him at the same time. The playwright has been very careful in *Enemy* to make sure that the "bad guys" are so bad that even though we do have to laugh loudly at the Don Quixote charging his windmills we must identify with him because opposed to him are only money-grabbing crooks and oily politicians. In *The Wild Duck,* the most despicable character we meet is the most sincere. The truth-bringer is the villain and though marshaled against him we have drunkards, fakers, lechers, and to be sure, one hard-working mother and one sensitive child, we feel more at home with the inhabitants of the world of the wild duck than we do with the sickly idealist Gregers. Then it would seem that an important, perhaps the most important, point in the drama is the necessity of the lie. When the drama was first presented it was met with puzzled frowns and worried expressions. Was the leader of the realistic drama lost in his own mass of twisted symbols? Or even worse, had the truth-seeker become the apostate, and was he denying his own teachings? Now most critics will agree that he was taking a broader and deeper look at the human comedy than he had done in *An Enemy of the People.* In *The Wild Duck,* Ibsen's view of people has softened a little; it is a warmer, more humane, understanding view. He is not only caught up with, he is in love with, the inhabitants of the photo shop. He is also taking a greater interest in the borderline cases. In fact, Gregers has been called Ibsen's first study in a pathological person. However, though Gregers may be, and I believe is, over the borderline as a result of his mother fixation, and though little Hedvig is one of Ibsen's softest characters, still it is the figure of Hialmar that dominates the play and makes it necessary for the director to lay the stress, not equally as the playwright had suggested, but more heavily on the comic side of the drama. Ah, but we have Ibsen's own words that the "tragi" is as important as the "comedy." True, but we have different circumstances within which to present the play than did the original producers. Perhaps the largest factor to overcome in the presentation of Ibsen is the stern, bearded face that glares from the dust jacket of too many of his books. In the United States today we think of the old Norwegian as lacking a sense of humor. He has been anthologized and martyrized on the cross of "good literature," hence he can't possibly be interesting or funny. A good many people have read *An Enemy of the People* as a serious drama of the individual against an insane society. Most have read both *A Doll's House* and *Ghosts* without seeing the humor in Nora or in Manders, and I remember getting what amounted to threatening letters when I once advertised *Peer Gynt* as a "rollicking comedy." Perhaps we need look no further than the play itself to find which way the piece should be played. Dr. Relling reminds us that most people are ennobled in the presence of death, and with that in mind we can let the tragedy take care of itself; the playwright has put it there and it can't be missed. But the comedy? It is all too possible to play Hialmar as a frustrated artist, and all too difficult not to see Old Ekdal as a pitiful old man, rather than a ludicrous furtive drunkard.

We will then think of *The Wild Duck* as a tragicomedy, but it is the comedy in Hialmar that we will stress, and it is as a besotted, dirty old man that we will think of Old Ekdal. We are now ready to analyze the play in terms of the rite-role approach. Whenever the analysis stalls or doesn't know which way to turn we will consult the critics, but we will not use them to back up what seems to be a good theatrical interpretation. The point of the following analysis is to direct a production, not to contribute to the mass of critical material already available.

Roles and Rites in *The Wild Duck*

It is difficult to read *The Wild Duck* without becoming at least aware of the fact that Ibsen is using symbols, and while one early critic, Storm Jameson, writes of the play's symbols being so irritating that she believes Ibsen to be ridiculing symbolism itself, an age accustomed to Eliot, Joyce, Ionesco, and Albee will hardly find the symbolism in *The Wild Duck* difficult. Ibsen is always very careful about his stage symbols—those actually seen on the stage—and is usually very explicit about his literary symbols. For our purposes in this analysis let us treat them when, where, and if, they seem to be a problem.

The Wild Duck might well be called the play of the satisfied role-players for it is, from one point of view, a story in which all but the newcomers have found, and are fully satisfied with, their role in life.

In stage terms, the play, and the characters who live therein, might be compared to a third-rate theatrical stock company. The director is Dr. Relling, a broken-down man of medicine, who moves in and out, keeping the production he has cast running smoothly while he not only ministers to the needs of his company but satisfies and, for the most part, justifies his own role and his own reason for being. It is Relling who has suggested that a man of Hialmar's stature and intellect must surely be the man to elevate photography to an art through a method he is sure Hialmar is capable of inventing. It is Relling who has encouraged Old Ekdal to continue in his role of sportsman, encouraged Hedvig to idolize her father and to live in the world of the wild duck, and finally has invented the life-saving illness for the drunken, defrocked clergyman, Molvik. Relling, as a director of psychodrama, has cast each of his mediocre company in the role which best compensates for his primary deficiency. The doctor has a light touch on the strings of his puppets, and is sensitive enough to let the play run smoothly when his help is not needed. It is, as is so often the case for the director, the helpful friend or the blundering critic who throws the entire cast into confusion by misjudging Hialmar's talents and expecting much more than the poor "ham" is capable of delivering. The fact that Hialmar is a "ham" actor of the first order is apparent only to Relling and, until the death of Hedvig brings his bitterness to the surface for a moment, he finds the father's melodramatic scenes only amusing.

It almost appears as if Ibsen himself were seeing this play in terms of a stock company, for he has presented the public not with one major role-playing character, as he had done in *Peer Gynt* and *An Enemy of the People,* but with an entire company. Hialmar, the lead "ham"; Old Ekdal, the character man lost in his role of "character man"; Gregers, the second lead, the professional reformer with a flair for the melodramatic himself; Relling, the director; Molvik, the proud demonic; Old Werle, the "heavy"; Mrs. Sorby, the ex-leading lady now relegated to character parts; Gina, the mistress of all trades who simply does her work without comment; and Hedvig, the child protégé who delights in her role as "daddy's little girl."

The comic elements of the drama are centered in the almost too obvious role-playing of Hialmar, the too serious unconscious role-playing of Gregers and the childlike, dramatic (albeit rather disgusting and at times even revolting) play of Old Ekdal. The most grotesque bit of conscious role-playing is reserved for a minor character, Molvik. In the final scene, as the bereaved parents carry the dead child to her room, he mumbles in his drunken stupor, "Blessed be the Lord; to the earth thou shalt return; dust to dust——" Relling takes over quickly and whispers, "Hold your tongue, you fool; you're drunk."

most memorable evenings, and woe to them if all is not ready when the hostess arises from her place at the banquet. There is an air of tension hanging over even this opening scene. This is a special dinner party, the son has not been home for some seventeen years. He and the father have never gotten along well, and the arrangement with Mrs. Sorby is a ticklish one for a father to explain to a son with a mother fixation such as Gregers carries. Mrs. Sorby herself must have been a bit on edge preparing for this particular dinner party, for not only is she to convince the son that she is "right" for the father, she must also help sell the "tableau of filial affection"—not an easy position to be in. Hence it is that the old servant at least is a little more particular, just a little on edge. The same tension mars The After-Dinner Drink. The ceremony lacks the casual quality that such a rite in such a surrounding might be expected to have. Even the guests are not quite at ease: "I hope Mrs. Sorby mayn't play us a tune we don't like, one of these days." And Old Werle is concerned over the fact that there were thirteen at the table. Hialmar is aware that he is out of his element, and doesn't know what role is expected of him. Gregers, too, could hardly be called the life of the party. He is always suspicious of his father's motives, and as he was called back from the works, something must be up. He must be a little lost in the bright and gay atmosphere of the Werle dinner party after his "delightfully lonely time of it" at the works.

It is within the rite of The After-Dinner Drink that the rest of the act is seen. The friendly conversation between Gregers and Hialmar is played against this formal background. Even what might be a rite in itself under different circumstances, that is the father–son conference between Gregers and Werle, is subdued and quiet because of the rite in progress. Old Werle is quite at home within the rite, but

Gregers is not as comfortable as he had appeared to be when contrasted with the fish-out-of-water Hialmar. The director must bear in mind constantly that though vital information is to be revealed, the formal, clearly recognizable ceremony of The After-Dinner Drink is the framework. Since we are later to see the principals in quite different circumstances, the Ekdal home and the contrasts in personalities must be clearly marked. Hialmar will be "cock of the walk" at home, but strangely enough, Gregers will be just as uncomfortable in a different way as he was at the dinner party. When Gregers sits down at the Luncheon Party in Act III, he should appear as if he would be more comfortable at a formal banquet, yet would give, at a formal banquet, the impression that he would be easier at an informal dinner.

Some twenty-nine separate dramatic actions make up The After-Dinner Drink in Act I. Each director will have to title them for himself, but they will run something like the following: "giving instructions," "pleasant conversation," "commenting on the thirteenth guest," "reassuring old friend," "describing melancholy," "explaining wife and marriage," "being suspicious," "caring for loved one," "clever conversation," "making apologetic exit," "denying father," "instructing servants," "defending self," "bidding farewell," "checking up on servants," "invitation to perform," "accusing father," "defending self," "accusing father," "discussing mother," "offering proposition," "being suspicious of father," "revealing plans," "accusing father," "leaving house forever," and "contemptuously commenting." In each case the task is to name what is happening at that moment, what the playwright is saying. The actors' goals can be drawn from the dramatic actions and the rites.

In Act I then, an analysis will show sixteen scenes—

scenes meaning "French scenes," each scene lasting until the entrance or exit of a major character, thirty-three different dramatic actions but only two major rites: Preparing the Room and The After-Dinner Drink. We move from the grandeur of the dinner party, with its set ritual of adjourning to more comfortable surroundings for The After-Dinner Drink, to the cheap living room/photography studio of the Ekdal home. The glitter of the formal gown and the dress suits fades into the dull housecoat wrapper of an overworked middle-aged mother trying to account for the pennies spent for the simple, if high-caloried, food Hialmar demands. The After-Dinner Drink has become the rite of Waiting. The three hours at table have shrunken to a cold dinner, the banquet complete with coffee and maraschino and the after-dinner punch is seen in retrospect against the background of a little girl who believes she is "a little hungry too."

Just as he interrupted but did not change the rite of Preparing the Room in Act I, so Old Ekdal now interrupts but does not change the rite of Waiting in Act II. The rite of Waiting changes quickly and easily into Homecoming as the now "man of the world" makes an entrance that is in considerable contrast to the exit we watched in Act I. During the Homecoming ceremony, the actions flow through "greeting father," "discussing grandfather," "discussing triumph," "changing costumes," "hiding bitter disappointment," and "discussing important improvements." Homecoming changes into Family Conference, and that rite changes with Gregers' entrance to Entertaining the Guest. It is important to note that it is Hialmar who sets both the Homecoming and Family Conference rites, and it is around Hialmar that the rites turn. It is almost as if the ceremony is staged by the two women, with a little help from Old Ekdal, for Hialmar's enjoyment. And enjoy it he does. With his flair for the stereotype in melodrama, Hialmar is quick to catch the word or phrase that does not fit the rite in progress.

It is Gregers who dominates the remaining rites in Act II. Once he arrives, contrary to Hialmar's wishes it should be remembered, Hialmar is forced to drop his roles of "loving father" and "musician" and play the "humble host." While the photographer–inventor manages to sprinkle his host role liberally with variations of "proud father" and use the visit as an excuse to swig a bottle of beer and eat a slice or two of Gina's excellent bread with "plenty of butter on it, mind," still he is primarily concerned with keeping the rite of Entertaining the Guest flowing smoothly, while arousing his friend's sympathy and admiration for his valiant struggle against overwhelming odds. Even after his Leave-Taking, quite a contrast from Hialmar's exit in Act I, Gregers dominates the dramatic actions in the final rite of the act: Retiring for the Night.

The opening rite of Working, in Act III, might well be called a maimed rite.[49] Hialmar accomplishes nothing and finally, with his father's help, convinces himself that Hedvig can do the work while he runs off to the attic to play. Again we see the rite of Entertaining the Guest, but this time it is Hedvig who attempts to play the hostess while the guest shamelessly pumps both wife and daughter for information. It is during the latter part of this rite, in the scene between Hialmar and Gregers, that Hialmar is compared quite specifically to the wild duck. The weakness in the comparison is that Hialmar has never flown free and has never wanted to try. The maimed rite of the Luncheon Party follows, and we meet for the first time the other members of the cast. The Ekdal Luncheon Party is a formal affair for this environment, but when one recalls the lavish display of the Werle dinner party, the herring salad seems quite insignificant. In both formal parties it is the old grandfather who manages to upset the rite. In the opening act, his inopportune appearance is sufficient to cause discomfort to those familiar with his former association with Werle, but not enough to affect anyone but Hialmar, Gregers, Werle, and Mrs. Sorby. His truly memorable faux pas upsets only Molvik. Old Ekdal's entrance from the garret in the middle of the Luncheon Party, as he proudly displays the bloody rabbit skin, draws a mild reproach from the "sensitive" Hialmar: "And you've gone and skinned it without waiting for me——!" Molvik exits quickly and the strong-stomached Dr. Relling proposes a toast: "Let us drain a glass to the old hunter." The Luncheon Party is interrupted by the arrival of the "founder of the feast," and the Father-Son Conference that follows spurs the "impatient reformer" to action. In the final rite of Leave-Taking, the "impatient reformer" and the "old friend" leave the truncated Luncheon Party with a "concerned psychiatrist," a "concerned wife," and a "confused little girl" wondering what Gregers' "acute attack of integrity" portends.

In Act IV the familiar rite of Waiting is in progress and it is the father who is under discussion. Upon his return we again find the Family Conference, only this time the father, instead of playing "romantic father" or "bread winner," is working hard at numerous variations of the role of "husband." His "hurt husband," "angry husband," "noble husband," "misunderstood husband," and several others make the rite of Family Conference quite different from the other conferences we have seen. The Informal Call, initiated by Gregers, is in the best tradition of the social worker making a follow-up call. The Formal Call of Mrs. Sorby, which interrupts the Informal Call of Gregers, hints at a strange and rather difficult relationship (difficult from the director's viewpoint) between Relling and Mrs. Sorby, but it is the gift that Mrs. Sorby brings that allows Hialmar to add up the evidence and make his dramatic exit. Gregers sets the rite of Comforting the Child after Gina's exit to find Hialmar, and uses it to suggest the blood sacrifice to Hedvig. Hedvig, lost in her unconscious role of "hurt little girl," is in no condition to examine the idea sensibly, and tries valiantly to become "resolute daughter." But the effort is too much for her and she throws herself into her mother's arms as soon as the meddling reformer has left.

Act V opens with the firmly established rite of Waiting, and though the characters change, Gregers and Relling are actually continuing the rite of Waiting when Gina and Hedvig leave to straighten up the house. Once again Waiting turns into the rite of Homecoming, but what a difference from the other two we have witnessed. Instead of the triumphant entrance in Act II where Gina and Hedvig rush to help Hialmar with his coat and hat, Hialmar is now hatless, ". . . *he is unwashed, and his hair is disheveled and unkempt. His eyes are dull and heavy.*" Even so, Gina and Hedvig are ready to greet the man of the house as the lord and master, but Hialmar turns his back on the child. His first act is to announce his immediate departure. It is this cruel action of denying the child that adds a touch of pathos to what has been called one of the most humorous scenes in modern dramatic literature.[50] The final rite of Laying out the Body is a wonderful example of Ibsen's

bitter comedy in the middle of a tragic scene. The dirty old
grandfather mutters meaningless phrases and runs to his
make-believe world, where Hedvig's blood is still fresh.
Hialmar plays his most grotesque scene as he shouts to
heaven, "Why hast Thou done this thing to me?" The
drunken, defrocked priest mumbles his canting phrases, and
the terrified reformer attempts to find a moral hidden in the
tragic action of a hurt, confused little girl. Here is a scene to
test any director and any group of actors. The bitter, dark
laughter in this final tragic scene is the laughter of the gods
on Mount Olympus at the foolish performances of mankind.
Weigand, in his book *The Modern Ibsen,* a Freudian interpretation of Ibsen's social and psychological drama and
one that any director should read carefully before attempting Ibsen, says of this final scene: "For the last time all the
warped and maimed existences of this household are gath-
ered together to act an ensemble so shockingly grotesque
that the reader must be steeled with an Aristophanic sense
of the comic in order not to succumb to the ghastly aspect of
the performance."[51]

The rites in *The Wild Duck* become steadily less formal
as the play progresses: from the rich, perhaps ostentatious,
surroundings of the Werle home to the tawdry surroundings
of the Ekdal studio, the dinner party to the luncheon party
with its bloody rabbit skin, the triumphant homecoming to
the bleary-eyed morning-after hangover, each succeeding
family conference degenerates a bit more until finally we see
Hialmar trying to go while he wants to stay.

With the exception of Act I, where Hialmar is out of
his element, the rites are, for the most part, established
either by Hialmar or Gregers. In any case, Hialmar is quick
to see the melodramatic possibilities in whatever rite is

bit under the weather. It is in Act III, however, just before
we meet him, that we get our first hint of his real function,
when on two occasions Hialmar uses the doctor's name to
back up his own statements: ". . . and Dr. Relling thinks,
as I do myself, that father may be allowed to wear his
uniform again," and just a minute later, ". . . But I can't
be goaded to it; it's not a bit of good; Relling says so, too."
Relling himself enters in the role of "guest" and quickly
identifies himself and his friend as doctor and clergyman.
He drops into his usual role of "psychologist" almost immediately as he strengthens the demonic identity for his
companion. Relling loses no time in needling Gregers and
his claim of the ideal, but the needling is done in a good-
natured manner, for he is still consciously playing the
"guest" and attempting to stay within the framework of the
Luncheon Party. The doctor hides his smile and proposes a
toast to the "old hunter" when Old Ekdal enters with his
fresh rabbit skin, but cannot resist testing Hialmar's reaction to his tongue-in-cheek toast: "To the gray-haired——
(*drinks*) By-the-by, in his hair gray or white?" He points
out all of Hialmar's treasures and prompts him when Hialmar forgets his daughter. One should get the feeling from
watching Relling perform his duties as "psychologist" that
he enjoys his role. The larger the pill he can induce his
patients to swallow, the greater his enjoyment. He is truly
concerned for his patients, however, and is sincere when he
attempts to dissuade Hialmar from accompanying Gregers
after the visit of Old Werle. Relling knows the dangers a
sick personality such as Gregers can have on the make-
believe world of Hialmar Ekdal, and when he damns
Gregers, in the presence of Gina and Hedvig, he is truly out
of temper. The generalization Relling draws, applying

Gregers' "attack of integrity" to Norway, shows he has regained his composure and is once more laughing at his own role as well as at the world in general.

In Act IV Relling, making a house call to his prize patient, finds the villian is still pursuing, and when he can neither shut Gregers up nor show him that he is a mistaken idealist, he attempts to use Hedvig to end the foolish experiment "to lay the foundations of a true marriage." It is the arrival of Mrs. Sorby in the rite of the Formal Call that completely shakes his composure. He changes from "family psychologist" to "rejected lover" and even more surprisingly to "spiteful ex-lover" with his remark, in regrettable taste, "Mr. Werle never gets drunk—so far as I know; and I don't suppose he's in the habit of thrashing his wives, like the late lamented horse doctor." It is a different Relling we see in the scene with Mrs. Sorby, the conscious role-player, the director, loses control of himself completely. His assumption of the unconscious role of "hurt ex-lover," announcing he will "go out with Molvik tonight," may well be the turning point in the drama. If Relling had stayed and aided Hialmar in keeping things in their proper rose-colored perspective, then quite possibly Hialmar would not have found it necessary to make the connection between Mrs. Sorby's gift and Hedvig's weak eyes. The good doctor has been very successful in his prior treatment of Hialmar, and it is not improbable that he could have headed off the suspicions. Certainly, had he not left involved in his own misfortune he would have stopped Gregers from making the idiotic suggestion of the blood sacrifice. But while Relling is evidently strong enough to accompany Molvik on his sprees, without the comfort and help of the illusion of an incurable illness, he is not strong enough *not* to accompany his friend.

It appears that this dispenser of illusions is not, after all, without his own life-lie. Relling seems to have been able to satisfy his own weakness for the stuff that cheers by further-ing Molvik's illusion. Thus, without casting himself as a weak "poor harmless creature" who is in danger of suc-cumbing to self-contempt, he is able to drink himself to ruin while doing his duty as a doctor to the souls of men. His loss of self-control as the result of learning of the coming marriage between Mrs. Sorby and Old Werle, and the invitation to Hialmar to join the night of drinking is a good example to directors who allow their own personal problems to keep them from concentrating on the problems of the play. Relling's production goes to pieces when he forgets to administer to the needs of his leading man. Relling sees his mistake and admits it in his only self-deprecating remark in the play, "Yes, I'm a brute," which he utters in the early minutes of Act V. He is a brute in his own eyes not only because he failed to report the whereabouts of Hialmar, but because he is primarily responsible for Hialmar's going out in the first place. The doctor soon gets back into character, however, and strips Hialmar naked in Gregers' eyes. He then proceeds to show the indignant Gregers an unadorned, unflattering image of himself. Molvik and the old Lieutenant come in for the same treatment, and all four role-players are left without a shred of the costume of illusion. For the first time, the audience should see clearly what they have suspected since early in Act II, that stripped of their illusions these mediocre actors are blobs of human-ity without rhyme or reason. It is to Relling's description of the characters that the director and the actors must turn when in doubt. It is Relling who sees them clearly and without their illusions. But the director must be careful to make the most of Relling's slip, for the only time we see him as an unconscious role-player is in the scene with Mrs. Sorby, and it is here that the audience must suspect that none of us, Ibsen and Relling included, is without his life-giving illusions.

There is little doubt that Relling fulfills the function of an abbreviated *raisonneur,* that character left over from the Scribean drama who stood outside and represented the author's view and comments throughout the play. Relling is certainly not outside the play but he just as certainly does represent Ibsen's view in this drama. The critics have called him everything from a "down-at-the-heels physician"[52] to "the incarnation of an idea, rather than a living flesh and blood person."[53] Relling is a cynic, but he is far from an "incarnation of cynicism" as one writer has called him.[54] His roles are, except for the aforementioned scene with Mrs. Sorby, conscious roles. His mildly sardonic smile is generally meant for himself as well as for the other poor souls he sees around him.

OLD EKDAL

The illusion-ridden (but contented) family of the Ekdals is led by the patriarch of the clan, Lieutenant Ekdal. The old gentleman is the first of the family we meet, and in a sense he typifies the entire family. There is great danger of treating Old Edkal as a charming, childlike figure, but the director will notice that it is only Gregers, "the mad, cracked, demented" fellow, who sees the "childlike mind" of the old man as a delightful asset. Dr. Relling sums Old Ekdal up as "one who has been an ass all his days." Though it is a distinct temptation to play this wonderful acting character as a cute old gentleman, it is a gross error to do so.

The grandfather is a consummate role-player. The most obvious bit of role-playing is the donning of the old uniform for special occasions, but the old man generally knows what he is doing when he is not "under the influence." Old Ekdal is introduced in the assumed role of "meek old man" and he plays the role with belief and conviction. He has no difficulty in deceiving the butler, Petterson, but the former bear hunter cannot resist a quick aside: "Thanks, Petterson, good old friend! Thanks! (*Mutters softly*) Ass!" His exit through the sumptuous dinner party is made in the same "meek old man" role; in fact he almost overplays the part here. There is no such meekness noticeable when he arrives home in Act II. With work in his hand and a bottle in his pocket, the "meek old man" has become "happy old man" as he peeks in at the sleeping livestock. The transparent role of "busy worker" fools no one as he goes to the kitchen to fetch hot water for his toddy. The old man falls into the role of "proud father" as he listens to Hialmar recount his triumphs of the evening, and finally he ends the act in his favorite, but unconscious, role of "tipsy old man." Later in the play we see him in such roles as "sportsman" and "worker," but his roles are always as "old" hunter, "old" worker, even "old" grandfather. Ekdal knows his talents and he never attempts to shed his years, he wants people to "do for him," and he enjoys the attention Hedvig gives her lovable old grandfather.

The grandfather is not without imagination. He has, as Relling tells us, "hit upon his own cure" and invented the wonderful garret. The idea must have come originally from the old man, for Hialmar has neither the imagination nor the perseverance to create a forest primeval from an empty attic. The director needs to take a close look at that wonderful garret with its menage of poultry and rabbits. Certainly it is an unusual extension, especially for an upper apartment, but the idea of chickens, pigeons, rabbits, and a wild duck living not only on the same floor, but in the next room, presents distinct possibilities of an unpleasant situation. We learn that Gina, "by no means without culture, mind you," is the only one who seems to object to the livestock straying into the living quarters proper. Hialmar remarks that the contrivances, all his own invention, are absolutely necessary, "For Gina objects to having rabbits and fowls in the studio." When one considers the home of the wild duck in light of Relling's description, as a room filled with rubbish, the morning walk of the "old sportsman" takes on quite a different aspect, to say nothing of a different odor. The director must see that the garret is introduced to the audience in the same manner it is to Gregers, first by the romantic light of the moon, and then in the clear, illusion-dispelling light of day. And the actor playing Gregers must make sure the point is made by his reading of the line, "It looks quite different by day from what it did last night in the moonlight." There is no wonderment in the reformer's voice as he watches Hialmar and Old Ekdal in the dirty garret, but the disgust must be evident.

The old man's roles are not well played, for just as Hialmar is prone to overplay the melodrama in his roles, so the old Lieutenant overacts his simple roles. The old man does not play well primarily because he lacks the mental power. While we must give him credit for sufficient imagination for the creation of his world of illusion, he must not be thought of as a clever person. His poor attempts at hiding the cognac, his unimaginative excuse of going to light his pipe, and his childlike petulance when Hialmar refuses to leave his work do not suggest a great amount of native intelligence. He has been, is still, and will be "an ass all his days."

HIALMAR

Hialmar, Old Ekdal's only son, has been referred to as Ibsen's most universal character creation, with the exception of Peer Gynt.[55] The corpulent clown is laughable primarily because he takes his trunkful of stock roles so seriously. In many respects one is reminded of a much earlier Ibsen creation, Stensgard, in his first realistic play, *The League of Youth*, but Hialmar lacks the young lawyer's driving ambition to get somewhere. The photographer has been likened to Peer, but as he lacks Stensgard's ambition, he is completely devoid of Peer's wonderful imagination. It is possible, even though one does not believe Peer's story, to see him riding through the clouds on a reindeer, but after seeing Hialmar recount his triumph to his family, it is impossible to even believe that he believes himself. Hialmar is a master at dodging the thinking process. He can convince himself of almost anything he wishes by simply not seeing the problem or fact from any but the most advantageous angle. It is because of this talent Hialmar has, not letting unpleasant subjects or facts into his life, that Relling has been able to cast him in the role of inventor. The fact that Hialmar has not as yet thought of what he might invent doesn't faze him at all. Relling has simply harvested what Hialmar's "two high-flown hysterical maiden aunts" had sown years earlier. The "two soul-mothers," as Hialmar describes them, had evidently cast their small nephew in the role of "sensitive genius" while he was still in toddling clothes. As the young "genius" grew older he had the misfortune to be looked upon as a shining light by his friends. Relling recounts, "He was handsome, the rascal—red and white—a shop-girl's dream of manly beauty; and with his superficially emotional temperament, and his sympathetic voice, and his talent for declaiming other people's verse and other people's thoughts——." The specific idea of becoming an inventor and making a magnificent contribution to the art of photography came from Relling, but obviously Hialmar had only been biding his time until someone suggested what he might do with his mythical talent.

The life-illusion that keeps Hialmar going is not, however, that of his invention. The life-lie of the invention is made possible by a much greater illusion, namely, that Hialmar Ekdal is an exceptional person. He can and does pass as a talented man for a number of years but this is a commentary on the mentality of his friends and associates, not his own intelligence. That Hialmar believes himself to possess remarkable mental powers and great depth of mind is not remarkable. Most of us, if pushed into an admission, would classify ourselves as, if not exceptional, then certainly above average. And one must give Hialmar credit; he generally manages to avoid any situation that calls for immediate results. It is important to remember that Gregers has not seen Hialmar for a number of years, and that he does not see him, as does the audience, when he is off his guard.

In the rites that he can control Hialmar is, as one critic has called him, "A colossal poseur" who "spends his life playing a succession of parts, deceiving himself into an imagined nobility of character."[56] In Act I, however, Hialmar is out of his element and has no control over the rites. In this situation he is incapable of finding the correct role,

even when Gregers gives him a gentle nudge. Hialmar has
enough theatrical consciousness to realize that his vast
repertoire of melodramatic roles would be ludicrous in these
surroundings. The ritual of the formal dinner party demands a polish and *savoir-faire* that Hialmar possesses only
in his own little world. While he is conversing with his old
schoolmate, who still accepts him as a shining light, Hialmar has no difficulty. He can wax sentimental, use his little
martyr's sighs, fill his well-modulated voice with emotion
when speaking of his benefactor, in short, play his favorite
role of "melancholy martyr" without difficulty. As soon as
the rest of the guests enter and begin the ritual of The After-
Dinner Drink Hialmar becomes nervous and ill at ease. The
"young genius" can do nothing but writhe and ask his
friend, "What am I to talk about?" When he finally does
enter the conversation with his shy question concerning the
effect of seasons on fine wine, he only succeeds in making
himself appear ridiculous. His denial of his father so shortly
after his sentimental words, "Of course my poor unhappy
father lives with me. He hasn't another soul in the world to
care for him," is followed by his melodramatic exit:
"Gregers——I am going! When a man has felt the crushing
hand of Fate, you see . . ."

Hialmar's view of himself is perhaps best suggested in
Act I when, without the necessity arising, he feels called
upon to explain and defend his spouse as "by no means
without culture." The photographer goes on to explain,
"You see, life is itself an education. Her daily intercourse
with me——."

In Act II, when Hialmar is seen in his own surroundings,
the events of Act I are painted in quite different colors than
we remember them. Now Hialmar is completely at home,

starring in the rite of Homecoming, and as he recounts the evening to his adoring audience of three, his halting attempts to join the conversation are transformed into glittering gems of wit in which the dinner guests were given their due "right in the teeth." Hialmar, safe in a familiar rite and secure in his role, replays the dinner party as he would have liked to have played it earlier in the evening. It is within this rite of Homecoming that the first concrete evidence of Hialmar's love of the stock phrase and the stereotype is found. When he learns that Old Ekdal has found a bottle, Hialmar declaims, "Oh, God! My poor old white-haired father!" Ibsen has, in his stage directions and in the lines, made it clear that Old Ekdal is not costumed in the white locks of a beautiful old age, but rather is almost bald but still vain enough to cover his growing baldness with a "dirty red wig." The son's great concern for the "shipwrecked father" is shown in its true light when after the dramatic "Oh, God!" Hialmar concludes the speech with, "Well, well. There let him sit and get all the enjoyment he can."

After strutting about the room fishing for compliments from his daughter, Hialmar is forced to drop his role of "handsome Bohemian" with his "sweeping" locks and "flowing" necktie and assume the role of "irritated, put-upon father" when his suggestion that Hedvig satisfy her longing for the promised treat by reading the menu while he describes how the various dainties tasted is met with tears from the disappointed little girl. Hialmar makes his first retreat into the realm of the wild duck when he uses it as a topic of conversation with Old Ekdal after Gina has attempted to ease Hedvig's pain of being forgotten with sign language. Gina steps into the Family Conference to remind

Hialmar that he will "hardly have time tomorrow," much to Hedvig's dismay, and Hialmar falls immediately into the "martyr" role of which he is so fond. The poseur is quick to call for the correct props when, after suggesting the flute to change the mood of the rite, the sensitive Hedvig stops the "melancholy martyr" as he is ascending his cross of misunderstanding with the suggestion "Beer." But Hialmar is no fool, he seizes the opportunity to put the family back on the desired sentimental basis, refuses the beer, and calls for his flute. One can almost see the tears streaming down the sensitive artist's face as he wrings every trill and every plaintive run from what was written as a lively peasant dance. For Gregers' benefit, Hialmar runs through a number of roles—"old friend," "proud father," "sorrowful father," "poor-but-willing host," "embarrassed man of the world" (when the old man insists on showing Gregers the garret), "proud man," "landlord," and finally the unconscious role of "confused man" when Gregers suggests he would like to be the dog that brings the wild ducks to the surface again. The act ends as he looks with confidence towards the morrow—he really needs a rising sun to silhouette him here—but manages nonetheless "(*takes a fresh piece of bread and butter*) As sure as I have a mission in life, I mean to fulfill it now!" . . . "Poor old white-haired father! Rely on your Hialmar. He has broad shoulders—strong shoulders, at any rate." But it is the practical Gina who brings him down to earth, and he falls into the role of "dutiful son" as the curtain falls.

In Act III Hialmar is so busy playing his roles that he has no time to work during the rite of Working. "Breadwinner," "superior husband," "man of affairs," "abused breadwinner," "busy worker," "dutiful son," "harried father,"

completely. On several occasions Hialmar slips and admits his knowledge of his playing. The inventor speaks of leaving "the everyday details of business" to his wife, "for then I can take refuge in the parlor and give my mind to more important things." Later, when he is railing at Gina for her black past, he moans in his martyrdom, "When I used to lie in there on the sofa and brood over my invention, I had a clear enough presentiment that it would sap my vitality to the last drop." Gina, however, is too down-to-earth to remember Hialmar's dramas, and she speaks of scheduling a business appointment in the afternoon when it would not interfere with his nap. Hialmar lets it go by without comment. Certainly, Hialmar comes very close to admitting his real satisfaction with the life he leads when Gregers persists in continuing his talk of his new-found mission, "That's all very well, but you will please leave me out of it. I can assure you that—apart from my very natural melancholy, of course —I am as contented as anyone can wish to be. . . . I am not used to that sort of talk. In my house nobody ever speaks to me about unpleasant things." His juggling of roles for Gina and Gregers, and his quick switches for his father, his daughter, and his wife during the rite of Working in Act III, all argue for the conscious role-player. Hialmar sees himself in a dramatic light when in actuality he is not in any such light. Cyrano and Hamlet and Peer play their respective roles with a dramatic flair, but they are in truly dramatic situations, or if not, they make them so. Hialmar attempts to magnify his afternoon nap into a hardworking session of inventing, his stumbling social attempts into great triumphs, his contented drunken father into a broken, white-haired patriarch, his comfortable home life, which he enjoys, into a life barely to be endured because of its hardships, his broken-down friends into men of the world, his daughter into a pathetic, hopelessly lost child, and finally, his dirty garret into a wonderfully interesting park. He has one great talent, "that of enacting the melodrama." From this talent stems the play's comedy and the tragedy.

GREGERS

It is as Hialmar's friend that Gregers takes on his importance to the play, but he is seen primarily as his father's son. He is introduced in the role of "old friend" but, in the rite of The After-Dinner Drink while they are alone, it is Hialmar who manages the dramatic actions. While Hialmar discusses his melancholy existence and explains his wife and marriage, Gregers drops the role of "old friend" and becomes "suspicious son." For the remainder of the act, except for a short speech as "helpful friend"—a trifle condescendingly: "You must join in, Hialmar"—Gregers plays some variation of the basic role of "son." Thus, in Act I Gregers is seen as "overstrained son," "helpful friend," "suspicious son," "bitter son," and finally at the first curtain, while he sees himself as "man with a mission," in reality he is still lost in his role of "bitter son." Throughout the first three acts Gregers remains close to the role of "son." Even as he is playing "meddler" in Act III, when he is pumping Gina for information, he thinks of himself as his father's son. It is Old Werle's inopportune visit that flings Gregers forward. Doubtless he would have found an opportunity in the near future to enlighten Hialmar, but it is seeing his wealthy father in Hialmar's house that makes it imperative for him to "get on with the job." His father's appearance unleashes the clever dog who is all too anxious to dive to the bottom and hunt around in the slime. Hialmar is not the only romantic; Gregers too finds it necessary to cloak his activities in shining armor. He is the knight sworn to protect his old friend and, incidentally, to avenge the wronged damsel, his mother. His veiled threat of suicide to his father, his invitation to Old Ekdal to return to the wilds of Hoidal, his visit in Act IV, timed to catch the sentimental domestic scene of forgiveness, his dramatic but asinine suggestion of the blood sacrifice to Hedvig, his request that Hialmar acknowledge and thank him for his help—"(*laying his hand on Hialmar's shoulder*) My dear Hialmar—was it not a good thing I came?"—are all symptomatic of the overly romantic soul.

Gregers does not play nearly the variety of roles Hialmar does and, more important, Gregers' roles are unconscious. The starry-eyed reformer is certainly sincere, and it is this very sincerity that makes him dangerous. It is the same sincerity that gives him his comic quality. While Gregers plays reformer and son, it is as savior that he sees himself. It is his mission, his manifest duty, to lay bare the lies, the deceit, the deception that he finds in "the depths of the sea." The director should strive to achieve a feeling of "being at home in the tangled ooze" for Gregers. Though Gregers is Relling's antipode, both seek the same end result—one by building illusions, the other by destroying them.

A word should be said in connection with Gregers' rather puzzling speech that his destiny is "to be the thirteenth at table." The critics have much to say about the underlying meaning, but a simple interpretation will carry as much meaning for the audience as all the scholarship in the world. It will aid the actor playing this role if he thinks of it solely in answer to Relling's observation that "life would be quite tolerable, after all, if only we could be rid of the confounded duns that keep on pestering us, in our poverty, with the claim of the ideal." If Relling is correct, Gregers may well be saying he is glad that his destiny is what it is, not to belong to any particular group. He will be unwelcome and unwanted, he will never become a part of that "tolerable life," but will return to the type of life he has so recently left where he can have a "delightfully lonely time of it——" and "plenty of leisure to think and think about things."

G I N A

The prime mover in the Ekdal household is the "wife," "mother," "servant," "cook," "daughter-in-law," "business woman," and "photographer," Gina. Her roles are all unconscious, all efficiently played, and all deadly serious. Gina is, at first glance, an exception to the general rule that the unconscious role-player is a comic or pathetic figure, yet, when viewed closely through the rite–role glasses, she is seen to be drawn as a pathetic figure. The idea of this hardworking, sincere woman being used so blatantly by her husband, looked down upon by that paragon of virtue and education Gregers, and put upon by Relling and Molvik, makes us pity her position even as we admire her for keeping the house running so smoothly. Ibsen has taken great pains, unfortunately, according to some critics, to place her in a low educational bracket, with her mispronunciation and misuse of words, but he has, on the other hand, made sure that it is obvious that it is Gina who is responsible for the household's functioning normally. Again, it is Relling's observation that best sums up the wife and mother: "And then you have your excellent wife, shuffling quietly in and out in her felt slippers, and that seesaw walk of hers, making everything cozy and comfortable about you." In fact, it is Gina's composure and dignity that bring a touch of the noble to the death scene. And while Gregers attempts to salve his own conscience with his remark about death ennobling Hialmar, it is Gina who sees the only thing that the death has actually accomplished: "We must help each other to bear it, for now at least she belongs to both of us." The most puzzling question the play raises is that of Gina and her premarital affairs. Is Hedvig Hialmar's child or is she actually the child of Old Werle? Gina, in her straightforward manner, albeit a trifle angry at the time, tells Hialmar that she does not know. She is upset and angry when Hialmar asks if Hedvig has a right to live beneath his roof, and rightly so. Hedvig spends a great deal of her time trying to make her father comfortable. She loves him beyond reason, and certainly she has as much right to live under that particular roof as does Hialmar. Gina is not, at that moment, concerned with the parentage, rather she is angry because she interprets the question literally; Hialmar should know better than to ask a question in such a manner. When he rephrases the question and asks, "Does Hedvig belong to me—or—? Well!" Gina answers, with "(*cold defiance*) I don't know." The director and the actor do not have the necessary information to decide who is the father, but such questions are often left up in the air. The audience can make up its own mind but the actors, especially the person playing Gina, must make up her mind whether or not she thinks Hedvig is Hialmar's or Old Werle's. The most dramatic situation is brought about if Hedvig belongs to Hialmar. Then Hialmar's dramatics are based on nothing, and the laughter of the gods rings loudest at the foolishness of man.

Perhaps it should be noted here that the entire play is

based on a lie. Gregers brings the news to Hialmar that his father had an affair with Gina while Gina was in service and the wife still living. Gina tells us, and we must believe her, that she did not give in to Werle until after she left the services of the family. Gregers knows of his father's indiscretions only through his alcoholic mother, and her suspicions were not founded in fact when she passed them on to Gregers. Hence, though Gregers' meddling and tale-carrying does bring out the truth, the story as Gregers knows it, and as he tells it to Hialmar, has no truth in it. Hence the truth-bringer is mistaken in his facts. His attempts to avenge his mother, based on the misinformation which his mother gives him, lead to possible truth, but if it be truth, it is truth that brings tragedy.

HEDVIG

The last of the Ekdals is little Hedvig, whom one authority[58] has aptly described as the tragic victim of the claim of the ideal. Hedvig is perhaps one of Ibsen's most poetically delicate characters and, from an interpretation point of view, one of his least complicated. Hedvig stays very close to her basic role of "daddy's little girl." It is this role she most enjoys and this role that Hialmar prefers to have her play. She is not, however, an idle dreamer who sits contemplating the wild duck. That an only child, who does not attend school and who has no playmates her own age, should spend considerable time in an imaginary world of her own is not at all unusual. But even so, we do not see Hedvig with much idle time on her hands. She is, if not attending to the comfort of her father, helping her mother or doing her father's work for him. True, she talks with Gregers about the garret and the various changes it goes through with the change in weather, and she confides that she is fond of going in there when she can manage, but only on one occasion do we see her enter, and when she does, her reason is death.

It is important to look closely at Hedvig's reasons for entering the garret. While her grandfather and father use it to "potter with and to put to rights when they get out of order," Hedvig is primarily concerned with the books in the old captain's (a former resident of the garret) belongings. "There are big cupboards full of books, and a great many of the books have pictures in them . . . And then there's an old paint-box and things of that sort; and all the books." "Daddy's little girl" may have to go into the attic when she wants to read or to look at pictures. We learn early in Act II that her father doesn't care much about reading, and if both her parents are continually reminding her not to strain her eyes, then quite possibly the attic is the only place where she can read in peace. To a child perched on the edge of puberty, any attic can be attractive, but one with wildlife, trees, and the treasures of a dead sea captain would certainly be an escape from reality.

Hedvig plays her roles easily and unconsciously. We meet her in the role of "daughter-companion," but she shifts to "mother's helper," "granddaughter," and, with the entrance of her father, "daddy's little girl." Throughout the rite of Entertaining Guest in Act II, Hedvig is enjoying her role as "daddy's little girl." She drops into "puzzled little girl" when Gregers leaves, and back to "mother's helper," and finally "daddy's little girl" as the curtain falls. Hedvig attempts quite successfully to play hostess to Gregers' visit in Act III and is unaware that the reformer is pumping her for information. Her final role of "hurt little girl" is a difficult one to play, for the director must make up his mind if Hedvig is, as one critic contends, "demonstrating the only free spirit among all the tame, rabbit-souled folks of the Ekdal menage" when she places the gun to her breast, "preferring when wounded to die rather than to live just for the sake of living,"[59] or, as seems more likely, reacting to Hialmar's remark, which she can well overhear (and perhaps should be seen overhearing), "Hedvig, are you willing to renounce that life for me? (*laughs scornfully*) No thank you! You would soon hear what answer I should get."

Hedvig goes to the attic, desperate and willing to attempt even Gregers' nonsensical suggestion of killing the wild duck, but she hears Hialmar, in his best melodramatic form, suggest her own life, and as she is feeling rejected and unwanted, the overly sensitive child might well in a moment of self-pity turn the gun on her own breast. Hedvig plays "daddy's little girl" right to the end.

WERLE

Old Werle is seen primarily in the role of father, first as Gregers' and then later as Hedvig's. He, Gina, and Mrs. Sorby seem to be the only level-headed, "normal" persons in the odd menage. Werle is always felt in the background, and most of the play's action can be traced back to his influence. In the final act he even manages to effect the life of Relling.

It is as Hedvig's father that he makes his greatest impact on the drama. Just as it will make for a more dramatic situation for the actors if they decide that Werle is not Hedvig's true father, so it will help the play and the character of Werle if he believes himself to be the true blood father, and the gift of the yearly income strongly suggests that he does think of himself in that light.

While the old man is seen as a villain by Gregers, Gina, and finally by Hialmar, it is not difficult to make a strong case for him. All the unsavory charges are originally made by his son, certainly a most prejudiced source. Mrs. Sorby (whom Ibsen presents as a sensible, understanding woman regardless of her past) believes, on the other hand, that her future husband is more sinned against than sinning.

The aged engaged couple, as Hialmar points out, will realize the true marriage. The "settling of accounts" scene between the old rake and Mrs. Sorby must have been a rather lively exchange of confidences, to say the least.

We first meet Werle in the role of "congenial host" and throughout Act I we watch him fluctuate between "congenial host" and some variation of "father." He tries vainly to set the stage for a Father-Son Conference which will iron out the bad feelings, or at least establish a workable relationship, in his last personal appearance in Act III. First as "distressed father," then as "dejected father," and finally as "disappointed father," he attempts to smooth the past. He succeeds only in hastening the coming tragedy. Each time the old man attempts to right real or fancied wrongs, he makes the situation worse by spurring his son to greater action. Only through the eyes of Mrs. Sorby do we see the otherwise villainous figure clearly. He may or may not be guilty, as Gregers suspects, of framing Old Ekdal, but the irony of the play will be greater if he did not and if he looks upon himself as guiltless in the timber-cutting case. On the other hand, the actor playing this rather difficult role will find his first act easier and more dramatic if he decides that Werle thinks he is Hedvig's father. Such a decision will also add to the visit in Act III. Old Werle is a man with a past, but he is not, and cannot look upon himself, as a villain.

MRS. SORBY

The last of the characters we will touch upon here is Mrs. Sorby. Her master role is that of "bride to be." The knowledge that she is soon to marry Old Werle will color all her roles. Her conscious role of "hostess" in Act I is replaced by the unconscious role of "old friend" when she visits Gina in Act IV. In this rite of the Formal Call, the "old friend" announces her forthcoming marriage and it is as a "bride to be" that she faces ex-suitor Relling.

The director must remember that Mrs. Sorby, too, has risen in the world. Her friendship with Gina, a real one apparently, as Gina is on a first name basis with her, leads one to think that Bertha Sorby may at one time have been employed by the Werles, perhaps, as Rebecca in Rosmersholm, as companion or nurse for the invalid wife. Her first husband, a "horse doctor" as Relling describes him, left much to be desired even though "he had his good points too." The guests in Act I seem to be more than a little aware of their past connection with her. It would seem then that this charming and witty woman, who by her own words has "come in for a great piece of luck," is bettering herself by the marriage. Though her own evaluation, that she is giving as much as she is getting, must be taken as a fair one.

SUMMARY

The rite-role breakdown found in the Appendix, and the brief observations on the rites and the roles played by the characters above, are not meant as a finished interpretation of *The Wild Duck*. Both are meant to show how the rite-role analysis works in practice and how it is helpful to the director. Completing a thorough breakdown is an excellent way of becoming familiar with the play, and studying the completed breakdown does reveal interesting and playable parallels and contrasts. The play's structure is bared in staging terms, and both director and actor have a point of departure. Each character can be assigned master roles that will give the actor something to hang onto until he completes his own study of his character. Such a handle will point him on the track the director wants taken, and cut short the days of embarrassed stumbling around in the limbo of the initial rehearsals. The director, regardless of experience, will never count the time spent in a rite-role breakdown as lost. The rites point the way to what is to be staged and set the background for the action, while the roles indicate the character's frame of reference and his mental set. When such a breakdown is completed, the director is ready to begin the trying, but exciting, test of staging the play.

Part III
THE DIRECTOR
AND
THE STAGE

Introduction

Remember the bright young director who did not believe in blocking a play but who, nonetheless, ended up by dictating all the movement? I am sure that had this gentleman been asked to explain the basis of his strong feeling against blocking he would have answered patiently that no one can block a play for an actor because no one can feel what that actor is feeling, hence no one can do that which will "feel right" except that actor on stage. He would have gone on to explain that he was, "God forbid," no puppet-master who sat back and pulled the strings which made the actors rise, cross, turn, and so forth, and that what he was doing in the later rehearsals was not blocking, but simply refining the movements the actors had found felt good and comfortable to them.

Few will deny that there is more than a grain of truth in the argument based on the actor's feeling right. Certainly, by opening night the actor must be comfortable in all his actions, and it is the director's job to see that he is. However, while the director must be sure that the actor feels right, he must realize that just because the actor *feels* right is no guarantee that he *is* right.

It follows, I believe, that if the actor is completely involved in his character in precisely the manner the playwright visualized when creating the role, if the actor is a good technician and has some real experience behind him, then probably he will be right in what he does. I use the word "probably" advisedly for there is no assurance that what he is feeling is being conveyed to the audience.

The director must continually bear two things in mind: one, regardless of experience and talent, any actor is prone to fall into the trap of confusing "feeling good" on stage— being lost in what he is doing—with being in character; and two, being completely in character is useless unless the desired emotions and ideas are conveyed to the audience.

All the "feeling" in the world is not worth much from a theatrical point of view if the audience can't see or hear the play. Nor is feeling of itself worth anything to the theater. All too often I have witnessed backstage scenes when the individual performer, still flushed and excited about the evening's work, awaited the director's dressing-room visit, sure that "tonight it happened——we really hit it," only to look stunned and a little hurt when the director's first words were, "Well, what happened tonight, what happened to our play?" Stanislavski warns of the grave danger of confusing "feeling in general" with feeling especially what is called for at a given moment in a play:

> Everyone at every minute of his life must feel something. Only the dead have no sensations. It is important to know *what* you are feeling on the stage, because it often happens that even the most experienced actors work out at home and carry onto the stage something which is neither important nor essential for their parts.[60]

All of which would seem to suggest that the director's principal role is that of acting as the actor's mirror. He should, then, sit out front and tell the actor not what to do, but rather, what he is doing. Many actors feel that this is the director's greatest responsibility and it *is* one of his primary functions. No actor can see himself on stage, and thus he must have a mirror, a mirror he can trust. However, any actor needs more than that mirror, for he has, or should have, his hands full with his own character. It is not the actor's job to be concerned with the balance, the stage picture, or where the audience is looking. His job is to act; the rest are directorial problems and should be handled as such. The director who does not have the techniques at hand to solve problems of this type is not worthy of the title. In spite of the opinions of our bright young director, methods and techniques of blocking a play do exist, and further, these techniques and methods are based on definite principles, as are the techniques and methods of any other art. Many of the directors in the professional theater today came up through the acting ranks and learned these principles the hard way, and hence scoff at learning the principles of direction in class. Such was the case with our bright young director, but *he used them all* even though he could not discuss them because he had no labels for them. I believe the danger at the other end of the scale is greater, for though it is often assumed to be true in the educational theater, knowing and labeling the techniques and methods will not make a director.

Contrasted with the bright young director, I recall a bright young drama department head in one of the better-known universities. This gentleman had made his name primarily in the realm of the textbook and the professional journal. He had an excellent and well-deserved reputation as a scholar, but unfortunately, he looked upon himself as a director. This gentleman had once written that anyone with a knowledge of the basic principles could block, and hence, direct an acceptable drama. Having seen one of his college productions, I can vouch for his knowledge of basic blocking techniques; in fact, it would have been difficult to find fault with the appearance of his stage at any given moment. Far more important, however, was that fact that it was impossible to find any of the drama. The director in question had turned one of Ibsen's greatest works into a long, boring evening. The stage itself never made the audience uncomfortable, just what took place on it. The director had mastered the methods of centering the attention of the audience on a particular person, his stage was in balance, the groups tied together nicely, and he had broken up his stage and played his scenes in logical areas without overdoing any one of them. Technically, it was a well-directed performance, except that there was no *play* there to see. If the director had mastered the drama, he had failed dismally in communicating any of it to his actors. Though his blocking was clean-cut and no one ran into another, there was no connection between the blocking and Ibsen's ideas and emotions, perhaps because none of the actors on stage had the slightest idea of what he was saying or doing.

It is true that anyone of average intelligence can learn to block. The principles touched upon below can be memorized and parroted back to the class instructor, but the artistic and meaningful use of the principles will come only with experience and sensitivity to the author's intent.

Our bright young director's objection to blocking is based on the sort of blocking our bright young drama department head called direction, and if the theater must make a choice between raw talent and academic sterility, then it had better continue in its choice of raw talent. Hopefully such alternatives will not always be the only ones available.

Certainly, blocking is a vitally important part of play direction and most assuredly it involves more than keeping the actors out of each other's way (no mean task in itself in some shows), but no matter what it involves, blocking is only a tool, one of many the good director must have at his command.

While this section will be concerned primarily with the skills of blocking, the student must constantly bear in mind that it is the author's intent he is staging; that blocking is considerably more than keeping the apex of the triangle in full view. Finally, the student must remember that "skill does not the artist make," though it can save any real artist worlds of time if the skill is available when needed.

Blocking

One needs to think in terms of blocking a play because an author writes a play primarily in terms of dialogue. It is, in almost every case, the dialogue that carries his ideas and hence, the ideas of the play, but a play is not read, a play is not heard. One thinks in terms of seeing a play. It is because the poet of the theater carries his ideas in the dialogue that so many literary analyses have little connection with the play proper. The literary claim to "see" the idea in the drama, but it is never there, or seldom so, as an idea; it is there as dialogue and action. This is the basic difference in the literature of the stage and that of the short story or novel. All can, and do, deal with ideas and emotions, but the dramatist gives his ideas life (and it must be admitted, often condemns them to sudden death) by voicing those ideas through a live being. An idea remains an idea until it is acted upon. It is true that an idea in a novel may act upon the emotions of the reader, but it is as Thornton Wilder says, "a past reported in the present," and whenever the writer attempts to leave this form—"Now as I finish this final page I can hear them coming for me, farewell"—he brings the reader up with a jerk by the incongruity of the then and now. The playwright's ideas are alive because they are *now*. Even as we watch them, they are being born:

> The novel is a past reported in the present. On the stage it is always now. This confers upon the action an increased vitality which the novelist longs in vain to incorporate into his work . . .
>
> In the theater we are not aware of the intervening storyteller. The speeches arise from the characters in an apparently pure spontaneity.
>
> A play is what takes place.
>
> A novel is what one person tells us took place.
>
> A play visibly represents pure existing. A novel is what one mind, claiming to omniscience, asserts to have existed.[61]

It is this "nowness" that gives the theater its life and its aliveness. On the stage an idea is acted out, it is tried and we see the result. We judge it not as thought or theory, but as an action. All ideas, all thoughts in the theater are converted into action and hence they become much more vivid and more startling.

It does not matter, as we have discussed elsewhere, that all action is symbolic and simply a matter of what conventions are in vogue at the time. If the play is well acted and well staged we only "see" the thought, the idea, clearly after we have thoroughly assimilated the action. Thus when the director blocks the play, he is translating the ideas and the emotions into direct action that is clearly and easily seen.

A play must be blocked if it is to have any form in its new medium. In other words, the reason for blocking is to give the written drama a stage, or action, form. But bear in mind that blocking serves, even as our bright young director suggested, a second, and in many respects, equally important function. That function is to clarify and make "natural" or "comfortable" for the actor the ideas and emotions we have been discussing. This second function of blocking is often overlooked by directors, and many actors have become so accustomed to poor blocking they deny the value of good blocking. But the fact is that no actor can read a line or perform a piece of business at his full capability when the blocking is wrong, either for him or for the play. As was stated above, the feeling that the actor is "comfortable" is seldom a sign that the blocking is right, but when the actor is uncomfortable, after giving it an honest try, the blocking is always wrong. The director who insists upon a particular bit of business of blocking, clever though it may be, when his actor is uncomfortable, will find both the idea and the bit lost in performance. Blocking, then, stages the ideas and emotions in a manner that can be seen from the entire house, and aids the actor by helping him find the "right" action in the particular play. It will be seen then, that in order to block out the design for a play, one begins by blocking actors and ends by helping characters in their search for the correct action.

Before the director can think in terms of blocking a play, two things must be clear in his mind. First, what is being attempted, that is, what is he trying to do with the blocking, what sort of overall design does he want his staging to have; and second, what effect is he striving for within the audience. The answers to these questions can come only when the director is thoroughly familiar with the play and is satisfied with his analysis of the playwright's intent. The problem of analysis we have discussed in a separate chapter. This chapter is concerned with the second element, that is, what effect will particular designs, movements, and lines have on an audience. And if the director knows what he wants to stress in the play, how does he make sure that those values are the ones that receive the stress?

The director acts as the camera for the audience. It is he who decides when they will come in for a close-up and when they will pull back to see the entire stage. In other words, it is he who controls and directs the attention of the audience. Where he wants them to look will depend upon his analysis, how he makes them center their attention on a particular spot will depend on how well he knows his methods and techniques. The director must never forget that he is responsible for what play the audience sees. Though the audience should never be conscious of the fact that their attention is being focused on a particular person or thing, the director must be absolutely sure *what* he wants them to see and hear *when*. Directing audience attention is pure technique, knowing where and how to do so at any given moment can be art.

Emphasis

The experience of hearing a large choir perform is a fairly common one for the student and will serve as an example without casting any aspersions on the music department. (Heaven forbid, maybe you'll have to do a show with them one day.) Often, unless one is acquainted with the individual voices, it is almost impossible to find the solo voice that has a short phrase in the middle of a number. Most of us have had the exasperating experience of missing the music while hunting for the one open mouth in the sixty before us. If the choir director would employ one of the methods of focusing the attention of the audience, perhaps more music would be heard. In the days of the large dance bands, the soloist would often stand, or an entire section would rise, thus using the principle of height to command the attention of the audience.[62] Each moment of the play has something happening that must be pointed, thus one phase of blocking a play is making sure that each pair of eyes in the house is watching the point of emphasis chosen by the director.

Most of the methods used to direct the attention of the audience come to the stage director from one of two sources, the art of painting or the art of the choreographer. Perhaps the choreographer is the more direct link, since that group of directors and inventors has been using the principles discovered first by the painter for a considerable number of years.

Always in a painting worthy of the name there is an organization that leads the eye of the beholder to a center of attention. This in no way detracts from the rest of the painting; rather it gives the painting a unity, a direction, if you will. In the same manner, the "picture" of the ballet has its center of interest, most often the ballerina. Recent years have seen a closer tie between the drama and the dance, while choreographers such as Helpmann and Robbins have crossed the two until it is often impossible to separate them. It is noteworthy, I believe, that the choreographers' forays

into the legitimate theater have been much more successful
in the field of musical comedy than in the drama. It follows,
I think, that while many of the ideas and emotions of a *West
Side Story* can be brought to life via movement per se, such
is not so obviously the case with *Mother Courage*. Be that as
it may, the stage director can learn a great deal from observ-
ing the artists of painting and the dance.

In most dances, ballet, modern, or musical comedy, the
choreographer has attempted to find a design, a form, that
will harmonize with the music, the emotion, and/or the
scene. Within that design he has brought to bear certain
principles to "point" the central characters, the lead dancer,
or the ballerina. The design of the director must fit the
written form, must underline the emotional qualities of the
play, and must center the attention of the audience on the
proper place at the proper time.

Methods of Achieving Emphasis (Pointing)

Everyone at one time or another has been cautioned,
"Don't point." Pointing is impolite because it draws attention to the object of the pointing, and it is for precisely that
reason that it is used so much on stage. Pointing, whether
done by a hunting dog or a small boy, is simply a method of
drawing a line from the finger, in the case of the little boy,
or the nose, in the case of the dog, to the object to be
noticed. It is a peculiarity of the human eye that it will
follow a line in an attempt to find its end. It matters not if
the line be real as railroad tracks in the country, or the
yellow-brick road in the *Wizard of Oz*, or the imaginary line
extending from the finger, or nose, to a particular object;

once set upon it, the eye will travel it to its end or until it disappears in the distance.

Focus: Visual Line

If you have ever played the old trick of standing on a busy street and pointing toward the top of a tall building, you will have noticed that there is an almost uncontrollable tendency for each person who passes to look up. It would seem that we automatically reason that if it is worth your attention, it is worth ours. Perhaps you did not notice that the heads or eyes did not snap to the top of the building; rather, they followed the imaginary line from the end of your finger in an attempt to find the object worthy of attention at the end of the line. Objects along the way, windows, bricks, pigeons, etc., were passed over, unless something was happening there which seemed to warrant studying, rather than a "passing glance." In this peculiarity of the eye is found one of the simplest devices at the service of the director.

Once the principle of the real or imaginary line as a directing device is thoroughly understood, it will be seen that the possibilities therein are almost limitless. As in the case of the pointed finger, the audience will pick up the line at its origin and will follow the line through fairly intricate designs until the object of the pointing is found. Provided what is happening is interesting enough, the audience will focus its attention there. Usually the origin of the point is not the finger, but rather the eye, for whenever an actor who has the attention of the audience looks at another actor or object, on or even off the stage, the audience will attempt to follow his line of vision. Thus it is apparent that the "focus" of the actor must be planned and cannot be left to chance.

For example, if actor A looks at actor B, B looks at C, C looks at D, actor E looks at C, actors F and G focus directly on D, then providing that all the actors can be seen from the house, and providing that D is doing something to hold the attention when it reaches him, no matter where the audience picks up the picture they will end up looking at actor D. Thus it will be seen that if there are several elements on the stage that are important, the director can make the audience aware of all of the elements and have them focus on the most important.

A son is leaving his home forever; the play is concerned with the son's decision to leave, so he will receive the principal attention of the audience. He stands by the door *d.l.*, looking at the floor, attempting to make up his mind; his mother sits center on a divan, reaching out as if to hold him; the father, the real reason for his leaving, is *u.r.c.* looking off *r.*, his back to the son who is on the opposite side of the stage; the older sister stands just behind the divan and to the left, looking at the mother; the younger daughter sits full back on a small stool *d.r.*, looking at the father; the teen-aged son kneels *d.r.* of the divan and focuses on the son at the door; the maid, *u.l.*, focuses directly on the son at the door. Here the three important elements, son, father, and mother, will all be seen but the audience will, no matter where they pick up the lines, end up looking at the son leaving, yet they will have had to be aware of the mother and the father. In this case the father looking off *r.* away from the son tends to soften the focus on the son. The possibilities of using the line of vision are indeed endless.

Focus: Actual Line

While it is the line of vision that is the most obvious, the real line also can be used to good effect. By the real line we mean the line formed by bodies or heads on stage. In the case of a real line the audience will pick it up at the point that is closest to them, that is the downstage end, and follow the line to its end. Hence a diagonal line from *d.r.* to *u.l.* will center the attention on the last person in line. Notice that if the line of figures is parallel to the footlights then the line as such does not carry a point of emphasis and has no focus. A line of figures perpendicular to the foots will emphasize the figure that is closest to the audience, a technique often used in the ballet. In this case two factors are at work: the line itself and the fact that a figure that is repeated is emphasized by each repetition. This repetition of a figure or of a line can be used in conjunction with the set itself. For example, a figure standing in front of a pillar will capture the attention of the audience. The same is true of a figure that is contrasted to a set line. Thus an actor standing by a long flat-topped table will be easier to point than one sitting at that table.

Still other types of lines at the director's disposal are the converging lines of the triangle. Whenever three or more actors are on stage simultaneously, they will, unless they are standing in a straight line, form a triangle. In general it is the upstage member of the triangle who will receive the benefit. In other words, in the case of an equilateral triangle, the apex will appear to be upstage, that is, if no other factors enter into the picture. It is quickly apparent, however, that through the use of the visual line, any two members of the triangle can point the other. The director must remember that whenever he has a large group on stage, he cannot avoid the use of a series of triangles, and it is vital that the apex of each triangle be used to advantage. Often the central figure in the scene will become the apex of several triangles and hence receive tremendously strong emphasis. No matter what the shape of the triangle, any one of the three points can become the center of attention by the use of visual line. Thus it should be apparent that the director has as many lines reaching out in as many different directions as he has people on stage and directions in which they can look.

Lines and Shapes

Lines and geometric shapes have, as well as a pointing quality, a second and equally important quality. As the painters and architects have long been aware, lines and shapes have a direct influence on human emotion. Thus it is that the curved lines drawn by the actor's movements or by the designer's pen will harmonize with the romantic comedy or drama, while the short, straight lines that turn at abrupt angles will fit the farce, and the long, straight line will have a majestic and often cold classical quality that can be used in the tragedy. The effect lines and shapes have on us is known to us all, but the director planning on using them (and remember, he has no choice, for they will be there whether he wants them or not) must be sure that the lines and shapes help rather than hinder the production. Think for a moment of how you picture a church steeple and how it can affect you, or visualize the cold, frigid woman, the jolly gentleman, or the current sex goddess. The soft, round (curved) line will have the same sort of effect on us whether it be found in a woman's body or in the imaginary line drawn by the actor's movement. The director must think in terms of what kinds of lines and shapes will fit the play. Some directors like to think of the play as being a certain shape; they then keep that shape before them during the entire rehearsal period. Once again the warning, certain lines and shapes must be on stage if there is either a set, or actors, or both; the director must assure himself that what is going to be there will add to the play and not detract from it.

As has been suggested, all movement has an emphasizing quality as well as a direct effect on the spectators' emotions, thus the line created by movement can point too, and should be used by the director.

Body Position

Though the real and the imaginary lines are always present and do provide a convenient way of directing the attention of the audience, there are even simpler methods at the director's command. One of these is the position the actor takes on stage. As a general rule an experienced actor will fall into a three-quarter position, that is, his upstage foot will be about half a step in front of his downstage foot. This allows him to have three-fourths of his face to the audience and yet appear to be within the stage frame. Just as in life we try to see the eyes of the person we are interested in, so it is on the stage. Actors learn quickly that it is the face the audience wants to see. As a result, and because acting is an exhibitionistic art, the natural tendency for an actor whose concentration is not on his role will be to turn full front.

If you place a group of amateurs on stage, whether they be aspiring actors or not, and tell them simply to wander until you call a halt, you will find that, more often than not, they will drift towards stage center and that, for the most part, they will keep their faces out front. Two useful techniques of directing the attention of the audience are involved in the illustration. One, because in life we tend to concentrate on the eyes, on stage the more of the face (thus, eyes) we see, the more important the character will seem at any given moment. An audience will, if no other factors are involved, tend to concentrate on the person who shows them the most face. It is, therefore, the full-front position that will take the audience's attention. Such a position tends to break down any barriers between actor and audience. The full-front actor is talking to us if he meets, or seems to meet, our eyes. It is a strong position and its strength is no doubt responsible for its being the preferred position for lecturers, ministers, or teachers who are attempting to reach their audience as individuals. Perhaps the best and most stupid example is to be found in certain comedians on television. All too often the spectacle of two actors (?) talking to each other and both staring directly into the camera greets us when we turn on the telly.

Stage Area

The second useful principle involved with our amateurs wandering on stage, is the principle of stage area. If one divides the stage floor into the nine traditional areas—*d.r.,* *d.c., d.l., r., c., l., u.r., u.c.,* and *u.l.,*—it will be found that the center area is the strongest, provided no other factors are working on the audience. The down center area certainly has an aesthetically harder quality, but it is doubtful if it is any stronger in terms of emphasis. It is often stated that the area just left of center is actually the strongest on the stage, but I would hold that it is simply more satisfying aesthetically. George, Duke of Saxe-Meiningen warns that, "It rarely works to have a figure dead center." He goes on to explain that it should never be used:

Scenery and other objects are placed whenever possible on the side, of course, at a certain distance from the wings so as to be visible to the audience.

The actor must never stand dead center directly in front of the prompter, but always slightly to the left or right of his box.

The middle foreground of the stage, about the width of the prompter's box, from the footlights to the background, should be considered by the actor merely as a passageway from right to left or vice versa; otherwise he has no business there.[63]

Obviously, if the two principles are put together then full-front dead center (or just to the l or r, if you prefer) is pretty hard to beat, and so it is. It is also pretty obvious and pretty boring and in general should be avoided.

Just a little experimentation will show anyone interested that, when no other factors are taken into consideration, the closer the actor is to the audience the more emphatic he will be. Thus we see that *d.r.* is stronger than *r.* or *u.l.* The relative strengths of *d.r.* and *d.l.* are, for all practical purposes, about equal.

It should be apparent by now that when speaking of the relative strength of the actor's position or of the area of the stage, we are considering the area or position as though no other factors were present, but of course they always are. For example, we have just discussed the relative strength of *d.r.* as opposed to *u.l.*, but now let us add our line of actors extending from *d.r.* to *u.l.;* we use the strength of *d.r.* to catch the eye of the audience, but we use the line to carry it to the *u.l.* area, hence in this case the emphasis will be *u.l.* and there the eye of the audience will come to rest provided there is something worth seeing. But if we keep our line of actors and have them all look three quarters *d.r.* and the actor *d.r.* looks straight out, he will have the attention of the audience. When one begins to add interlocking triangles, it becomes apparent that the director must analyze his picture closely to make sure which methods are combining to capture the audience's eye.

Many other ways exist to focus the audience's attention, and once more the neophyte is referred to Dean's[64] book for a very complete listing. I shall touch upon three more of the most obvious ways of handling this important part of blocking.

If the reader will place a small pencil dot in the center of a plain sheet of typing paper, he will notice that from, say, an arm's length, the dot is rather difficult to find, but if he will circle the dot so that it now becomes the bull's eye of the circle, the dot will seem to jump into notice. The same principle holds true for the stage. Defining the space around a figure will make him stand out. Both the movies and television make great use of this principle. For example, the situation in which a person in the center of a crowd is pointed out as having some undesirable quality, the crowd draws away, as does the camera and we see the long figure surrounded by many others. The space around the figure has been defined and the figure becomes the center of attention.

Height presents another method of centering the audience's attention. Generally speaking, when nothing else is interfering, the figure whose face is the highest will be the face the audience will choose to focus upon. Thus it is that a standing figure is easier to emphasize than a sitting figure. Notice that this will hold true without the use of levels provided by the designer, for the director always has a number of levels at his disposal. He has, in fact, as many different levels to use as one face will occupy if its owner is standing on the shoulders of the tallest member of the cast down to the level of the same face lying with one cheek on the stage floor. Very often, beginning directors overlook levels that are always at their disposal: the tops of tables, arms of chairs, mantles, and window sills can always be made practical and used to good advantage. Even the floor should not be forgotten. A word of caution here, however, for if the director is working in a house with a flat floor, his stage floor will be visible to only about the first three rows.

Finally, for a highly effective method of capturing attention the director need only think in terms of contrast. Just as in life, where our attention is attracted to that which is different, so it is on the stage. The contrasting figure will almost always take the scene. Any sort of contrast is extremely strong. Thus it was that the stars of earlier days liked to carry a fan or a small handkerchief, and whenever the attention of the house slipped from them to another, a few flits of the hanky or waves of the fan would bring it back. This obvious method of scene-stealing is seldom seen now, but dealing with amateurs, the director will do well to warn his cast of the dangers inherent in a moving object on stage. The light dancing on a necklace or reflecting from a shimmering dress can cause havoc with a well-planned scene.

Let's go back to our line of actors from *d.r.* to *u.l.* again.

Let any one of the actors in the line take a very weak position that is in contrast with the rest of the line and he will receive the emphasis. The full-front position is strong, as we have said, but let one person in the line turn full back to the audience and he will immediately become the center of attention. The sitting figure if all others are standing, the standing figure if all others are sitting, the kneeling figure if all others are lying down, and so it goes; the moving figure if all are still, the still figure if all others are moving, etc. The greater the deviation from the norm on stage at any given moment, the greater the emphasis on the contrasting figure will be.

If there is one key word which the director must bear in mind during his blocking rehearsals it is *variety,* variety in everything. The director must continually look for new ways to combine the various elements which will help him center the audience's attention at the desired spot. The director who is working with experienced actors will find that they will be quite conscious of their body positions and will automatically fall into positions which differ from the others on stage, but if the cast is made up primarily of amateurs, or singers with little acting time under their belts, he will often have to make a point of giving each actor a position. As a general rule, the more body positions in evidence at a given moment, the better. It is obvious, but often overlooked, that variety, like everything else on or off stage, can be overdone. The director's guiding principle must always be "Will it aid the idea, the emotion, and will it help to make clear the author's intent?" The director must return again and again to Stanislavski's dictum: "Whatever happens on the stage must be for a purpose."[65] And just as the actor must not "run for the sake of running, or suffer for the sake of suffering,"[66] so the director must not block for the sake of blocking, must not attempt variety for the sake of variety, and must not direct for the sake of directing.

It is, I believe, seeking variety for its own sake and blocking for the sake of blocking that is referred to as "overdirection." Good direction cannot be overdone, but any direction that stands out as direction is bad direction. (I would maintain that there are only good direction and bad direction and the shades of gray which lie between. Overdirection, as used by the student in his marginal note referred to earlier, is an impossibility.) Any direction given by the director and made his own by the actor is good direction, provided it fits the play and character; any direction not assimilated by the actor is bad direction and should be cut. Overdirection is like too much help; as long as it is a help there can't be too much, but when there is too much it is no longer a help and becomes a hindrance. I fail to see how there can be too many good suggestions for a production, although certainly some of the good suggestions may be badly timed. If there is always a reason, and if the reason always helps the play, the director need not concern himself with overdirection. Overemphasis and unimaginative use of the methods of focusing the attention of the audience is, however, often a glaring fault. Again I would remind the reader that the artist is revealed by the result he obtains with his techniques and that "Great art conceals art."

Thus far we have been discussing the pointing of one figure on stage, and certainly the audience can be concerned with only one thing at any given moment, but it is apparent that this center of attention must change often within a scene and hundreds of times within a play. If the audience is to follow the play at all, it must shift its attention with the dialogue and the action.

Most often a scene is shared between two actors, but

almost every play has a climactic scene involving most of the cast. In such a scene many methods of directing the attention of the audience will come into play. Each important character must be placed in such a position that it is possible for the audience to locate him without searching. In general, a different method of emphasis should be used on each character.

When a scene is shared by two characters, the director must be careful not to fall into the "tennis-match trap" and let his audience wear itself out following the bouncing ball back and forth between the two actors. He must also be extremely careful about any extras in such a scene. If, for example, he places the extras up center and allows them to point the speaker, he will surely find that some of them, as they learn the lines, will anticipate the change and shift their focus just before the correct moment. Few things destroy the illusion of reality as quickly or as devastatingly as having the chorus, for example, tennis-match the dialogue and get a bit ahead of the actors.

A stage director needs all the help he can find, and the methods of directing the audience's attention discussed above will be of immeasurable aid. They are discussed, however, not as the be-all and end-all, but rather to demonstrate some of the problems facing the director, and to give him a start toward solving them. If the director knows where he wants the audience to look and can make it look there, he will have fulfilled one of his responsibilities. The novice is strongly recommended to read and memorize the list of "Methods of Obtaining Emphasis" in Dean, and to use them consciously in his first few attempts at direction. He will not become a competent director until the ways of centering the attention of the audience are second nature to him. He can no more direct with his mind on such technicalities than the painter can paint when he is concerned with the way he is holding the brush. As in any art, the tool must become an extension of the artist if it is to be used effectively.

Balance

A few years ago I had the unfortunate experience of sitting through a badly directed high school play. I was interested to note from my seat in the rear of the gymnasium, close to the exit, that by the middle of the second act almost the entire house, at least that portion that was still following the play, was sitting on the left hip, trying in vain to bring the stage into balance. The director, following the floor plan found in the back of the "acting edition" of the play, had placed his main entrance up left and he was not skillful enough at, or did not recognize the necessity for, getting his actors out of that area, and almost the entire play was played there.

As human beings we want to see things in balance, and woe be unto the director who does not cater to that wish. The picture hanging askew can destroy the evening for many playgoers, while a stage continually out of balance will destroy the play for all.

For blocking purposes it is wise, I believe, to think in terms of three kinds of balance—formal, informal, and character.[67] Formal balance is simply equal weight on either side of the stage. Each figure is balanced by another figure on the opposite side of the stage as children of the same weight are balanced an equal distance from the center of the teeter-totter. As can be imagined, this type of balance can grow tiring if used too obviously or too often. It is, however, wise to consider formal balance when tackling a Greek tragedy or a French neoclassic. A courtroom scene or a throne room scene will generally call for a very formal feeling. Balancing weight against weight will often help to achieve this overall feeling.

Informal balance retains a trace of the formal feeling, but is not nearly as obvious and offers more possibilities than does strictly formal balance. Using informal balance, one figure can balance three or four by simply moving away from center. In order to visualize this type of balance, think of a little boy teeter-tottering with his father. The father sits in front of the handles, close to the fulcrum, while the little boy sits as close to the end as he can. The further away from the fulcrum the little boy moves, the more weight he can balance. On stage, the director uses the center line as the fulcrum and the side wall ends for the end of the teeter-totter. A figure, say three feet from the right-side wall, will balance a figure three feet to the left of center. In the case of one figure balancing three or four, the single figure need only balance the last figure on the opposite side of the stage. That is to say, if A is balancing B, C, and D, then A must be the same distance from the right-side wall as D is from the left. When one figure balances more than three, the distance the single figure moves from center decreases with each figure added. The single figure will never reach the side wall, in other words, and, somewhere over three (probably between four and seven, depending upon the play), the addition of more figures will not materially add to the weight, as far as the audience is concerned. The director can see this principle clearly only by sitting in the middle of the house and asking five or six friends to try various positions for him, until he "gets the feel" of one figure balancing three or four.

The most usable and most used type of balance is character, or emphasis, balance. Here the director can, either by using the inherent weight of the character or by using the weight he has added by focusing the attention of the audience upon a particular character, bring a stage into a satisfying balance regardless of the weight left and right of center. Thus one man can balance a hundred if the one man is Cyrano holding back the hundred assassins. The weight of a Hamlet or a Peer Gynt will balance a stage full of lesser characters. The character weight will be determined by how interested the audience is in the character. Peer Gynt has no difficulty holding down stage right while stage left is filled with mourners for the boy who cut off his finger, but Peer might well have difficulty in holding his side of the stage if the other side was filled with the troll king and his followers.

A word of warning here: When one is speaking of character balance, one is talking of weight built in by the playwright, but some actors have such a magnetic quality that they carry their own weight. There are some women, for example, so startlingly beautiful that the audience cannot keep its eyes from them. In such cases the director is wise to use the built-in weight to throw the attention of the audience to the desired spot, and even then it may take considerable experimentation to find the solution. Fortunately, or perhaps I should say unfortunately, for it is always pleasant to work with such a personality or such a beautiful woman, there are few such actors, and when the director is faced with the problem he need only be aware of its existence to devise some way to overcome it. It is when he is unaware of this problem that his design is ruined.

Balance problems seldom arise unless the full stage is being used. In smaller scenes, where only one or two areas of the stage are being used, the audience automatically cuts the stage down to the areas being played. It is important, however, to think in terms of a balance for the overall play, and in small-cast plays it is necessary to plan the various scenes in such a manner that all areas of the stage are used. All areas do not have to be played an equal amount of time, rather it is often wise to save an area for one of two "big" scenes. Just as a Hamlet or a Peer may carry an inherent weight, so may an important scene. Thus, an important scene played in an area used only a few times during the play will balance an area used often for less important scenes.

Stability and Sequence

Closely connected with the problem of balance are two factors: stability and sequence. To give a stage stability in terms of actor placement means simply to tie the composition to the stage. A stage grouping placed center will seem suspended, it will seem to float off into space. In other words, it will not have a stable quality. To anchor the grouping to the stage, one has only to add figures down left and down right; the number will depend on the size of the group center, but in most cases two or three will suffice, and often one or two will tie the group to the stage. Sequence, too, is used in terms of stage groupings; that is, sequence ties groups together while still allowing the groups to retain their individuality. Sequence problems are solved by adding figures between the groups.

The size of the stage is a problem that often bothers directors with more than a little experience. In many of the secondary schools across the country, plays are presented in a space some fiend of the architectural world has labeled the "all-purpose" room. In actuality the term "no-purpose" room would come closer to fitting these monstrosities that enthrall so many administrators in our public schools. Very often, in such rooms, the architect has decided to be generous and give the director lots of room. As a result, he has run the stage along one side of the room. Hence the director will find himself with a fifty-foot proscenium opening and ten feet of depth, with no backstage room, and no access to the stage except through the house. No matter how much experience he has, the director will find that such a playing area gives rise to serious problems. But though such a stage limits the director drastically, it must not stymie him completely. Generally he is wise to cut down the opening, simply by not pulling the curtain all the way. This will give him some off-stage space, and if it makes for sight-line problems, simply cut some seats along either side. Better to run an extra performance, if seats are at a premium, than try to fill the entire space with furniture and action.

In general the stage should be just big enough to handle the particular play, and in my opinion a director is better off with a stage a trifle too small rather than one that is too large. The more limited the playing area, the more carefully must the director plan his blocking and the more exacting must the actors be. An appearance of spaciousness can be achieved upon a small stage, but a large space filled with furniture can only slow down the action. Long crosses to exits and long entrances can slow down and deaden the pace of the play faster than any other single fault. Hence, I would advise that the director plan his action in as small an area as is suitable to the particular play.

The depth of the playing area will depend on the play. As a general rule, the lighter the play the further down stage it will be played. The action of most farces, for example, will take place on, or just above, the curtain line. The heavier the drama, the deeper it will be played. It is an easy rule to remember: The deeper the thought or the emotion, the deeper the staging. Obviously this does not imply that a farce cannot have a good deal of its action take place upstage, or that a tragedy will be played against the back wall, but for the most part there will be a direct relation between the depth of feeling and the depth of the playing area.

Where various scenes are played is often dictated by the furniture arrangement. Whether or not there is any value in assigning certain "tonal qualities" to the various areas of the stage, as has been done by Dean and others, we will not go into here. It is sufficient to say that knowing the tonal qualities listed by Dean[68] can be helpful if the director is in a quandary about where to play a certain scene.

Stage Picturization

While I have discussed the type of play being blocked and, in general, the effect that such things as line and shape may have upon the mood of the audience, thus far the discussion has been in terms of form only. But if blocking is the process whereby visual form is given to the written work, as I have stated I believe it to be, if it is the transferring from the page to the stage, then it is the transferring and the transforming of the basic plot line as well as the form. The blocking must not only make the action clear to the audience, it must interpret that action as well. The director-artist creates the form and within that form interprets the playwright's intent. It is his responsibility to see that the playwright's story is told not only through the dialogue, but also through the staging.

In the field of dance it is possible to present highly individualized character through the artistic use of dance and mime, and to reveal incredible depth of character. In the legitimate drama it should be the aim of the director to aid, not supersede or repeat, the dialogue. Blocking is not choreography; it should not try to do too much. I recall working in stock with a young woman who had spent most of her stage life in the dance. She was playing a role in Coward's *Hay Fever,* and as it was the first time in years she had spoken a word on stage, she found dialogue quite difficult. Her movement was superb and left nothing to be desired. When I complimented her after a rehearsal, she answered, "Oh, yes, both my body and I know . . . perfectly; it's those damn words that keep getting in the way." The director must bear in mind that he is using movement to aid the words, not to take their place. Thus it is that only the broad outline of the plot should be pictured. It is the essence of the story that the director should strive to achieve. If the director is successful in picturing the essence of the scene, the dialogue and action will particularize the show.

Regardless of the hallowed reputation of the dramatist or of the intellectual content of his drama, it is important to remember that any good playwright is first and foremost a storyteller. When he is absolutely satisfied that he knows what story the dramatist is telling, the director is ready to outline that story with his blocking. He will then stage, i.e. create, a moving picture that is the essence of the dramatic actions that go to make up the rite.

I recall once talking with a man, fairly well along in years, who had just witnessed a dress rehearsal of the children's play *The Indian Captive*. He told me that as the curtain went up his hearing aid had "quit on him." Though he could not hear a word of the dialogue, he maintained he had enjoyed the production considerably. Here was an excellent opportunity to check the storytelling quality of blocking, and I asked him to tell me the story he had seen. He did so with more than a little insight into the characters. He was stymied at one point only, the relationship between the Indian girl, Eagle Feather, and Cornplanter, the Indian Chief. Those familiar with the play will remember that the girl is the chief's wife. The hatred of Eleanor is based on Eagle Feather's prejudice against white people and not, as our deaf watcher had thought, on feminine jealousy. After thinking it over I attempted to picture this relationship, but without success and, as I later decided, without justification. The relationship is spelled out clearly in the dialogue and needs no help from the blocking. The student will remember that the example is that of a children's play where both plot line and relationships are usually strong and simple. I do not believe such a result could be achieved with a complicated comedy without getting in the way of the play, nor do I believe that a director should attempt it.

How much of the story will be told by the blocking and the pantomime of the actors will, once the basic outline is there, be dependent on the abilities of the actors. With the help of a few simple principles the director should have little difficulty in building a series of pictures that will spell out the broad outlines of any story.

Good storytelling blocking is often as much aid to the actor as it is to the audience, because it will clarify and define relationships for him, as well as dictate many line readings that might otherwise be troublesome.

Arriving at the story that the blocking will help tell is a problem of analysis, but staging the essence of the story is a problem in blocking where art and technique must blend.

This book takes the view that all scenes in modern and other drama are staged rites. We will assume the director knows the rite and the dramatic actions he is to stage. His problem is to build his picture around the essence of the rite. How does he go about solving this problem?

Let us assume that the rite is that of Confession. Now, a scene built around the rite of Confession would undoubtedly have a series of dramatic actions that would build to the confession proper, but for our present purposes let us take only the act of confession itself. Confession carries the implication of admitting, or owning up, to something. It implies a relationship that, for the moment at least, places the one hearing the confession above the one making it. Generally it has a quality of repentance about it. Whether the quality is one of defiance or humbleness, whether the confession is rejected or accepted, will be revealed by the dialogue, but for our example let us say that it is seeking forgiveness from a loved but feared authority. This much we can and should include in the blocking.

If one thinks of confession, one of two examples will spring to mind, either confession in the church or a criminal confessing a crime. As we have stipulated a "loved but feared authority," let us take the church, though, depending upon the dialogue, the criminal confession would suit as well. Having decided upon the church, next I would attempt to imagine as typical and stereotyped a picture as my mind could invent. A man on his knees before a crucifix which hangs fairly high on a wall. He looks up at the crucifix, but does not gaze at it directly, almost as if he dare not meet the eyes. His hands are clasped in the traditional pose of the supplicant. He tells his story with the tears of true repentance streaming down his face, but with fear in his voice for the retribution he expects to follow.

Now, to stage the scene this way when our principals are a teen-aged boy and a headmaster would be absurd, but in the imagined scene we can find the essence of pictorial confession. We put the boy in a chair, instead of kneeling on the floor. One foot, the left, is under his chair with the toe only on the floor. He leans forward with his right arm on his right knee; his right hand is extended with the palm open and up. The head is bent slightly down, but the eyes look up. The headmaster is standing a short distance away from him, perhaps behind a desk. He stands straight and tall; perhaps he holds a book or a pencil in both hands at waist level. His head is bent slightly, eyes looking down on the boy. Such a picture might easily be too much for the scene, but the position of the boy and the headmaster alone could, with the help of some dialogue, suggest confession.

Let us take one more example, Reading the Will. The director will have two factors to mix here. Again the church can be of help as this scene evokes, as it were, the voice from beyond the grave. Though this ceremony is for the living, it is the dead who hold all the cards, and the reading is a solemn and formal rite partly in honor of the departed. But in spite of the "religious" quality, the reading is in reality a legal rite. Thus the director might well decide to attempt a picture that will be reminiscent of a funeral service and a courtroom scene. Again, of course, it will be dependent upon the dialogue, but let us suppose that in our play the widow is in for a tremendous surprise because the money and estates have been left, for the most part, to the mistress. We will need to have considerable distance between the two women. As this is a big family and all are present, balance, sequence, and stability may well create problems. Certainly, with the stage full of relatives, the director will make sure that at least the three principals— the lawyer, reading the will; the widow; and the mistress— are all easily seen and heard. He will take pains to use a different means of directing the audience's attention for each of the three and probably provide for the lawyer to fade into the background once his contribution is made.

The distance between the two women will be horizontal rather than vertical, and as any conflict is usually strengthened by having the parties face each other over some barrier, suggesting that they might well come to blows if they were closer, it might be wise to place the two in such a position that the rest of the family acts as that barrier. With the family in such a position it would be possible not only to use them for purposes of emphasis, but also, by their body position and line, to indicate which side of the dispute they favored.

Our scene has been set in the library, and previously we have watched the butler and the maid arrange the chairs for the ceremony. The desk over left will serve as a pulpit and/or judge's bench. If we wanted to stress the funeral side of the picture, the stand that holds the large dictionary might well replace the desk. The church and funeral atmosphere can be forwarded with the entrances—the first person entering alone slips into the back row, all who follow enter with a solemn demeanor. The lawyer (judge–minister) enters last with the widow on his arm. They walk down the aisle of chairs and the lawyer places a chair beside the desk, facing the family, for the widow. Now the widow is facing the family, close to the will and last testament of her husband, but also facing the family as a witness might face the courtroom in a trial scene. The mistress enters last and takes a seat near the back on the downstage side. If, when the revelation comes, the widow rises in anger and the mistress in surprise, we are into the dramatic action that follows the reading proper.

Neither of the two examples is taken from a play, but both picture ideas might be used in several different plays. It is the essence of the rite we are attempting to suggest through the process of picturization, not each word or syllable of the dialogue.

Notice that neither of the examples is meant as a tabloid, for the director should never think in terms of static pictures. His pictures must fade, blend, melt into one another until the play is one continuous flow of action. The director who cannot visualize the flow of continuous pictures is very apt to fall into the trap of maneuvering his actors around until they fall into the correct relationship for the picture he has in mind, and freeze there until the next picture comes up. Such a technique can be used to good advantage only when one is directing an old melodrama and making fun of the style used in an earlier day.

For highly imaginative use of storytelling pictures the student should make it a point to see some of the early silent movies of D. W. Griffith and the early comedies of Charlie Chaplin.

Movement

Thus far a great deal has been said about where to put actors and how to use them to point, balance, picture, etc., but almost nothing has been said about how to get them into a position where they will accomplish the desired effect. Obviously, they move to these positions.

One of the most pleasant and relaxing ways to spend an evening for me, as well as for many others I am sure, is to sit in front of an open fire and listen to good music. The intricate harmonies for the ear and the ever changing, never repeated pattern of movement in living flame for the eye almost hypnotize the mind; a fascinating attention-holding study in abstractions.

For the eye, an open fire or a body of water are restful and at the same time interesting. The surface of a small creek or the interesting waters of Puget Sound, before me as I write these words, both have an always changing, always satisfying fascination. No matter what basic innermost impulse is responsible for our universal interest in water and fire, one of the attention-holding factors in both cases is movement. It is movement that will catch and hold the eye. As it is in nature, so is it on the stage. Movement will capture the attention of the audience more quickly than any other method. If the movement is not carefully planned, it will, in its attention-capturing power, prevent the audience from seeing the play the author wrote.

The fact that movement has an emphasizing quality of its own, and that the line movement creates will affect the mood of the audience has been touched upon above. It is necessary, however, to examine movement much more closely than has thus far been attempted if the director is to have any mastery over this, the most powerful of tools. While movement is, in my opinion, the director's most powerful tool, it is, judging from productions I have seen, the least understood.

Too many beginning directors are of the opinion that the movement suggested in the "acting editions" is sufficient and adequate, but in the vast majority of cases, it is neither. One has only to remember that such movement is, for the most part, designed by a particular director for a particular production with a particular actor playing a particular role. It is always designed for a particular set and a particular size stage with particular pieces of furniture. In short, such movement is highly particularized and will seldom do the same job when any of the particulars is changed.

True, the playwright will often have definite movements and definite business written into his script. At the risk of displeasing some budding young playwright and many older ones, I would strongly advise that such movement be looked upon as sign posts only, never as commands. Most playwrights are not familiar with the principles of direction, and a good director can usually come up with a better move or bit of business than the one suggested by the author. If he cannot, and if the line or situation does call for a move or bit of business, then certainly the director should not hesitate to use suggestions from the author, or from anyone else for that matter.

How, the reader may well be asking, can I discuss the problems of staging the playwright's intent, and then about-face and say ignore his directions? I can do so for two reasons. The first, already mentioned, is that the director should, once he is sure where the intent lies, be able to come up with a better move, or at least one that will better fit his particular situation, than will the playwright who is thinking of an ideal situation instead of the particular one facing the director at that given moment. What Bert Lahr, for example, could do with a move or a piece of business, your actor may not be able to touch, and very often in today's theater, as well as in the Shakesperean theater, the author writes with a particular person in mind. The second reason I feel free to advise using the author's directions as suggestions rather than commands is that many authors write directions to help themselves visualize the action and many do as Shaw has written he did, write directions for the reading public while expecting the director and actor to come up with much better ideas.

Having read a great many original scripts, I am almost inclined to generalize that when the writer is not writing for a reading public, as Shaw certainly was, then the more experienced and skilled the writer, the fewer directions he writes in.

Often the director has no choice but to use the business or moves that are written in, and this will hold true most often in farce, where the plays are rewritten during rehearsal to fit the business that develops out of the rehearsals. To invent clumsy moves or business when the author has provided the director with good ones is, of course, pure foolishness and must be avoided. By the same token, to treat as a royal command a playwright's idea for blocking can be just as foolish. They are only sign posts, but they are valuable ones.

Finally, the director who relies solely upon the directions printed in the "acting edition," or on the suggestions included by the playwright, is denying both himself and the actors one of the most enjoyable and creative activities that either direction or acting has to offer.

Several distinct tasks are accomplished through movement: first, from the viewpoint of both the actor and the director, movement is an important part of the character being portrayed; secondly, again from both vantage points, movement interprets the play; and thirdly—and this is more the director's problem than the actors—movement gets the actor on and off the stage, and positions him for particular pieces of business. The three qualities, three kinds, or three uses of movement are separated only for purposes of discussion, since obviously the actor must interpret and get on and off with character movement. Any one move may well fulfill all three tasks. For purposes of our discussion, we will talk in terms of character movement, interpretive, or storytelling movement, and technical movement. All three must come from, and be inherent in, the script.

The overall quality of the movement, i.e. the kind of movement, will be dictated by the type of play being produced. While it is true that the terms "comedy," "tragedy," and "farce" are often almost meaningless when combined, e.g., "a tragicomedy drama in three farcical acts,"[69] in general a play will lean more heavily toward one of the usual classifications.

Comedy will call for a faster, livelier quality in the movement than will tragedy, while the farce will demand a zany, insane quality throughout the play. (When discussing the quality of movement, it must be understood that I am speaking of the feeling of the move, not the energy, the vigor, and freshness that must always be present regardless of the type of play being performed. There must be an energy under even the most tired defeated move. That is to say, the actor must always have energy in reserve, must always be underneath the role, even when the character is tired, worn out, and defeated.) Both comedy and farce will be filled with short crosses and quick entrances and exits, but the comedy will often call for the curved cross that will give a softer quality, a more languid, almost liquid quality to the blocking. Movement in the farce will be abrupt, sudden, hard, and brilliant. The difference in the quality of the movement between comedy and farce might be likened to the difference between a kitten's play with a piece of thread and a great dane puppy saying Hello to the family after being left alone for a few hours. It is that difference which the ballet accomplishes so beautifully, the headmistress in *Graduation Ball* or the light-hearted movement in many of the dances performed at Aurora's Wedding.

The classic tragedy, on the other hand, will be filled with long, stately crosses and the movement will have a deliberate, inevitable quality. The realistic modern tragedy or drama often lends itself to a heavy, almost labored, quality. But I would again stress that no matter how slow or how stately, no matter how heavy or labored the movement, there must always be a vital, alive quality underneath the character movement. Failure to insist on this quality will mean playing to an empty house by the final curtain.

The importance of the basic quality exhibited in the movement was brought home one evening while watching a civic theater production of *My Three Angels*. The director, probably because of the unusual situation created by the presence of three convicts in a family household at Christmas time, mistakenly conceived of the play as a farce and blocked it accordingly, this in spite of the author's forewarning that it was a "Gallic fairy tale." The evening was a complete bore and the play completely missed. When this play is handled lightly and delicately, with what might be called the Peter Pan quality of that never-never land just out of reach, it provides a delightful, light evening of entertainment. Playing this particular play as a farce destroyed its fairy-tale quality. By his blocking and movement design, the director had taken a situation in which three lovable French convicts bring Christmas joy to a badgered family by cheerfully murdering the mean rich uncle and the cowardly sneaky nephew who would, with the uncle's backing, force himself upon the ingenue. The farcical handling of plot, that is, the fast, hard playing, placed the whole idea of the play within the realm of bad taste.

The quality of the movement will be dictated by the type of play, and the director who misses the quality called for will miss the play.

Of course, it should be evident that much of the quality is left finally in the hands of the actor. For example, the line, "Stop in the King's name," might well take the same basic move in a tragedy, comedy, or farce, but the difference in the execution of the move would be tremendous.

Because the stage is a place for action and because movement has such a strong interpretive quality, the director has an excellent opportunity in the early rehearsals to set the actor upon the "correct" road insofar as line readings are concerned. In fact, in the amateur theater, where the actor is often not at all familiar with the play until he comes to the first rehearsal, the director can, with his blocking, settle many problems of interpretation before they ever arise. Almost any line in any situation can be read in a number of ways, but when the actor is moving toward the object or person his line refers to, the choice of readings is considerably narrowed. For example, an actor saying, "You don't dare touch me," will automatically interpret the line one way if he is moving toward the person, quite another if he is backing away, and will mean something still different if he is edging up or down while reading the line. Once again, the execution, that is, the manner in which the actor accomplishes the move, will depend upon the kind of play being produced. The backing away move might well bring a laugh in a farce, a slight chuckle in a comedy, tears in a drama, and fear in a tragedy. The basic interpretation given the line by the move would be the same; the audience response, however, will depend upon the method of execution.

Not only will the move command the attention of the audience, it will be, in many cases, the deciding factor in the interpretation of the line. The director must remember that the play the audience sees depends completely on where its attention is focused and what it sees there. He cannot depend on the line alone, for in any battle for attention between the eye and the ear, the eye will emerge the victor. Thus if the actor says, "I am not afraid of you," in a strong, brave voice, but at the same time backs away, the audience will believe the move, not the voice, and in its mind he will be afraid. If, on the other hand, he advances toward the other party, even without a line, the audience will conclude that he is, indeed, not afraid. On the stage, even more so than in life, actions do speak louder than words.

Every director is faced with the problem of "when and where do I move them." When the actor moves and when he "stays put"—that is, when he "holds"—depends upon first, his character; second, the situation; third, the line itself; and finally, the technical requirements. "On the stage," says

Stanislavski, "you must always be enacting something; action, motion is the basis of the art followed by the actor." Later he amends that statement to, "On the stage it is necessary to act, either outwardly or inwardly."[70] The director might well paraphrase this to, "On the stage there is always movement, either inner or outer, and if it is inner, it can be made outer if necessary." Just as Stanislavski warns his students never to "run for the sake of running, or suffer for the sake of suffering," so the director must resist the temptation to use a move for the sake of movement. The important thing to bear in mind is that, if absolutely necessary, any line can take movement. Most lines have an inherent movement and often the director, by close observation, can catch the beginnings of a gesture, a leaning into or away from in an actor's reading and build that gesture into a cross or an exciting move. The test for any move is simply, does it add to the meaning, the intent, of the drama. If the move adds, it is a good one; if it does not add, it will detract and should be cut.

The playwright's dialogue, then, is the true basis for any and all movement and even the most technical move must be justified by that dialogue.

When one speaks of justifying movement, a word of caution is necessary. I recall an experience early in my own directing career when, in the middle of a tense scene, I was shocked to see one of the minor characters, whom I had given a move, yawn quite noticeably. The actress was not receiving the emphasis at the time, as the move was a purely technical one making possible a quick exit demanded by the situation. When I hurried backstage after the performance and demanded to know what she thought she was doing, she, rather testily, replied that she was simply following incomprehensible direction. I learned, much to my chagrin, that she had, early in the rehearsal period, asked me what her motivation was for the move. Apparently, with my mind on the exit about to take place, I had replied that I didn't have the slightest idea; maybe she was tired of standing still. As a director I learned two valuable lessons from this experience: one, that every move is vitally important and two, so is every actress. The girl was correct in what she was trying to do, the move needed some justification and while she had, with my help, chosen an idiotic motivation, she had at least tried to make the move believable through justifying it. If the actor cannot justify a move, and if the director cannot help him in his search, the move must be changed to one in which the actor can believe.

In the rather general discussion that has gone before, I have spoken of the "quality" that a move or a movement design sometimes carries, and of movement that is inherent in a line. I have also touched upon the necessity for justification or finding motivation for even the technical movement. It follows, therefore, that finding the movement in a script is, in the final analysis, dependent upon having a "feeling" for, or a "sensitivity" to, the author's intent. More so than any tool or principle thus far discussed, movement is difficult to talk about away from a particular script. Movement is the action, the essence, of the theater, and while it is possible to communicate the meaning and to give examples of such tools as balance, stability, picturization, and sequence, movement is so closely bound up within the character as portrayed by a particular actor that there are few, if any, generalizations (including this one) that will hold true. It is, I believe, this vagueness about teaching movement that is responsible for so many directors believing that it is impossible to teach direction. The director will, with study and experience, discover the lines that will take strong, long movement and those that will not. He will, with experience, think in terms of a particular kind of movement for a particular kind of play. If the student lacks even the beginnings of a sensitivity to movement, then the theater is not for him. Achieving any sort of success with any sort of play depends upon understanding the underlying action within that play. The job of the director is to use his art to transfer the play from page to stage. Movement is his chief and most powerful tool; he must eventually reach an understanding of stage movement or change his profession.

General Rules for Movement

Actors generally move on their own lines. As has been stated, movement is a strong emphasizing agent. Movement will capture and hold the attention of the audience; hence, as the ear cannot compete with the eye for attention, a moving actor will receive the emphasis. In most cases the move and the line will be simultaneous; however, whether the move comes on, before, or after the line will be dependent on what the director is attempting to point. If the move itself is vital, then the director will use the spoken word to focus the attention of the audience on the actor about to move. If the line is the vital ingredient, the move should be used to focus the attention of the audience on the actor before he begins speaking. A single moving figure on stage will attract every eye, and as the ear will follow where the eye leads, the audience will be ready to catch the important line. Notice that in each case the line or the move is vital to the play. If, as in a vast majority of cases, neither the line nor the move needs special pointing, they will begin simultaneously.

Movement towards a person or object to which the line is directed has a positive quality; movement away from the person or object carries a negative quality. As was discussed above, the line "I'm not afraid of you" will be positive if the actor is moving toward the person or thing, and will become negative if he moves away from it. This simple and rather obvious rule has hundreds of variations within its confines. Thus, the negative line "I really don't like to stay here, the room frightens me" will take on a positive determination if, during the line, the actor advances into the room and sits. The line will become much more negative if the actor moves toward an exit during the reading.

Movement into the audience tends to be strong and positive; movement away from the audience tends to be weak and negative. The basis for this rule is the same as the one for strength and weakness of the various body positions: the more face the audience sees, the stronger the move becomes. The negative line "I really don't like to stay here, the room frightens me" will be much more emphatic and much more positive if, when the actor moves into the room, he is moving from up center to down center than if he is moving from, say, stage left to right center. A little experimentation with crosses into and away from the audience will bear interesting fruit. The line will become much weaker and much more negative if the actor moves directly from down center to up center. It will become stronger, but retain its negative quality, if the actor tosses it over his shoulder into the audience while moving up. It will be very strong, but very negative, if he backs from down center to up center while reading the line. He can start his line down center, looking around—"I don't like to stay here"—cross full back up center, turn, and finish the line directly into the audience —"the room frightens me"—and make the line strong and positive with a slow deliberate turn, or weak and negative with a quick frightened turn. The variations are endless.

Exits are generally more important than entrances. Because the direction of the actor's movement is important, the placement of doors, arches, etc. is vitally important, and a director can save literally hours of rehearsal time if the means of entering and exiting are thoughtfully placed in the set design. Remembering that the more face the audience sees the stronger the move becomes, it follows that an up-center position is best for important entrances but difficult for important exits. The strongest exits are made down right or left but, as many sets have only one entrance and the demands of the script place it up center, the director must know how to make the best of a rather awkward situation. Actually, an up-center exit can become quite strong if the actor will save part of his line until he reaches the exit, then turn, deliver the line, and take his exit. It is important to notice that strong and weak, positive and negative, do not carry the implied meaning of good or important, or bad and unimportant. A negative exit is often temendously strong and can be made to be very emphatic. A strong move is strong because it is easy for the audience to "look him in the eye"; a weak move is weak because it is difficult to see the eyes. However, a weak, negative move can be emphasized and is often an important part of the drama. For example, think of Shylock's final exit. Shakespeare has not even given him an exit line, for he cannot leave on his final line; he must wait for the Duke to grant him the permission he begs:

SHYLOCK: I pray you give me leave to go from hence: I
am not well. Send the deed after me,
And I will sign it.

DUKE: Get thee gone, but do it.

GRATIANO: In Christening thou shalt have two godfathers:
Had I been judge, thou shouldst have had ten
more,
to bring thee to the gallow, not the font.

(exit Shylock)

Here is a case where the exit is, in effect, the plot's end. In a professional production with a star in the role of Shakespeare's Jew, the final exit would have to be pointed even if the situation did not call for such an emphatic exit. In this example the character is completely defeated. It is a broken man who leaves the courtroom and the exit must be weak and negative. An up-center exit could be made to work very nicely, especially if the set were so designed that the upstage area was on a level. Such a design would let us have Shylock climb up out of the arena where he had lost all he had owned. Shylock might well start his exit as soon as the Duke gave him permission and walk through Gratiano's line. If the exit was a short one, he might hold until the line was finished. In either case he would probably pause and at least start to turn back to the court at the exit; he might start a last plea and then change his mind. Regardless of the interpretation, the exit would have to be a "big one" with lots of emphasis on it, but at the same time it would have to keep its negative and weak quality. A play that demands strong, positive exits will work best with the exits located down left or down right. There is probably more than a grain of truth in the theory that a cross made against the normal eye pattern, that is, left to right, seems more positive than one made in harmony with the eye pattern. At any rate, it does seem to be true that a cross or an exit made from stage left to stage right, that is, against the normal eye pattern which moves from stage right to stage left, is more positive than a cross moving the other way.

Exits must be kept short. The actor who is allowed to speak his line from his position and then start the exit will almost always kill his exit. Except in a situation as described above, in which Shylock's exit is all-important, the longer the exit, the more ineffectual it will be. The greatest danger in the long exit is not, however, that of killing the exit; rather, it is in slowing down the tempo and action of the play. In most cases the dialogue cannot continue until the exit is completed, and it takes an unusual situation and a rather unusual character to sustain a long cross to the exit. In general, a good rule to follow is *line and off.* If either the set or blocking is so designed as to necessitate long crosses to the exit, the director should ask the actor to split the lines and to save the tag of the speech for delivery at the exit.

Entrances must be timed to bring the actor into position when the cue comes up. Most amateurs are prone to wait in the wings until they hear their cue, then start the entrance. The action cannot proceed until the next line is delivered, and either the entrance itself must be tremendously interesting or the reputation of the actor must be such that the audience has been waiting to see him to justify holding for the entrance itself. Thus, either the actor must hit stage and begin his line at the same time, or he must be in his position when his line comes up.

All entrances must start at least six feet off stage, and all exits must continue for at least that distance after leaving the stage. All too often the audience is subjected to watching an actor don his character as he makes his entrance or to seeing him drop his character as he is disappearing in the wings.

A cross is seldom longer than the line. The length of a cross will, of course, be determined by the necessities of the design, the furniture placement, the business which must be accomplished, and the situation itself, but in the majority of cases, as an actor moves on his lines, the length of the line will determine the length of the cross. An actor is often asked to cross as far as the line will take him. It should be borne in mind, however, that when necessary, as much or as little of the stage can be covered as is required at the moment. Thus it is that a very short line can be broken, read slowly, haltingly, or explosively, as the need requires. "Oh, nooooooooooooooo youuuuuuu don't," can, if need be, take an actor all around the stage or can be read as quickly as the actor can deliver a right to the chin.

Cues must be picked up immediately. Very seldom is a cross, a reaction, or a piece of business worth holding up the flow of dialogue. Many professional actors seem to feel that they are achieving a deliberate quality by holding their line until either the move or the business is completed. In most cases they have only made the play drag.

Crosses, head action, turns, and gestures should be used to punctuate lines. A turn, a pause in a pacing scene, a gesture stopped before completion can be a much more effective form of punctuation that the comma or the period, for in general, the body position will shift as the thought shifts. The actor has a great aid here in cueing the audience to the character's line of thinking.

When two or more actors enter simultaneously, the speaking actor will enter last. On any except an extreme downstage entrance, this order of entrance will allow the speaker to throw his line downstage rather than back over his shoulder. The entrance of the nonspeaking actor also helps to point the entrance of the speaker.

Any unusual move will carry its own built-in emphasis. An entrance through a window, crawling, running, backing on, sliding down a banister, doing a flip, dancing, or stumbling will make for emphatic entrances as well as help define character.

Crosses which follow the set line will seem weaker than those which are at right angles to it. Not only is the actor apt to blend in with the wall, but unconsciously the audience is likely to place him in the wallflower class much like Kipling's water rat, who was always trying to get up enough courage to go out into the middle of the room. Inexperienced directors seem prone to line up their casts around the walls of the set, possibly keeping center open just in case anything interesting does happen.

The actor making the cross should be downstage of the other actors on stage. As has been pointed out several times, we are interested in the faces of those we watch. As an actor takes his cross the audience will tend to follow his face, and if the line of the cross is interrupted momentarily by another face, valuable words may be lost while the audience catches up with the moving actor.

Most of the action should be down of the furniture. When left to his own devices, an inexperienced actor will play upstage of the furniture. He seems anxious, often with just cause, to get a barrier between himself and the audience so that he won't be hanging out there all by himself with no protection. Whenever possible the director should bring the actor out into the open where the whole body can be seen. Of course this does not imply that one never blocks behind furniture, very effective scenes can be played there, but in general, keep the actor out in the open.

Don't allow furniture grabbing. Many actors, regardless

and while a show may well be produced in many different "manners or ways," it is difficult to conceive of one being produced without any "manner or way," that is, without any style. As in all other facets of the theater, so it is with style; "The play's the thing," and from it must come the particular style. Specifically, the writer's style is found in the dialogue and it is from the lines that the movement style must come. No actor of any sensitivity can speak noble lines with a hoodlum's slouch. No actor worthy of the name will "feel" the same realistic movement demanded by Miller's realistic dialogue in *Death of a Salesman* in the poetic lines of Christopher Fry's *The Lady's Not for Burning*. The actor who "feels" to "move normally" while reading the lines of Sir Fopling Flutter in Etherege's *The Man of Mode* has either got big personality problems or is no actor. Likewise, it is almost physically impossible for an actress dressed in the style of the late 1800s to move with the freedom a modern girl is allowed. I say "almost" because I recently watched an off-Broadway production of Strindberg's *The Creditors* in which the leading lady not only managed to achieve the movement of the modern girl, but was equally successful in "modernizing" the line delivery. Though her reviews were good, Strindberg was destroyed. While the actor should feel the style of movement from the style of the writing, the final responsibility, as always, falls on the director, and he must work with the actor until he has achieved movement within the original style of the author.

This is not to imply that a style should be forced upon a production, as Vsevolod Meyerhold was fond of doing, though in some cases this may improve the drama. For before the director can begin to experiment with a style, he must understand exactly what it is he is departing from.

Movement can help build a scene to a climax. There are several ways in which movement can help build to a climax: increasing the speed of the movement, increasing the number of people moving, starting with an individual movement and enlarging the particular movement to a group movement, increasing the tension underneath the various moves, increasing the hand movement, increasing the number of people crossing one another, increasing and shortening the number of crosses, moving the figures further downstage, and increasing the number of figures on levels—any and all of these will help build to a climax. The young director will do well to watch good ballet and musical comedy choreography for interesting and exciting ways of using movement to build scenes to a climax.

The smaller the playing area, the more precise the movement. Working on a small stage often calls for considerably more ingenuity and authority on the part of the director than does working on a large stage. While on a large playing area it is possible to let the actors play a given area, on the small stage with a crowd scene it is often necessary to be exacting in the placement. A small stage can be made to seem quite roomy providing the blocking is so designed to let actors cross each other without edging by. While the audience is quite aware of the width of the stage, they have a very vague idea about the depth used in any production; thus with careful blocking, a shallow stage can appear to be spacious.

While discussing the matter of playing space it may be helpful to some to mention the problem of the character who is confined by the role to a particular piece of furniture—a bed, a chair, or a davenport. In these cases, and they occur more often than one would think, it is wisest, I find, to treat the piece of furniture as a stage itself. The face can play in many different positions and in many different areas of the reduced stage.

Explain your terminology at an early rehearsal. Not only must the director be thoroughly familiar with the various terms used on the stage, he must be sure that the actors understand his meaning. The time it takes to explain these terms will be time gained in the long run. I am once again reminded of our bright young Broadway director. One of his favorite directions (remember, he did not believe in blocking) was "take stage." Within my experience, to "take stage" has generally meant to move upstage in order to receive the emphasis. My term for that is "take the scene," not "take stage." In the particular circumstance, I had been directing six to eight of the usual ten plays produced per year and the company was familiar with my use of the term "take the scene," but when the phrase "take stage" would ring out, with some fifteen on stage, the actors became confused. The director was continually telling the character man, with forty years professional experience behind him, to "take stage." After several wasted rehearsals it developed that "take stage" to the director meant to invent a way to take the emphasis, to play the area or to gesture, to "play the scene bigger." To the character man the direction "take stage" meant only one thing, move center. So time after time he would move center for his speech. Finally, after the director complained to me about the particular actor not knowing his business, the two got together on their terms and the problems disappeared.

When working with amateurs, it is wise to assume that they do not know their stage right foot from their stage left, and in such a case it is best to spend thirty minutes or so going through the most basic terms: up, down, center, left, and so forth.

Some of the more generally used terms on stage are as follows:

to counter: to take the position just vacated by the moving actor; to balance him in his new position.

to dress the stage: to bring the stage into formal balance or its approximation.

to share the scene: to stand on the same plane in approximately the same body position as another actor on stage.

to take the scene: to move up to receive the emphasis.

to give the scene: to move down to throw the emphasis upstage.

to steal: to move normally, but without taking the attention from the speaker; it is generally accomplished by keeping the eyes focused on the actor receiving the emphasis.

to curve the cross: to use a slight curve in an upstage or downstage cross in order to fall into an easy three-quarter position when the object of the cross is reached. Without this slight curve in such a cross, the moving actor, if he stops on the same plane as the object of the cross, will be facing upstage when he stops and have to make an awkward adjustment.

to move in: generally, to move closer to the person or object you are addressing.

to cover: to block another actor from the audience's view. In general it is the responsibility of the covered actor to move out into view.

to open it up: to turn more of the body or face to the audience.

Blocking the Play

All of the elements of blocking a play—the balance, the emphasis, the picturization, the stability, and the sequence —depend upon the use made of movement. What a director does with the movement he finds in the script will have a

vital effect on the final production. Either his use of movement will add to, and help clarify, the author's intent or it
will muddle and detract from it. There is no middle ground
here. The director can be sure of very little in the theater,
but this much he can know with an awful certainty: If he has
not helped the play, then he certainly has hindered it.

To block a play is to use movement in order to achieve a
satisfying composition, a vivid picturization that will help
interpret the drama. But lest it seem as though too much
emphasis is being placed on the blocking, let the director
bear in mind that it is a play he is blocking, not a dance he
is choreographing. He is staging a play that carries most of
its meaning as well as most of its emotion in the dialogue.
Whatever he does with his staging is to aid, not hinder, the
dialogue.

When the director attempts, as is all too often the case, to
be as clever in his blocking as an author like Shaw is with
his dialogue, he is doomed to failure. And even if he were to
succeed, he would be, by his very cleverness, destroying
Shaw's dialogue by matching its brilliance with his blocking. If this is the director's aim, then let him dance the play,
not act it.

All the action stems from the dialogue, and if blocking is
giving a visual form to the written drama (as I suggested at
the beginning of this section), if it is indeed transferring
from the page to the stage, it is transferring the idea intact,
simply placing the idea, the concept, in another form.
Blocking a play is a process of choosing the correct movement design, the movement blueprint, for the basic intent.

The type of play and the style of the script will dictate the
type of balance that will dominate, the methods used princi-
pally to achieve emphasis, the style and the individual

quality of the movement, and the style and individual quality of line readings.

The director must see and understand the original form of the script if he is to discover the one form that is right for that script on his stage with the cast which has been chosen. Failure to see and understand the playwright's form is disastrous to the production.

While even the nontheater person wouldn't think of staging *King Lear* in the same manner that he might stage a farce, the choice when a play such as *Twelfth Night* is the problem is not nearly as obvious.

While writing this book I was fortunate to see two professional companies perform *Twelfth Night*. Both companies were more than competent, and both directors experienced and justly famous within the theater world. In the first production the director had seen fit to treat the play as a classic–romantic comedy. He used formal balance, a slow tempo, and stately, highly romantic use of line. His pictures were pretty, the groupings beautifully architectural, the entrances formal but sweeping. On the other hand his play was staged with very little depth and with all the action right on the curtain line. All the characters in the show had been given, or had developed, slapstick business, and the actors' attitude was one of tongue-in-cheek. It was light and it was gay. The direction, and hence the action, had what might be called an "aside" quality. Everyone seemed to be rather consciously having fun, but saying at the same time, "Come along with us. We know the plot is unbelievable, we know Viola doesn't look or sound anything like a boy and that no one in his right mind could possibly mistake them, but isn't the whole idea charming and fun?" I found that this treatment made it impossible to become involved with either the characters or the plot. The director had decided to use a very artificial approach in his staging of the comedy. I am convinced he reached this decision, consciously or unconsciously, because the play is based upon a convention no longer in vogue. The convention of mistaken identity between twins of the opposite sex is, at best, an artificial device, and one that present-day audiences will have difficulty believing. With this in mind, the director, it seemed to me, used a like design, that is, one that frankly said the situation was artificial and impossible from start to finish, but charming nonetheless. He forgot that when the play was written the confusion on which the main plot is based was a completely acceptable convention and, as such, believable as far as the audience was concerned.

The director of the second production treated the play as one might treat a modern comedy set in romantic surroundings. He based his design upon the convention of the play, found a way to make that convention acceptable to his audience, and staged the comedy for its plot as well as for its slapstick. The fun, the beauty, and the sense of the play all came through in this production. The comedy characters were played as such; the rest of the characters were interpreted as real people in an extremely odd situation. In the first production the actors did not accept the plot and hence the audience could not. In the second production, because the plot problems were solved, the actors developed believable characters acceptable to the audience within the framework laid down by Shakespeare.

Both directors love and respect Shakespeare. However, in this case, one director trusted him and found a dramatic and exciting way to transform the original form of the play intact from the page to the stage. The other director at-

tempted to change the play's form into what he thought
would be acceptable to a modern audience. As a result, his
blocking design was a comment on the play rather than the
playwright's form translated into a movement design. In the
one case we saw Shakespeare's play; in the other we lost the
play in the staging.

Before leaving this important subject of blocking, a word
should be said about planning that blocking. Most students
who take a course in direction have had a considerable
number of hours in rehearsal as college actors and have
developed opinions about directors who pre-block and those
who don't. Whether or not the director should plan out his
movement and his business in advance depends upon the
director. Personally, I do not believe in pre-blocking. On the
other hand, I have several friends who achieve brilliant
results with pre-blocking. There is little doubt that the
beginning director will need to do all the advance planning
he can. Certainly he should have his basic movement pattern worked out in as much detail as he is capable of before
he meets his cast for the first time. Pre-blocking in this case
is necessary in order that the director himself gain confidence and that the cast have a chance to gain confidence in
the director. Few beginning directors will have the confidence to take their time and think before a cast of waiting
actors. Even if they do have the confidence it is doubtful if
they will have the know-how, and any thinking done under
such pressing circumstances is very apt to be confused and
foggy, to say nothing of wasting the actors' time. Until the
new director has mastered his techniques he will be wise not
to depend upon that will-o'-the-wisp, inspiration.

I find my own pre-blocking dry and uninteresting, and I
much prefer the spontaneity and the give-and-take between

actor and director that a rehearsal can provide. While I have often failed to come up with the right answer at the right time, I have also watched directors who have pre-blocked experience great difficulty leaving their preconceived play for a better one suggested by the rehearsal process. The question of whether to pre-block or not to pre-block is, as are so many questions in any art, a question of individual preference. The beginning director must find his way by continual experimentation. There is no better way than your way, providing that you know your business, know where you are trying to go, and know when you arrive there.

Part I V
THE DIRECTOR
AND
THE ACTOR

The Actor

The first time a teacher steps from behind the desk to the front of the class, the speaker to the podium in front of his audience, the actor to stage center—the first time for almost anything can be a nerve-shattering experience. No first time is tougher on the nervous system than when a director meets his first cast. Few "first times" are as challenging or as exciting, for always, whether it be the director's first play or his hundredth, two extremes are waiting in the background —fantastic success or dismal failure. The excitement of the first rehearsal for a new play never seems to pall. Regardless of the success or failure of the previous effort, here is a new opportunity, a new challenge with, at best, new problems, at worst, new slants on old problems.

First Meeting

The first meeting for a new cast is bound to be a nervous occasion for all concerned. The director at such a meeting must appear fairly calm and businesslike, but he will be making a mistake if he masks his own excitement completely. His excitement, his love, or, conversely, his distaste, for the play will show through to the actors and may well color the entire rehearsal period. The director who does not feel the tingle of nerves and the underlying excitement is not a brave man, he is an insensitive clod and has no business in the theater. His responsibility to the actors sitting around him, to say nothing of his responsibility to the author, producer, and audience, is awesome. By their presence there, the actors have demonstrated that they are willing to trust themselves, their reputations, and often their livelihoods to the director. They, too, will be nervous, but as there are more of them than there are of him, the actors will have more means of hiding their nervousness.

The director has the authority, and everyone there knows it. How he will use that authority is the question that will be lurking in the mind of every actor who is not acquainted with the director's methods. They're all there, at almost every first reading: the smiling, seemingly confident ones, hiding their apprehensions beneath a pseudosophisticated *savoir-faire;* the studious, serious ones, hiding their fear behind their concentration on the script; the group that hasn't seen each other since the last tour, or the last production, talking a little too loudly about old times; the ingenue primping in the corner; they're all there playing their conscious roles, but excited and anxious to get started. One thing they all have in common, the director, and they're all watching him out of the corner of one eye and the stage manager out of the corner of the other waiting for him to catch the director's nod that will cue in his request for "quiet, please." Though actors are often noisy at such a time, the stage manager's quiet call will get amazing results, for few groups are so anxious to get down to real work as a group of actors at their first rehearsal. Every one there knows that he is about to enter a new land. Every one is only too conscious that the first company call can be the call to excitement and creativity or the summons to drudgery and a nervous breakdown. Which it is to be depends almost solely on the director.

The experience level of the cast will make little difference at the first reading; all will be anxious to get started. If it is a professional company, any waste of the Equity-allowed rehearsal time, barely adequate for even the most experienced actor, will be severely resented by the actors as it should be by the director. The college cast will be used to a particular technique and will be anxious to know what they have to deal with now. The actors in the civic theater will be dying to know how the new man is going to work out. At that moment, before the reading actually begins, the director is the star. He had better put the moment to good use, as it will not come again until the next production. It is a short-lived moment too, for by the time the reading ends each actor will be concerned with his role. During the preliminary arrangement, however, it is the director who is the number one worry or curiosity.

Possible ways of organizing a rehearsal schedule are touched upon later; now it is the actor—the individual in that group of individual men and women, boys and girls who sit expectantly around the director—that we wish to consider. No matter how one looks at this strange being, historically, morally, professionally, artistically, or technically, the water quickly becomes deep and muddy, and unless one watches oneself closely, too hot for comfort.

The Actor–The Agent

The actor, the agent, is the means or instrument through which a play is born or aborted. He is the artist with whom the director must work most closely and whom he must convince if the play is to bloom. When the moment of truth comes, when the chips are down and the curtain is up, whether the directorial approach has been permissive or dictatorial, the play is in the hands of the actor. The director, on opening night, is just another member of the audience. Hopefully he has given the play its unity and its overall interpretation, but it is the actor who is "out there" laying his artistry and craftsmanship on the block. I can imagine no more frustrating experience than that of the director, standing at the back of the house watching the work of weeks disintegrate before his eyes. Though he may silently rant and rave at "those idiots" on stage, he is helpless. It is at such a moment, I believe, that a director worth the name admits his responsibility for the production. At such a moment a director true to himself knows the blame is his and his alone. He either got the performance he was after, or he did not. If he was successful in bringing the actor up to the performance level he desired and on opening night decides that level is the wrong level, then obviously he has failed. If, on the other hand, he did not bring the actor to the desired level, then he has failed in his most important job. Granted, this is a difficult moment for any director to face, but face it he must if he is to improve the show in question and his own technique and artistry. The natural tendency in such a situation is to shift the blame, and the actor is the logical person to bear it. Certainly the director is in the most favorable position at such a moment of disaster for he, at least, is in the back of the house in the comforting darkness, while the actor stands in a glare of light that can reveal his most secret weaknesses. Oh, yes, the director may catch it next day in the reviews (usually for the wrong thing), but the immediate figure for blame or praise is the actor. He is, as Jacques Copeau has said, "the very warp and woof of the play." Because it is the actor who is directly before the audience, and hence his body and voice upon which the audience concentrates, the actor is understandably concerned about how he appears and sounds to that audience. He, too, looks upon himself as a creative and interpretive artist even as does the director. The actor wants a chance to do his job well. He wants help, all the help he can get, but he seldom wants a demigod who will usurp all creative responsibility and manipulate him like a puppet.

The director, on the other hand, knows he has a duty to the entire play, not to a particular actor or character. With such a responsibility the director cannot be as singly concerned as the actor who is devoting all his energies to a particular role. The seemingly different ends, which are in reality simply a difference in emphasis, can lead to much misunderstanding between actor and director. An actor who is sincere in his art is attempting to interpret the role within a play honestly and at the same time look good personally, that is, to look good as an actor. He would not be human if he did not occasionally forget, in the heat and frustration of rehearsal and the frenzy of the approaching opening night, that looking good personally and honestly interpreting the play are one and the same thing. The actor would not be human if he did not, under such conditions, occasionally resent being told that he had forgotten that the two ends were really one. Then too, the director is not God; he is not infallible. He can be, and often is, wrong. The actor, with the intensity of his work on a single role, has a different outlook on the play than does the director. The actor is attempting to see the play through the eyes of the character he is playing, and rightly so. Very often, aspects of the play that are obvious to him will be missed by the director. Finally, no one likes to be wrong, especially if one has put a great deal of thought and effort into a particular idea. Both the actor and the director have put that time and effort into the play, both are trying to bring the play to life, both are necessarily straining the experiences of the play through their own past experiences. The view of the play and the past experiences are different; it is not surprising then that often the initial interpretations are different. Under such conditions, with the actor exposing himself to the public but the director having the final authority, differences of opinion are very apt to become violent arguments. A relationship that has these built-in differences is potentially an explosive one, and it is these differences, plus the strain of modern production schedules, that make the actor-director relationship the most tenuous and volatile one in the theater.

A great part of the director's job is to keep the actor-director relationship on an even keel. This does not mean that he always wears kid gloves, for he must often "get tough," but the basic respect between actor and director must not be allowed to disintegrate. If differences of interpretation cannot be ironed out, then the director must exert his authority. In such a case, if the actor has lost confidence in and respect for the director, he is prone to execute the disputed direction halfheartedly. The director, in such a case, must then either convince or reach an understanding with the actor, or he will never convince or reach an understanding with the audience.

The Actor's Evolution

Who is this all-important agent; this difficult, exciting, "liveliest part of the theatre" who is, as Stark Young says,

". . . of all theatre elements . . . the closest to the audience."[71] His history is long, often murky, often questionable, but always interesting.

The desire to act must be almost as old as man's consciousness of himself. The instinct, if you like, must go back, as Robert Edmond Jones describes it, to "Ook and Pow and Pung and Glub and Little Zowie and all the rest . . . sitting close together around the fire," listening and watching as the leader of the tribe of Stone Age men describes, then, because words are not enough by themselves, acts out the exciting lion hunt.

Since the dawn of history man has donned roles. He has pretended, engaged in make-believe, to get outside himself and to enlighten others. Always, it seems, man has found it necessary to put on ritualistic masks, to stain his face a color other than his own in order to represent powers he feels should exist. He has been forced by some inner compulsion to make his feelings, hence the felt powers, real through symbolic actions. Both the dark and the light side of his nature have found expression and a reality in the make-believe world where man can so forget himself that both he and his audience believe for the magic moment that he has become another. To make real through make-believe, to create a make-believe reality outside of reality, to create the idea in his own mind and in the mind of others through the use of make-believe action, has always been the actors' goal.[72]

Three thousand years before the birth of Christ, priests in Egypt were acting out episodes in the life of their gods, were donning the masks and preparing their inner beings that they might, in the rituals of life and death, be believable in their assumed roles. But it was the Greeks, with their passion for knowing more about man, who first conceived the idea of hiring a person to act so that an audience might be thrilled by the make-believe it watched. Most theater historians name Thespius as the first professional actor and place him in Athens around 534 B.C.

Thespius appears to have been a poet-actor, interpreting his own lines for the audience, and hence, in all probability, he was bothered neither by a director nor by theoretical problems of the whys and hows of acting. When Aeschylus (525–456 B.C.) introduced the second actor into the script, apparently Cleander by name, direction got its start. Cleander was, as far as we know, the first actor to act only, that is, the first actor-actor rather than a poet-actor. With the introduction of the second actor, the stage was set for the actor's view of the play.

Until the professional actor came along, most acting, with the exception of the comic strain, was performed as a magic art. That is to say, its purpose was to "generate in the agent or agents certain emotions useful or detrimental to the lives of these others."[73] With the advent of the professional actor—one who made his livelihood by acting rather than one who acted as a part of his priestly duties—the purpose of the art necessarily changed. Acting still generated emotion, but now the emotion was discharged (the catharsis) in such a manner that it would not "interfere with the practical life."[74] Acting, then, attempted to generate an emotion that would be discharged within the framework of the play. To generate an emotion for its own sake became, and remained, the purpose of the theater.

Shades of the old magic art are still to be found in certain schools of acting and within the mysticism of the creative process, but the break is a well-defined one. Perhaps some of the confusion in theories of acting could be traced to the probability that though the purpose has changed, the method may not have. The process of preparation in the magic art must have been much the same as the process of preparation for the amusement art, and this sameness in preparation may well have obscured the differences in the ends. At least I have often thought, while watching certain method actors perform or rehearse, that they were more concerned with generating their own emotions within themselves than generating the character's emotions within the audience. However, before attempting to discuss the actor's view of the play or the actor's view of acting, let's take a quick look at the actor himself.

All through his long history the actor has been suspect, a not-quite-acceptable person. Aristotle and Plato questioned his morals, Julius Caesar and Augustus "forbade senators or their sons to take to wife women who had been, or whose parents had been on the stage."[75] No Christian could be an actor or marry one, nor could an actor be baptized unless he left the theater. In India, in the Hindu theater, the actors were "reputed to live on the price of their wives' honor, and Manu imposes only a minor penalty on illicit relations with the wife of an actor,"[76] and in Japan the actors and actresses have fluctuated from the top of the social scale to its dregs.

Even today the actor is not considered a thoroughly "respectable" person. He still has more difficulty getting car insurance than does a factory worker, and the announcement that a boy or girl is going to make the theater his life's work will still raise eyebrows and voices somewhere in almost any family. Why is it that so many persons appear to look down their noses at the actor? True, in our Puritanical society, all the arts are suspect, but not to the same extent as the performing arts of theater or dance. Both the actor and the dancer are charged with being immoral, untrustworthy, and unstable citizens. The world of theater and the dance is supposedly packed with homosexuals, lesbians, nymphomaniacs, and satyrs. When one loves the theater, and most of those people who have made it their life's work do love it, it is difficult not to come out swinging at the charges made against the theater. Yet the charges have been made, not only in the Puritanical society of the United States, but in every country in every part of the world. Where there is so much smoke, one cannot help suspecting there is more than a spark of truth.

The sentimental, old-fashioned conception of the artist's life— long hair and flowing ties, garrets, tuberculosis and grisettes—is no more than a cheap color lithograph of the idea; yet it expresses in its own way this attitude of separateness. The artist, any artist, must suspend the purely normal course of his own individual existence and separate himself from something in order to grow closer to something else.[77]

The artist does, it seems, very often find it necessary to separate himself from the rest of society. He sees and experiences life from a different vantage point, so it is not surprising that his actions are often at odds with the rest of society. If this is true, and apparently it is, in the life of the poet, the painter, the playwright, and the sculptor, all solitary arts, how much more obvious is this truth going to be in the performing arts, which are of necessity group arts?

The theater attracts all sorts of people because it has glamour and a togetherness that few of the other arts offer. The theater demands short periods of highly concentrated work, and often that work takes one from home and familiar surroundings. The theater is now, and has always been, built on passions, and the workers within the theater work directly with their emotions. Actors working in a theater or on a particular production are thrown suddenly into very close contact and, out of self-defense, form their own little society. I say "out of self-defense" because though the public loves to talk about the theater, and always knows all about acting (haven't they all been in a high school play?), an actor, or any theater worker, soon learns that nontheater people are not really interested in the work side of the theater. They are interested only in the glamorous, exciting side. Hence, if an actor wants to talk naturally, he must talk with another member of the profession or be prepared to be listened to as if he were some sort of freak. It is not surprising then that the folk of the world of entertainment often both work and play together. Because theater people deal primarily in emotion, they soon learn to treat those emotions in quite a different manner than does the non-theater person. In ordinary life, emotions are something which are hidden, in ordinary work, emotions must be kept outside of the job, and in the usual situation one tries not to let his emotion show on his face, but because emotions are the stock and trade of the actor, he cannot treat them in such an indifferent manner. He must develop them, work on and with them in order to use them. Because of the close contact and the highly emotional nature of their work, theater folk are prone to view emotions from a different set of values.

Actors tend to be a self-centered group of individuals and seldom are very concerned by values outside their own little world. As a result of this unconcern, they often seem to be flaunting their "freer morals" in the face of the public at large. Actors (and directors) generally work hard during rehearsals and are often wound up as tight as the proverbial watch spring at the end of a rehearsal day or after a performance. They do not, as a rule, want to hurry home and jump into bed, even though the hour is often late. They feel a real need to unwind, to relax, and to talk over the day or the performance with people who see life from their point of view. Often this unwinding involves late hours and intimacies that would not otherwise occur. The entire social setup within the theater world is looser, one may call it freer, or immoral, depending upon one's point of view. No matter what you call it, it is different. While no one forces another into a particular line of activity, the temptation, or the opportunity, again depending upon the viewpoint, is always there.

I have heard it stated time and time again that life in the theater is no different than life in any other sort of work. I do not believe this to be so. The moral climate is quite different. The theater is as safe a place as the person in question wants it to be; it is also as reckless a place. Sometimes it seems as if actors were pushed into a sort of life they would prefer not to have by a public that lacks excitement in its own private life and demands to live vicariously through the artist's. It seems often as if the public demands that the actor be different. He is different, not because the public demands it, but possibly because, as Dostoevski says, "There can be no art without the collaboration of the devil." At any rate, the arts have always had their own standards, and genius has always been outside the normal rules and regulations. In the theater the difficulty may well stem from the fact that too many think they are geniuses and attempt to prove their right to the title by their social behavior rather than by their art. Finally, most people in the theater, though they will not admit it, are badly stagestruck. They know the theater is glamorous and exciting, though they pretend it is not. They enjoy their work, and often play at their work like children, and, like children, work at their play. I am convinced that few professionals outside the arts so enjoy their means of making a living. Actors do take their life on stage with them, they do use their personal experience in their art, so it is not surprising that the line between work and play, life and make-believe, is not nearly so clearly drawn in the theater as it is in other professions. To be a good actor is to live and explore life. Always the urge to live makes for difficulties socially.

To those who would say that the theater is just like any other profession I would say, "No, it is unto itself." The moral standard is different, the working hours different, and the stimulation received from the work is quite different. No one need avoid the theater for fear of corruption, for if the theater will corrupt, the chances are any other line of work will corrupt also. In the theater, however, fewer eyebrows will be raised and the temptations may be easier to find. If one is truly looking for temptation I would suggest the theater world, but if one is truly looking, he will not need suggestions, he will have found his own brand long before he comes across this book. There is a greater license in the theater and because of this license those whose inclinations may deviate from the norm are apt to be attracted to the theater rather than to the teaching profession, but if their deviation from the norm is all they have, they will not last long. For those who do not love the theater the hours are too long, the work too exacting and strenuous, but for those who do there are not enough hours for the work-that-is-play to be accomplished.

Two Theories

Though there are almost as many acting theories as there are acting teachers, all would seem to stem from the two basic approaches of technique or emotion. When one has examined the various schools of thought on the matter, the conclusion seems to be that all theories actually stem from one basis, technique *and* emotion, or, if you prefer, emotion *and* technique. In the final analysis, it is where one puts the emphasis that makes the difference. No theory of any value attempts to do without one of the two elements, for it is obvious that technique with no emotion to transmit would be valueless, and emotion without the means of communicating it to an audience just as worthless. The differences in opinion concerning the technique or the emotion approach to acting, in all probability, appeared shortly after the second actor was introduced into the drama, and perhaps long before that event. One can almost hear an ancient priest complaining, after performing parts of the ritual concerning Osiris and Seth, that the gods did not truly inspire him that day, that he was left to his own resources and had to pretend in order not to disappoint the public. Plato, in the dialogue with Ion, speaks of the actor as being divinely inspired:

Really, as I said just now, this is no art in you to speak well about Homer; no, some divine power is moving you, such as there is in that stone which Euripides called the Magnesian, but most people call it the Heraclean stone. This magnet attracts iron rings, and not only that, but puts the same power into the iron rings, so that they can do the same as the stone does; they attract other rings, so that sometimes there is a whole long string of these rings hanging together, and all depend for their power on that one stone. So the Muse not only inspires people herself, but through these inspired ones others are inspired and dangle in a string.[78]

Then do you know that the member of the audience is the last of those rings which I described as getting power from each other through the magnet? You, the reciter and the actor, are the middle ring, and the first is the poet himself; but God, through all these, draws the soul of men withersoever he will, by running the power through them one after another. It is just like that magnet! And there is a great string of choristers and producers and under-producers all stuck to the sides of these hanging rings of the Muse. And one poet hangs from one Muse and another from another—we call it "Possessed!" and it is very like that, for he is held fast.[79]

Plato holds that "no art, but divine dispensation" makes the great interpreter, while his pupil Aristotle tells us that "Dramatic ability is a natural gift, and can hardly be systematically taught." Yet Aristotle goes on in his next sentence to inform us that "The principles of good diction can be taught," thus, while the actor is born, and not made, he can be improved by diction. Aristotle, however, goes considerably further in his argument for technique as opposed to the "natural" talent. His *Rhetoric* is concerned with the public speaker, but must have applied to the actor as well, since the style of acting was, as far as we can determine, declamatory. Certainly, in the following excerpt, what holds true for the public speaker holds true for the actor:

Our next subject will be the style of expression. For it is not enough to know what we ought to say; we must also say it *as* we ought; much help is thus afforded toward producing the right impression of a speech . . . It is, essentially, a matter of the right management of the voice to express the various emotions—of speaking loudly, softly, or between the two; of high, low, or intermediate pitch; of various rhythms that suit various subjects. These are the three things—volume of sound, modulation of pitch, and rhythm—that a speaker bears in mind. It is those who *do* bear them in mind who usually win prizes in the dramatic contests.[80]

There in ancient Greece, where the theater had its birth, the two theories of acting appeared, and the seeds for the seemingly never ending argument about feeling or faking, emotion or technique, representational or presentational, being or pretending, real or make-believe, living or acting, were planted. Down through the centuries they have grown, withered, almost died away, then been given new life by the scholars, the critics, or the more explicit actors of a particular age. At times the dispute is evident only when one examines the different styles exhibited by the tragedians and the comedians but always, it seems, it is there: How should the actor act? Quintilian and Cicero discussed the actor-orator for the Romans while Bharata canonized the laws of acting for the Hindu theater in his *Natya-sastra;* Seami Motokiyo set down the secret rules for *No* acting in the fifteenth century while the Confreri de la Passion et Resurrection in France were just receiving the right to produce religious plays from Charles VI; and though Shakespeare touched upon methods and techniques of acting in his advice to the players in Hamlet (as Molière was to do in his *Les Précieuses Ridicules* and his *L'Impromptue de Versailles*), it was not until Dryden's *An Essay of Dramatick Poesie* that a serious and original piece of dramatic criticism appeared in English. The discussion blossomed in the eighteenth century with Charles Gildon's *The Life of Mr. Thomas Betterton,* in which the author was desirous of forming "a system of Acting." Remond de Sainte-Albine, both Riccobonis and Denis Diderot writing in France, and Goethe and others in Germany added their observations to the growing debate. The following century gave us actors of all types and critics to discuss the methods, along with theories of realism in both writing and acting.

The great influence in the United States was that of Constantin Stanislavski; it was brought to bear on the theater through the Group Theater in the early 1930s. When *An Actor Prepares* appeared in 1936 the Stanislavski system, or "the method" as Lee Strasberg's version came to be called, swept the scene, and for a few years it was a brave teacher indeed who would oppose the system.

For the director it really matters very little which road the actor finds best for his particular talent, providing of course that the road the actor chooses is taking him toward the author's intent. While it is not the function of this book to examine closely the merits or demerits of the two schools of thought, it is necessary to touch upon both methods, for the director must work with his actors where he finds them, time seldom allowing him to teach a theory of acting. Indeed, to teach a particular theory is outside the director's province. He must teach a theory if the actor has none, but he must teach within the actor's theory when he finds such a theory present.

Both approaches present difficulties and pitfalls for the actor; both are filled with traps for the unwary. If the actor is a technician, he is likely to become more interested in his technique than in the play, but if, on the other hand, he is "method," he is apt to become lost in his psyche rather than involved in the play. Any school of thought is liable to become more important than the result it is designed to achieve, any theory of acting can tempt the actor to make the means the end. The method actors must often be reminded that it is not the play in the actor that is the end, and the technician must remember that it is not the actor in the play. In all cases *it is the character as written in the play that the playwright conceived that is the goal.*

For the college actor to talk of being a technician is, I believe, absurd, for to develop a technique requires years of study and opportunity to work before an audience. Likewise, to talk knowingly of living the role every minute on stage is just as absurd in the rehearsal time generally available. The young, inexperienced actor must rely upon his intellect, his emotion, his youth, and his vigor, in short, upon all he can call on. If he is going to think seriously of making the theater a life's work, he must find his own method of creating a role. If the young actor has read *An Actor Prepares,* then the director will do well to loan him *Building a Character* and suggest dance and voice training. On the other hand, if the young actor has had a lot of speech and dance training the director must concentrate on the inner feeling.

On any level, amateur or professional, the director will meet all types and all sorts of acting theories. He must work with them all—those who act instinctively (and they do exist, these natural actors who don't seem to have to know the why or the wherefore, they simply are) and those who find it necessary and helpful to work out each little detail. He will find that those who think about their art and their craft will tend toward one side of the method-technique scale or the other, and as the director, it will be helpful to recognize the pitfalls in the two extremes.

The Technical Actor

What is meant by the phrase "technical actor"? Is it a compliment or an insult to describe an actor as a technician? Generally, of course, it depends upon who uses the word, but to have a good technique as an actor literally means to possess a good command of the special knowledge and methods necessary to the art or the craft of acting, in short, to know how, and to be able, to carry out the ends of acting by using the tools and knowledge available to the actor. In its literal sense, then, any actor is a technician, and he may be good or bad, expert or inexpert, but either he has a command of the tools and knowledge available or he has not. He may, it is true, have that command instinctively, that is to say, he may make use of the knowledge and the tools without being aware of it, or he may disdain to use them consciously, but either way, if he is an actor, some techniques of acting must be used.

The technical side of acting is concerned with the voice and the body, and few would deny that some use of both is necessary in the art and craft of acting. Again the distinguishing element is the amount of emphasis that is placed upon voice and body, and how the voice and body are brought into use. The difficulty arises with the technical actor only when he *seems* technical. When an actor is, during performance, more concerned with *how* a turn is made than he is *with the reason for* the turn, then he is in danger of being labeled a technical actor. In reality, however, if it is evident to the audience that he is concerned with the *how* instead of the *why*, then he is not only a bad technician, he is a bad actor. If acting is indeed symbolic action, whose end is the creation of an idea within the mind of the audience, then all acting is technical, but if the technique draws attention to itself rather than to the idea it is attempting to create, then acting becomes symbolic action for symbolic action rather than for the creation of the idea. The phrase "Great art conceals art," while true of all the arts, is most obvious to the public in the performing arts (*everyone* knows good acting). And as acting always is attempting to create a real idea through make-believe real actions, it is important that the technique of the make-believe be hidden.

Go back, for a moment, to our actor who is more concerned with the how than the why in performance. Certainly he must make the turn without falling on his face and generally, he must make it without drawing attention to the turn itself; the actor must use the turn to point an idea or a bit of action. To be able to do this the actor must be able to execute a clean, graceful turn—no mean trick when it must often be executed into the audience and actually is an "unnatural" move. The skilled actor must execute the turn in such a manner that it does not draw attention to itself, but does accomplish whatever the director is using the turn to achieve, and to do this the actor must have a good technique. If the above is true of a stage turn—and it is— what of a stage kiss, an entrance, a drop-sit in comedy, a double-take, or, vocally, a stage whisper, crying or laughing through a line, holding for a laugh, and the thousand and one *techniques* that any actor must learn to handle? Any good actor is a good technician.

The extreme example, that which gives the technical actor his bad name, is best represented by the beautiful girl who has been too long before the cameras and too often in the magazine ads. Such persons are accustomed to thinking in terms of the stereotyped, but "unnatural," poses. So great is the impact of the advertising world, and so used to the "unnatural" but eye-catching poses have we all become, that it is difficult to draw a line between the "billboard pose" and the acceptable stage convention. All poses are artificial, but the billboard pose goes beyond a studied attitude, it is always "in general." Always such poses convey the idea that the pretty girl and/or the good-looking man go with such and such a product and, of course, behind that, the hidden suggestion that if you buy the product you will look like the pretty people in the picture. Such poses are meant to be "in general" and consequently they will not work for the stage. The difficulty is not that the model's pose is artificial or studied (what acting isn't artificial?), but rather that it is a generalized pose for a very unspecific purpose. The model becomes unimportant to the meaning of the picture, he or she is a "happy," "glamorous," or a "dangerous" type that has a vague, unspecific connection with the product. The poses will carry the same message on stage, vague and unspecific, in short, "in general."

An inexperienced director may easily fail to recognize such actors during rehearsals. Because of the wide acceptance of such poses it is not difficult to be fooled by the ease and naturalness with which some actors fall into such patterns. When this happens, the director is in for a rude awakening on opening night. With an audience in the house the "fakeness," which in this case may well be simply the wrong convention, becomes glaringly evident. Such an actor will automatically and, as far as he is concerned, "naturally" fall into one of the popular poses that will show him off to the best advantage, regardless of how the character is meant to be seen. Actors of either sex who are physically beautiful are prone to "naturally" parade their beauty and are perhaps more apt to ape the "beautiful people" of the billboard world. These are technical actors at their worst. A director is faced with not one, but generally two problems in such a case: one, to make the actor conscious of his habit and recognize such poses kinesthetically; and two, to take the emphasis from the actor physically and place it on the character emotionally.

How the director accomplishes this feat depends upon the actor in question, but Stanislavski's technique of building to the emotional through physical action is one method. In effect, this appears to be an adaptation of the James-Lange theory which, as stated by James says, *"the bodily changes follow directly the perception of the exciting fact, and that our feeling of the same changes as they occur is the emotion."*[81] In other words, we do not jump suddenly from the path of an oncoming car because we are afraid; rather, we are afraid because we jump, or as James says, "We might then see the bear, and judge it best to run, receive the insult and deem it right to strike, but we should not actually feel afraid or angry." The scientific truth or falseness of the theory need not concern us at all, the fact is that such an idea does work for the director and for the actor. We need not be concerned whether or not the induced emotion, if indeed it is an emotion, is a true one, for finding the right physical action can often produce a feeling within the actor that will help him to forget himself and convey the idea desired.

Perhaps the best example is that of allowing the actress to "get angry" by slapping or kicking the object of anger (of course this can raise problems if the object happens to be another actor, but even in such cases, most actors will put

so-called method actor has, especially during the 1950s and
'60s, insisted upon putting himself, rather than the character, into the play. He has, it seems, taken Plato's "possessed" theory a step further and instead of being possessed
by the poetic muse, he has become the muse and possessed
the character. He seems too often to believe that the actor
must absorb the character, that is to say, instead of pouring
himself into the character, he pours the character into
himself. The character then becomes lost in the perplexities
of the actor's personality. Perhaps, as Duerr suggests,[82]
this tendency can be attributed to one of Stanislavski's
students, Vakhtangov, who wanted the actor to start with
himself rather than with a preconceived image. The actor,
according to Vakhtangov (who seems to have been an important factor in the Group Theater's technique), must play
himself in the position of the character. The method actor
often seems to believe that one should live his own temperament on stage rather than the supposed temperament of the
character. The temptation to follow such ideas, along with
Stanislavski's idea from *An Actor Prepares*—"never allow
yourself externally to portray anything that you have not
inwardly experienced and which is not even interesting to
you,"[83]—has tended to turn the stage into a dull classroom
for group therapy and has allowed too many actors to
confuse the theater with the psychiatric couch. Such an
approach to acting becomes an exercise in self-indulgence
rather than a creative experience through self-expression.

Method actors often appear to think of the play as having
been planned for the actors', rather than the audience's,
benefit. Such actors like to use the performances as experimentation. When a director is confronted with an actor of
this kind, he must be firm and insist upon a consistent,
steady performance. The rehearsal period is the time for

experimentation, and unless a scene is in trouble, it should be played as it was set in rehearsal. The director should make clear to his cast that he expects consistency in performances and what procedures should be followed when an actor feels that he or a scene is missing. In the professional theater, where a director generally leaves a show on opening night, any actor who finds himself having difficulties knows that he should go directly to the stage manager. In the amateur theater the actor should go to the director. Ad-lib experimentation is always a hardship on the rest of the cast and almost always on the play itself. Any actor who engages in such behavior is putting himself above the play and should be warned, and if he continues, disciplined as severely as possible under existing circumstances.

Few would deny the fact that an actor must use his own experience on stage. After all, his talent, his life, his voice, his body, and the director's help are all he has available for his task of interpreting the play. These he must bring to every role, but he must adapt his experience, voice, and body to the author's play. His inner struggles may or may not be interesting, but they are not what the audience pays to see. Any attempt to realize oneself on stage when such realizing does not forward the action or the thought of the play will hinder the thought and the action of the play.

An actor may, for one reason or another, find a particular line difficult to read. Such a discovery is not license to change the line itself. The actor's job is to read the playwright's line, and if he cannot do so, let him resign his role. A tremendous ego, it seems to me, is necessary before an actor could even consider changing a line simply because he found it difficult. Such an ego used in such a manner would, it seems, always interfere with the playwright's intent.

One of the most interesting developments in the method

school of acting is the difficulty its actors appear to have
with comedy and farce. In earlier days, comedy was that
acting that was close to life. Duerr suggests that the comic
acting of the Greeks may not have been considered an art
because it was "perhaps too close to life,"[84] and all through
the history of the theater it is the comedians who are "realistic" while the serious actors have a much more elevated
style. In the modern theater it is the comedian who often has
the style and the technique, while the serious actor, from the
method school at least, "lives" on stage. It is certainly true
that the method has not turned out comedians and, from the
method point of view, the acting difficulties found in
comedy also seem to be present in any nonrealistic drama.
When the director is faced with the problem of using a
method actor in a comedy, farce, or a nonrealistic play, a
private talk with the actor in terms of Stanislavski's "magic
if" and his "given circumstances," along with great emphasis on his chapter entitled "Adaptation,"[85] will often bear
surprising fruit.* Here too, the concept of playing roles
within well-defined rites can often be helpful, for when the
actor is aware of the incongruity between the rite and the
role he can often play the comedy and still be believable.

For example, in the final scene of *The Wild Duck*, the line

* The "magic if" is one of Stanislavski's methods of stimulating the
actor's imagination: "If I were in such and such a situation with such
and such a background, what would I do?"

The "given circumstances" are all those details, conditions, and events
that the author, the director, and the other theater artists have given the
actor. The age of the character, his profession, the time of year, the
particular events leading up to the moment in question are all part of
the given circumstances.

"Adaptation" is Stanislavski's term for the means that an actor uses
to attain his goals. Finding the correct means of attaining the objective
within the given circumstances of the play is one of—if not *the*—biggest
problems that an actor faces.

"O Thou above—if thou Be indeed! Why hast Thou done this thing to me?" Hialmar, even though the body of Hedvig lies in full view of the audience, is playing to his on-stage audience. If the actor can be made to see the self-centeredness of the line, the automatic "melodrama hero" response of Hialmar to the tragedy, then the comedy in this scene will come through. In the same manner, if the actor playing Molvik can be made to see the incongruity in a drunken, defrocked priest attempting not to be drunk and trying to play the role of "comforter" with his asinine, "The child is not dead, but sleepeth," the bitter comic element of the play can be played believably and come through the sentimental picture of the dead child and the bereaved parents.

Often the problem with actors of the method school is making them see the form of the drama, and always the stress must be on acting within the confines of the play, not the confines of the actor's experience. When the director can convince the actor that the form chosen for the play is the correct form, and that the correct form is not necessarily a copy of life, but rather a visual and auditory transformation of the author's intent taken directly from the author's texts, then, and only then, can the director hope to convince that actor that his realistic style of acting will not fit the play. The difficulties presented by the nonrealistic play and by farce and comedy are generally very real ones for the method actor. I am convinced that an intelligent interpretation and use of the "magic if," the "given circumstances," combined with the correct "adaptation," and the rite-role analysis can ease the difficulties considerably. The type of actor so often encountered is concerned with "believing" the role, the business, the action, and very often such an

actor cannot "believe" simply because he is not imagining
the correct "given circumstances." If he believes that he
must believe before he can be believed, then believe me, the
director should believe him. His difficulty generally stems
from not seeing that, just as in a realistic play he must be
believable only within the framework of that particular play,
so in the nonrealistic play must he believe and hence be
believable only within the idea of that play. For in any type
of play, it is the idea that must be created in the audience's
mind.

The matter of "justifying" or of believing in each bit of
business can be carried to absurd lengths by both directors
and actors. Most directors have had the exasperating experience of having to stop and hunt for "motivation" when their
immediate problem was balance within a complicated picture. Often, by placing the emphasis on "justifying the bit"
rather than on "a sense of truth," valuable cast time can be
wasted:

Once at rehearsal, for example, Daly directed Clara Morris to
cross to a far side of the stage out of hearing of two other
players—and told her to motivate the cross. "Here," as she later
explained, "are a few of the many rejected ideas. There was no
guest for me to cross to in welcoming pantomine; no piano on
that side of the room for me to cross to and play softly; ah, the
fireplace! and the pretty warming of one foot? But no, it was
summertime; that would not do. The ancient fancy-work, perhaps? No, [the character I was playing] was a human panther,
utterly incapable of so domestic an occupation. The fan forgotten on the mantlepiece? Ah, yes, that was it! You cross the
room for that—and then suddenly I reminded Mr. Daly that he
had, but a moment before, made a point of having me strike a
gentleman sharply on the cheek with my fan. 'Oh, confound it,
yes!' he answered, 'and that's got to stand—that blow is
good!' The old, old device of attendance upon the lamp was

suggested; but the hour of the day was plainly given by one of the characters as three o'clock in the afternoon. These six are but a few of the many rejected reasons for that one cross of the stage; still Mr. Daly would not permit a motiveless action, and we came to a momentary standstill. Very doubtfully, I remarked, 'I suppose a smelling-bottle would not be important enough to cross the room for?' He brightened quickly—clouded over even more quickly. 'Y-e-e-s! N-o-o! At least, not if it had never appeared before. But let me see—Miss Morris, you must carry that smelling-bottle in the preceding scene, and—and, yes, I'll just put in a line in your part, making you ask someone to hand it to you—that will nail attention to it, you see! Then in this scene, when you leave these people and cross the room to get your smelling-bottle from the mantle, it will be a perfectly natural action on your part . . .' "[86]

Interestingly enough, the scene above did not come from today's realistic theater, rather, the Mr. Daly referred to is Augustin Daly, the playwright responsible for the old melodrama *Under The Gaslight* and the "realistic" motivation for Miss Clara Morris' cross was found in the late 1870s.

The mistaken idea that one can be believable only by revealing one's own character stems, I feel, from the modern conception that character in drama is all. Aristotle pointed out, when drama was still in its infancy, that character was subservient to plot, and so it is. The actor, and all theater workers, are subservient to the playwright's intent.

In summary then, regardless of the school of acting the director is handling, his task is to make the actor see the playwright's intent and the "rightness" of the stage form chosen to make the shift from page to stage. The actor need not be concerned with self-revelation if he is sure of the idea that he must work from and the goal he must work toward. True, a certain amount of acting technique will be necessary since the actor, to be effective, must be seen and heard. Also true is the fact that the actor will have to be concerned with himself to the degree that he can easily identify with the idea and with the form to be used. But he must manipulate himself to fit the idea and form, not the idea and form to fit him. It is not necessary that he believe in the real-life possibilities of the play, but he must bring himself to believe in, or at least identify with, the idea. This does not imply that he must agree with the philosophy of the idea; it does imply that he must bring himself to accept the idea as dramatically interesting. His personal beliefs and feelings can and should be used if they help and if they fit, but in the final analysis they are extraneous to the playwright's idea. The actor, hopefully through the director, must find then "the characteristic quality" of the play and he must find the means whereby that quality can "be translated into the acting," otherwise, as Stark Young says, "the whole performance will be pretty much rubbish."

When acting carries us out of ourselves, it is not that we are deceived by what we see; we are swept by the poser of the actor's ideas; it is not so much someone's actually dying that we weep over; we weep over the agony of death. One often hears people say that the illusion in some scene was so perfect that they were carried entirely out of themselves. In a torture scene, for example, acted by Rejane, one might get so strong a sense of reality as to be made sick by it. But what makes us sick is not that we think someone is really being tortured, but rather that the sense of suffering and strain is made so powerful and so compelling that we are overcome by it.[87]

With the technical or the method actor the director must find ways of convincing him that it is the play and the idea which count and not, for the technician, the actor in the play; nor for the method, the play in the actor. For both, it is the character as the author intended him to be that is the goal. If, in any case, the director can turn the actor's concentration from himself to the play and can help the actor find an acting style which fits the stage form, then, and only then, does he have a chance to see the play the poet wrote come to life on the stage.

Professionals and Amateurs

Though the differences between the amateur and the professional theater have been mentioned, those differences have not yet been stressed. While certain differences do exist in any and every branch of the two theaters, it is in the director-actor relationship that the greatest differences are to be found.

Each theater seems to be misunderstanding the other. That the two theaters do exist is, I believe, often overlooked by the educational theater; that the purposes and the risks involved in the two theaters are quite different is often overlooked, or resented when not overlooked, by both theaters.

There appears to be, unfortunately, something about the word "professional" that rubs too many within the amateur theater the wrong way. Some sensitive nerve end in both educational and civic theater people seems to be touched when the word is mentioned. In all probability it is not the word "professional" that bothers; rather it is the implied application of the word amateur.

One of my favorite between-act pastimes in recent years has been to find the college or university drama school group in the lobby and eavesdrop on their comments about the play and the production. Almost never do such groups like either the play, if it is a new one, or the production, new or old. As a matter of fact, almost never do they see the production, for they are much too busy pulling apart the work of those "professionals" on stage. It has always been interesting to me that I cannot recall being in any way associated with an amateur production that someone did not believe was the best show he had ever seen—"And I've seen a lot of Broadway shows too!" At the same time I have almost never heard that sentiment expressed in regard to a professional production. Everyone, it seems, has seen better professional productions.

I recall hearing, retold in quite a proud manner, that when one rather famous Midwestern department of drama was discussing a revamping of that department, someone made the suggestion that perhaps the training should be more professional. One member pointed out that, to his way of thinking, the words "professional" and "whore" were synonymous. I refrained from asking what he would equate with the word amateur. On the other hand I have heard a famous critic and a well-known stage manager revel in the fact that they could not stand anything that was done by amateurs. Such views are not unusual.

I encountered both views, not once but time after time, in my association with a resident professional company. The rift is an unhealthy one and must, I believe, be laid at the door of the educational theater director. The university and college departments of speech or drama that have welcomed the resident companies as an addition to the underpopulated world of producing theater do exist (and seem to be increasing), but are still few and far between. Rather, the general pattern has been of noncooperation and, in some cases, outright antagonism.

All too often the schism would seem to stem from the men and women in the academic life who, at one time or another, wanted a career in the professional theater, but who did not, for a variety of reasons, follow such a desire to its conclusion. Having spent a good deal of my life in academic circles I can hardly subscribe to the old saw that "them what can't, teach," for talent is not the distinguishing factor. Both the professional and the amateur theater are loaded with talented and with untalented personnel. When one truly wants a career in the professional theater, that person must be ready to take the total risk, and the risk is a tremendous one. Jobs are scarce and conditions are often impossible. No director need feel ashamed that he chose the amateur theater where life is certainly more sane, and paychecks regular. True, some would hold that life there is duller, and perhaps it is, but I would maintain it is simply different. To live within the world of the professional theater and to enjoy it takes a particular personality, just as to live within the walls of academia takes a particular sort of personality. The director who chooses the safer life of the amateur theater, in a school or in a civic organization (thought the latter is an entirely different world), need not feel ashamed that he knows where next month's paycheck is coming from, or that his future does not depend upon the opinion of a reviewer or a fickle public, for whatever else it may or may not be, the job of the university director is not that of selling tickets. Since box office is not the primary concern of the university director, he need hardly adopt standards that are set with the intent of selling tickets, but rather he may select standards of his own. I am convinced that a good many educational directors do feel ashamed of their own security and their supposed retreat from the insecure world of the professional stage. When the educational theater director can look himself in the eye and not wish he were in the

professional theater, then perhaps he will stop maintaining
that there is only one standard of excellence regardless of
the level of the participants. When the director sees the
absurdity of asking to be measured by the same yardstick as
the professional company and sees that by such a demand
he is attempting to classify himself as a professional, then
perhaps he will stop turning out students who consider
themselves fully trained in the techniques of the theater
because they have degrees in their pockets.

Few academic departments in colleges and universities
attempt to compete with professionals, yet theater departments often do. Students majoring in dance, painting,
music, business, sports, or what-have-you all expect and
plan for years of work after college in order to achieve
professional status, why not the theater? There is no valid
reason why an amateur production should be judged as a
professional production. There is no sensible reason why the
standards of one theater should apply to the other. Do not
misunderstand; the amateur production may be, indeed,
often is, a fresher, more interesting and more spontaneous
one but it will not be as smooth, nor as polished, nor as
technically correct, in short, not as "professional" as the
professional production.

If it is true that the amateur director envies the professional his standing, his opportunity to work with better
actors, and his chances of having a superior product, so the
professional seems to envy the security and the chance to
produce the better literature that the educational theater
person has. He too adds to the schism by damning the
college productions because they are not professional. The
role of the two theaters is so obviously different that it seems
foolish to waste time pointing it out, but since this text is

directed primarily at young and would-be directors, perhaps the space can be justified.

The educational theater has an important and difficult job to do in the background training of would-be actors, in exposing the student body to the great literature, in the discovery and the encouragement of new playwrights (and this is where they are noticeably deficient), and above all, in setting standards of entertainment for the public. For the professional theater—movies and television included—is pretty much stuck with the public where it finds them. The universities, and even the high schools, can help to set high standards of taste in both their choice of material and presentation of honest productions based upon integrity toward the playwright's intent. They can prepare a public that will insist on good theater when they leave the confines of the university. They can give would-be actors and directors a wide background upon which to build a professional career.

The professional theater, on the other hand, can and must branch out from the Broadway claptrap and look to the great literature of the stage. It can attempt to bring prices within a sensible range. Then, perhaps, the total experience of theater will be enjoyed, and the purpose of all art—the enrichment of man's life—will be achieved more fully in that most human of all arts, the theater.

The distinguishing factor between the professional and the amateur is simply that the professional makes his living through his art while the amateur uses his art as a pastime. It is a difference of commitment. The professional commits himself totally, the amateur commits his spare time. The risk is proportionate: total for the professional, little for the amateur.

Handling the Professional and the Amateur

It is the difference in commitment, training, and experience that necessitates a different handling of the professional and amateur as far as the director is concerned.
When an amateur, especially a student actor, faces his
director across the footlights or the table, he is looking at
the expert who is going to teach him not only about the play
and the role but, because the actor is a student, about the
theater itself. All directors are, to one degree or another,
teachers. They may be good ones or bad ones, but teachers
they are. In the professional theater the director teaches
primarily the play (sometimes, of course, he instructs in the
niceties and the craft of acting) and his responsibility to the
actor ends there. The director is justified in doing anything
that he needs to do to get the performance he wants from the
actor. The actor is bound by his profession, and even by his
union, to give the director what he wants. Ideally the
director lets the actor know what it is that he wants from the
role, and the actor takes it from there. If the director is not
happy with what the actor comes up with, then he tells him
so. He helps the actor find the right path and sends him
home to study. When the actor returns, he has the new idea
going for him on stage. The director supposes that the actor
is a trained professional and knows his job. The director
does not have time for coaching and should not have to
indulge in it. The director does not teach acting technique.
The actor is expected to have mastered that end of his
business, and there is seldom time to teach acting technique
when a professional production is readying itself. In theory
at least, the actor either produces the desired result within

the time the director expects him to, or he is replaced. Actually some union contracts, better fitted for nonskilled laborers than artists, can make replacement an extremely expensive proposition. Because of such hindrances, and because acting is a nebulous thing at best, the director often must spend a great deal of time with the actor in informal situations that are not union rehearsal, talking the character and the play through until agreement is reached, for above all, the professional actor must be treated as an artist. He cannot be ordered to perform a particular bit of business, even though both his contract and his union say he must. For if he is to perform well, the actor must be happy and confident in his work. In the professional theater the director starts with the basic assumption that the actor knows his job; in the amateur theater he generally starts with the opposite assumption. In the professional theater the actor and director meet as equals, both specialists in their own work. In the amateur theater the relationship is more often that between expert and student.

One does not order a colleague about; one makes suggestions and works with him. This does not imply that the director in the college theater simply orders his actors about, but certainly he will not take the time discussing the pros and cons with a student that he will with a proven artist. The professional must be catered to, to a degree, where the student need not be. For example, when dealing with an amateur cast I can feel fairly confident that my directorial experience will exceed the total theater experience of any of my cast. With a professional cast there is an excellent chance that I will be dealing with actors who have been on the boards longer than I have been out of high school.

Any actor must be given respect, but the respect due a student actor differs considerably from that due a professional actor. One is the respect due a student by a teacher, the other the respect due a colleague. The student is there to learn, and it is an important part of the director's job to teach him, but the professional, by virtue of being a professional, has learned, is an expert, and quite naturally wants to be treated as such.

As a concrete example, I will work considerably longer with a professional actor before reading a line for him than I will with a student actor. If I still cannot, after a reasonable length of time, get the reading I want I will, as a final attempt, say, to the student actor, "All right, copy my inflection; the sound I want is *da-da-de-da-de-da-da-da,* not *da-da-de-da-da-da-.*" I would have to be completely frustrated and angry before I would say this to a professional.

Finally, the student does not (rather, should not) pretend to be an actor; he is a student attempting to help stage a production and at the same time learn something of the art of theater. The professional is doing his life's work.

The results the director is after are the same, whether professional or amateur, but the methods of reaching the actor and the attitude toward the actor differ considerably.

Actually, the problems one meets are apt to be the same regardless of the type of actor concerned. Generally speaking, the acting problems will be solved more easily and quickly, and much more satisfactorily, with the professional, but the personality problems encountered differ only in degree. Many actors are basically insecure individuals who need their confidence reinforced continually. Treating any actor as though he were a piece of furniture or a prop naturally tends to undermine his confidence in himself and his talent and build up a resentment that will be difficult to overcome. Most actors on any level will listen and will try desperately hard to please when they think they are working for an understanding and competent director, but they, along with the rest of the free world, are certain to resent simply being told.

Any actor is apt to be extremely hesitant about asking for individual help. Either he does not want to intrude upon the director's time or he feels he should be able to lick the problem on his own. In any case, it is a wise policy for the director to find time to ask the actor privately how he feels he is coming along on the role and if he has any problems he wants to talk over. I have had actors who have worked with me for years become quite angry with me for not taking time to work on a particular scene in which they felt ill at ease, but which in reality was coming along in fine shape from my point of view. Often the first indication of their feeling will come offstage rather than on. For example, I recall a particular scene that was going very well for that stage of rehearsal, but which had reached a high point in its development fairly early and was seemingly coasting along on its merits, waiting for the rest of the show to catch up to it. I had, for several rehearsals, all but ignored the scene and concentrated on a portion of the play that was in real difficulty. I noticed that one of the actors in the scene, one who had played for me for a number of years and was a good friend offstage, was becoming almost surly in his offstage behavior. I put it down to rehearsal nerves, if I thought about it at all. When I finally had the troublesome scene on the right road, I turned my attention to the scene that had moved so rapidly and was amazed to find the particular actor furious with me for ignoring him and his problems. He felt that he had simply been standing still and had lost the quality that had originally made the scene move. I apologized to the actor and to the company for allowing my concern with a particular scene to overshadow my view of the rest of the production.

The incident above is set down simply to demonstrate that an actor, although working with a director for years and in the face of a longstanding friendship, could not bring himself to come to the director and ask for help. This is not an unusual story. Actors are very apt to complain to anyone who will listen that the director is ignoring them, yet they will seldom simply come and ask for aid. Since this is often the case, the director must take it upon himself to make it as easy for the actor as is possible.

Actors, and even nonactors playing at being actors, can be an extremely odd and difficult breed. They are not, as Alfred Hitchcock is quoted as saying, "cattle"; they are, as he goes on to say in the same article, "children, and they're temperamental and they need to be handled gently and sometimes—slapped." I would agree with the movie director, especially on his final thought, for in any medium the director must at times take a firm stand and simply "lay down the law." Such a technique is not called for nearly as often in the professional theater as it is in the amateur; that is understandable and casts no aspersions on the amateur actor. For the professional, acting is a vocation; for the amateur, it is an avocation.

In the final analysis, handling any actor is the problem of handling or working with any human being. Mutual respect is a must, and if the director will remember that the professional is his colleague and the amateur, in most cases, his student, he will have the general rules of behavior laid down for all concerned.

The Community Theater

I have spoken of the two worlds of the theater, the professional and the amateur, and I have, for the most part, divided those two worlds into the academic and the professional. There is, however, another and completely different world, one that does not fit into either the academic or professional, but is definitely amateur. That is the world of the civic or community theater. In the civic theater one cannot apply the standards from either academia or the professional theater; it is a world apart and must be treated as such. The purpose of the civic theater is quite different, the type of audience is often different, and certainly the method of handling the actors is different.

The purposes of the civic theater will change from one community to the next, often depending on what other theater offerings are available to the public. The audience may range from sophisticated to "plain country." The actors are housewives, young hopefuls, businessmen, clerks; people from just about any walk of life that one can name. With few exceptions, however, all the workers in the civic theater have one thing in common—the theater as a hobby. It does not give them an income, nor does it take them toward a degree; it is a hobby, a time-consuming one no doubt, a blood, sweat, and tears one, often an expensive one, but still, when all is said and done, it is a hobby.

The fact it is such need not damn the civic theater. One could, of course, point out at great length that such theaters as the Moscow Art Theater and the Théâtre Libre were only hobbies when they were founded. However, few civic theaters today have any aspirations, nor would they have any desire, to turn "pro." The community theater fulfills a much needed function, and it can bring joy and art to an audience that would otherwise never have a chance to see live drama.

In the civic or community theater the director is faced with quite another sort of problem, to say nothing of another sort of actor. Of course it goes almost without saying that all types will be encountered in any and all fields, but nonetheless certain representative types do exist. In the civic theater the director is in quite a different world. It is not, as it seems at first, a world between the academic and the professional world; rather, it is a world unto itself. For in the civic theater the director must remember that his actors are indulging themselves, they are using the theater as one might use a novel or a bowling team. To the director the play must be all-important, regardless of the kind of theater he works in, but in the civic theater the director must remember that his actors have already put in a full day of work at their respective jobs. To ask, or rather to expect, them to "bring something new" to rehearsal is generally asking the impossible. The "actor" has put in his eight or nine hours, rushed home, had a quick dinner, tried to fulfill the duties of his homelife in twenty or thirty minutes, then hurried out the door and, if fortunate, made it to rehearsal on time.

The director must, however, keep his own standards high, must know where he and his actors are missing the character, and must continually push the cast toward the best they are capable of. His task becomes one of continually exciting and interesting the cast in the drama, of *making* the show a vital and important part of their lives, for the time they spend in rehearsal must "pay off" for them just as the time the professional puts in must pay in dollars and cents for him. For the amateur in the community theater the payoff is in satisfaction. This satisfaction can be achieved in two different ways. First, it can be achieved in the satisfaction that comes in exhibitionism and in a "good time" at rehearsals. Secondly, and all too rarely, it can be achieved through satisfaction in a true, artistic experience, one that not only enlarges the amateur's knowledge of the theater and of the art of acting, but one that also reveals the heart of a play to the cast and to the audience.

The satisfaction of the cast and audience is not, however, the only factor to be considered, for the director must find satisfaction in his work, or he must leave the profession. Just as actors' purposes change in the civic theater, so must the director's, for seldom will the civic theater director who is honest with himself achieve the quality of performance that the play demands. Seldom will he be able to watch his own work without flinching inwardly. The finished product as an artistic product will not give the director much satisfaction. Since that is the case, the director in such a position must find his satisfaction elsewhere in his work. In the community theater he can find a great deal of satisfaction in watching how far his actors progress. His shows will be uneven and inconsistent, but he can still find his artistic satisfaction in knowing that his actors are 100 per cent or 500 per cent better than they were when they started. He can have the great satisfaction of watching the standards of a community change, or seeing lawyers and doctors grow as actors while they grow in theater knowledge and appreciation.

Another great difference between this world of theater and the other two worlds lies in the director's role within the theater. In the community theater position he must be more concerned with the organization, the committee work, the extent of participation of the community, more concerned with the image of the theater than he is with any particular play.

Though typing in or out of the theater can be dangerous, and though in any field of theater a director does meet all types continually, still, in the civic theater I believe the types are more easily recognizable. Community theater actors appear to fall into three main catagories. One is the housewife or businessman who, during his or her college career, was a drama major and vitally interested in the art of theater, but has found it necessary to leave the joys of the stage for the tasks of homemaking or making a living. This actor is a joy to work with, for he has usually developed good work habits while in school and is anxious to continue learning about his favorite field. In contrast to this actor is the person who is interested in the theater only insofar as it feeds his exhibitionistic tendencies. Stanislavski describes the best of this type when he discusses Grisha in *An Actor Prepares*. These local stars often can be classified as "prop actors" or "costume actors." The director should not, however, discount these persons, for they are important to the theater and him. Often their performances are among his best, and most often their interest in the theater as an organization, though selfish, is great. The director cannot and should not concern himself with their real or imagined motivations. Knowing the type can often help him in handling the actor, but looking down on the exhibitionist can only hurt the theater he is attempting to build. The third type to be encountered in the civic theater is the lawyer, the clerk, or the secretary who needs some sort of creative outlet and is generally interested in experiencing the stage. Often, rather remarkable theater talents will be discovered hidden silences and forms an invisible bond between subject and object."[88] Most sensitive persons have had the experience of sensing an emotion, a feeling, or perhaps even an idea from another person or, more often, from a crowd. It is not unusual, for instance, to walk into a room occupied by two people and "sense" that they are in the middle of an argument. Certainly, most persons have "sensed" the air of excitement at a large sporting event or backstage on an important opening night. Whether the feelings experienced in such instances are picked up by some little-understood physical or mental faculty or whether they are triggered by some small action, smell, noise, etc. on the fringe of the attention, is still a matter for conjecture. One can hardly doubt that emotions can be transferred from one person to another. Plato, in the aforementioned dialogue, likens the transfer of emotion, or of inspiration if you prefer, to the pieces of iron hanging on a magnet: "So the Muse not only inspires people herself, but through these inspired ones, others are inspired and dangle in a string. . . . Then do you know that the member of the audience is the last of those rings which I described."[89] Regardless of the view of the subconscious and the communion between actors and audience on the nonspeaking level, it would be difficult to deny that theater and acting are built on the transference of emotion from author to actor and from actor to audience. The question is whether or not such transference can occur without the aid of the visual and/or the auditory. If such "inner, invisible, and spiritual" aspects of communication do actually exist, then it would seem that the prime factor for the actor might well be, as Stanislavski suggests, the actor's concentration on "some interesting, creative problem on the stage." I would suggest that the actor and the director, rather than using valuable time attempting to manufacture or control such "rays," concern themselves with the problems of stage concentration and let the rays take care of themselves. Acting is such a nebulous thing, and the "right" performance so evanescent and so difficult to dissect, in any event, that the director is wiser, I believe, to think of the art of acting as *a symbolic process by which ideas and emotions are transferred from the author via the actor to the audience through the artistic use of accepted stage conventions*. While I would not deny the possibility of some sort of direct transfer from person to person via Stanislavski's "rays," I would contend that if such does exist, at present it is of little use to the working director or actor. The artistic use of the accepted conventions is, however, of vital concern to both. The discussion of blocking centered upon the broad visual elements of the play, and while the actors' character business and pantomimic action, combined with the scenic and costume designers' contributions, round off the visual aspects of any production, the auditory remains.

Vocal Interpretation

Though all phases of staging a play are interpretive, it seems wise to build one phase of the rehearsal period around vocal interpretation. Though I prefer to break my rehearsals up so that the work on line reading is postponed until the actor is acquainted with the play and has his rough blocking in mind, many directors prefer to work on both aspects at the same time. In any event, for purposes of discussion it is helpful to treat the line reading rehearsal as a separate process, though of course the actor is continually adding to his business and his pantomimic interpretation of the play. It is while working on the vocal interpretation of the lines that the director is closest to his actor and generally, if the director does indeed understand the play, closest to the author's intent. "For it is not enough to know *what* we ought to say; we must also say it *as* ought; much help is thus afforded towards producing the right impression of a speech," says Aristotle; and further, "It is essentially a matter of the right management of the voice; of high, low, or intermediate pitch; of the various rhythms that suit various subjects. These are the three things—volume of sound, modulation of pitch, and rhythm—that a speaker bears in mind."[90] The right management of voice, the right rhythms and the right modulations, the right volume of sounds—when all three are right, any line is apt to be right. But once again, none of the three areas of voice management has more than a random chance of being "right" in any given line unless the reader knows exactly what is meant by the line. To know what is meant, he must know what emotional overtones the line carries and in what "given circumstances" the line is read. In other words, he must know what role the character is playing in what rite and whether he is playing his role consciously or unconsciously.

Prior even to the "right management of the voice" comes the necessity, often overlooked in today's theater training, of the right voice to manage. The importance of a good voice cannot be overstressed, for even in the day of such eletronic miracles as the neck and chest transistor mikes, the basic instrument is still the human voice. If the audience cannot hear the author's words, or if the voice is so unpleasant to listen to that the audience does not care to hear, then all else is useless. "You need only three things," said the great Salvini while discussing the requirements of a tragic actor, "voice, voice, and more voice."[91] "The first requisite for the male Greek actor was a strong, resonant, clear voice. Not that the vast theaters in which he performed demanded excessive vocal effort: they didn't; the acoustics of most structures were quite satisfactory. But acting anywhere and of any kind demanded a better-than-average voice."[92] Acting still demands that better-than-average voice if that it is to be of a superior quality. Nothing so moves us as the human voice. Words, with their intellectual and emotional qualities, are of course vital to the theater, but the sound of the human voice alone can bring us to laughter, tears, anger, or terror. In fact, when the extremities of any of the basic emotions are expressed, words cease and lose their little meanings while that which words cannot express is communicated in pure sound. Perhaps the former insistence upon pure vocal training, to the exlusion of the other aspects of acting, is at least partially responsible for the limited vocal training deemed necessary in today's "naturalistic" theater. The old maid elocutionist who taught "the right management of voice" with her monologues of "A Mother Visits Her Son in the Death Cell" and "Aunt Ethel's Easter Hat," along with the stress on the declamatory and melodramatic style demanded by the writings of the last century, turned many serious students of the theater away from such "mechanical and false" training. The new drama and the "slice of life" theater seemed to require little beyond being "real." Nonetheless, a pleasant-sounding, resonant voice is, and always will be, a plus for any actor. To be "natural" under unnatural circumstances requires a technique of handling the voice; further, the problem of being "natural" on stage should not be confused with the sin of being casual and sloppy on stage. Even in Aristotle's

Maxfield Parrish's excellent book on interpretive reading, *Reading Aloud.* The actor does read his line and often speaks of a particular "line reading." There is, of course, a difference between the art of reading aloud and the art of acting, but reading is the basis and acting simply an extension of oral reading. Indeed, the origins of the performed drama appear to lead directly to the single rhapsode who held the ancient Greek spellbound with his recitations of the great epic poets.

Though recent years have seen a decline in the art of reading aloud, down through the ages it has been an honored practice. Reading reached its zenith, as far as the number of listeners is concerned, during the brief but active career of radio. The advent and complete triumph of television has, for the moment at least, taken the emphasis from the spoken word and placed it upon action and tricks of the camera, hence stress on the reader has diminished considerably. The movies too, with their natural concern for the visual, have virtually ignored the spoken word. Only in the theater is line reading still important, and because of the lack of stress in the other entertainment media, less important there than it should be.

The principal difference between the interpretive reader and the actor is in the doing. Acting is doing, reading is suggesting. The difference is summed up in the type of action called for in the two arts. Acting calls for the overt action, reading requires and will absorb only the covert action. The covert action is the action of muscular tension and tone, and the overt an extention of that tension and tone. The covert action will be present in the overt action used by the actor, just as the interpreter's vocal inflection which suggests sadness is present in the actual crying of the actor. The distinctions between the two arts are much more important to the reader than they are to the actor, for the actor does read, but the interpretive reader does not act. Far too few young actors are trained in the art of reading and almost none, it seems, are trained in the art of analyzing words and sentences. If, no matter what level the actor, the director finds himself with a noninterpreter on his hands, he had better know how to help that actor. In any event, the director must know how to get the effects he seeks.

The word is, as Justice Holmes once described it, "the skin of living thought," and for the actor the real word must be, as Plato says, "graven in the soul." Stanislavski tells us that "to an actor a word is not just a sound, it is the evocation of images. So when you are in verbal intercourse on the stage, speak not so much to the ear as to the eye."[94] All (at least for the actor) are saying, know exactly what you mean, know exactly what "living thought" you are expressing, and more than that, know what the author intended by the use of the particular word. True, a word is nothing except a vocal symbol, a noise to which the hearers attach a certain meaning and intent, but always the voice will color the word, even when there is no such intention. Rest assured that if the voice does not add to the overall picture and overall meaning, it will detract from it. For many actors a word, almost any word, is simply a noise, a symbol, a dry, meaningless, sound rather than a clear, transparent covering for lively exciting thought or emotion. The director, and through him, the actor, must follow the advice of John Ruskin: ". . . get into the habit of looking intensely at words, and assuring yourself of their meaning, syllable by syllable . . . nay, letter by letter."[95] Knowing exactly the intended meaning, with all the connotations of a particular framework, is not only, as Ruskin tells us, the mark of an educated gentleman, it is one of the distinguishing marks of the truly good actor.

Once again we see that the director, in his search for the key to transferring the author's thought and emotion from the page to the stage, and thence to the audience, must return to the intent: the rite, the role, and the use of one particular word rather than another, and how the sound of that word will carry the playwright's intent where another sound would not. The director, though not always the actor, must be aware that often the effect the author is attempting to create in the audience is not the effect one character is attempting to create within the other characters in the play. For a simple example, the character may well be striking terror in the hearts of the other characters in the play while provoking sidesplitting laughter in the audience. The readings must be such that they will seem "believable," that is, artistically true to the actors, without interfering with the author's intent. This is, of course, the difference between seeing a play through the eyes of the character and seeing it through the eyes of the director.

Though there are many ways of breaking lines down into easily understood segments, one of the best I have ever come across is found in the aforementioned text by Parrish. Much the same sort of technique, as far as word groupings are concerned, is suggested by Stanislavski in his second book, *Building a Character.*

The newer, and hence more primitive a language, the simpler it will generally appear. Primitive people do not have need of a complicated language pattern, thus we often find in primitive societies the sentence word, such as, *go; come; beware; stay; wait;* and *run.* These words carry total meaning, but in a more complicated society they would be used as meaning-carrying words in a group of words. The command "Come," for example, might be changed to, "Would you mind stepping this way, please?" Complete meaning is carried in the two words "this way," but politeness demands the additional words though they do not add to the meaning. In present-day language thought is generally expressed not in single words, but rather in groups of words. The first step in conveying emotion or meaning is that of finding the word groupings. "The first work to be done with speech or with words is always to divide into measures, to place the logical pauses where they belong."[96]

Punctuation will help to fix groupings, but punctuation alone will not delineate to the extent necessary for the actor. Most of us have been taught in grade school that the pause indicated by a comma or the sentence by the period is the unit of thought to be expressed vocally, but such is not always the case. Often the true meaning will extend beyond the sentence and usually beyond the phrase. There is only one criterion for testing the grouping—the author's intent. A group may well be composed of one word or of many. To group falsely is to destroy and often to change the author's meaning completely: "Joe called while you were out to lunch with your wife" can read, "Joe called while you were out—to lunch with your wife," or "Joe called——while you were out to lunch with your wife." Or there is the old story of the barber who hung the following sign in his window:

What do you think
I'll shave you for nothing
and give you a drink

and when he was asked for the drink, informed his customer that the groupings should have been read:

> What
> do you think I'll shave you for nothing
> and give you a drink

Or finally, the children's riddle, "Which would you rather, a lion ate you or a tiger?" The correct grouping is obvious when one perceives the answer, "I would rather the lion ate the tiger."

The subtleties of grouping become more evident when one listens to a foreign language. If one is not familiar with the vocal patterns, neither phrases nor sentences nor even paragraphs can be distinguished. To the unknowing ear there will be no stops, no pauses, and the uninitiated will not even be able to tell one word from another, indeed, the voice may sound as if it is stopping only to breathe.

Examine for a moment the first two sentences that King Claudius speaks in Act I, scene ii of Hamlet:

> Though yet of Hamlet our dear brother's death
> The memory be green, and that it us befitted
> To bear our hearts in grief, and our whole kingdom
> To be contracted in one brow of woe,
> Yet so far hath discretion fought with nature
> That we with wisest sorrow think on him
> Together with remembrance of ourselves:
> Therefore our sometime sister, now our queen,
> Th' imperial jointress to this warlike state,
> Have we, as 't were with a defeated joy,—
> With an auspicious and a dropping eye,
> With mirth in funeral and with dirge in marriage,
> In equal scale weighing delight and dole,—
> Taken to wife; nor have we herein barr'd
> Your better wisdoms, which have freely gone
> With this affair along. For all, our thanks.

Here we have sixteen lines divided into two sentences, one fifteen and a half lines long, the other, one half a line, and certainly the thought does not stop until the end of the second sentence. From the audience's viewpoint, the thoughts in the first sentence are many and varied, but from the king's point of view the basic thought is the simple, "I thank you for going along with my marriage at a very difficult time for all." Shakespeare is not only revealing a great deal about the character of the king, he is passing along a great deal of information to the audience. First, though we have just seen the ghost in the first scene, we now learn that the death is a recent one, so recent in fact that the memory has not begun to wither and is still "green." Second, we find that the new king and the entire kingdom are in mourning for the former king, Hamlet. Third, that in spite of the recent bereavement, life must go on, and thus the new king has not allowed his "wisest sorrow" to blind him to his present needs. Fourth, the new king has taken his sister-in-law to wife. Fifth, that the emotions of joy over the marriage and grief over the death of the king have balanced each other out. Sixth, that the court has freely gone along with the new marriage performed so quickly after the king's death. And seventh, that the new king is highly appreciative of the court's blessing and understanding of the whole affair. Within these seven thoughts Shakespeare has spelled out some eighteen facts or images which must register with the audience: (1) King Hamlet has recently died, (2) the dead king was the new king's brother, (3) the new king bears his heart in grief, (4) the entire kingdom is "contracted in one brow of woe," (5) the king's discretion has fought with his natural desires, (6) wise sorrow will not lose itself in itself, but (7) it will, instead, combine with the needs and wishes of the living, (8) that the bride was sister (in-law) to the new king, (9) the sister is now queen (10)

that the whole state is prepared for war, (11–15) a series of
antitheses describing his mixed emotions, all worthy of
remark by the audience, (16) that the king has, if not
sought, at least allowed his court to advise him, (17) that
the court as a whole agreed with his actions, and (18) the
new king is thankful. To get the seven thoughts and
the eighteen facts or images, plus the speaker's feelings for
his words, his queen, and his court across to the audience is
no small grouping problem, to say nothing of the acting
problems involved in this, the character's first speech in the
drama. One method of grouping the speech might be as
follows:

Though yet of Hamlet our dear brother's death/the memory
be green,/and that it is befitted to bear our hearts in grief,/
and our whole kingdom to be contracted in one brow of woe,
Yet/so far hath discretion fought with nature/that we with
wisest sorrow/think on him together with remembrance of
ourselves:/Therefore our sometime sister,/now our queen,/th'
imperial jointress to this warlike state, Have we as 't were with
a defeated joy,—/with an auspicious and a dropping eye/with
mirth in funeral/and with dirge in marriage,/In equal scale
weighing delight and dole,—/taken to wife;/nor have we
herein barr'd your better wisdoms, which have freely gone with
this affair along./For all,/our thanks.

Another grouping that might make the speech flow a little
more smoothly, but would need excellent diction and not a
little breath control, could be as follows:

Though yet of Hamlet our dear brother's death
The memory be green, and that it us befitted
To bear our hearts in grief, and our whole kingdom
To be contracted in one brow of woe,/
Yet so far hath discretion fought with nature
That we with wisest sorrow think on him

> Together with remembrance of ourselves/
> Therefore, our sometime sister, now our queen,
> Th' imperial jointress of this warlike state,
> Have we,/as 't were with a defeated joy,
> With an auspicious and a dropping eye,
> With mirth in funeral and with dirge in marriage,
> In equal scale weighing delight and dole, /
> Taken to wife;/nor have we herein barr'd
> Your better wisdoms, which have freely gone
> With this affair along./ For all, our thanks.

Groupings are not necessarily set off by the use of the pause as Stanislavski seems to suggest in his discussion of "Intonations and Pauses."[97] Any device that will allow words within the desired groupings to be heard and thus thought of as a unit will serve the purpose. A raise in pitch will often suffice, as will a drop, a change in tempo, or a hesitation. Even the speaker's attitude toward the groupings, for example, scorn or agreement, can help to make them clear to the audience. The final word grouping that the actor and director decide upon will be dependent upon the overall interpretation and the particular actor playing the role. The more flexible and expressive the actor's voice, the less actual break there will be between groupings. The final criterion for word groupings will be the meaning and emotion that the actor and director have agreed upon. For example, in the role of Claudius the degree of expertness in conscious role-playing the interpreters have assigned to the king will affect the word groupings to a considerale extent.

Once the word groupings have been decided upon, the actor must learn to show the relationship between the various groups. As Parrish points out, the "interdependencies among phrases are so various and so complicated that no rule of elocution can be formulated to cover them."[98] The only sure way is to understand and know exactly what the author's purpose is in using the relationship. The usual relationship of groups will be that of the principal and the subordinate groups. "Most modifying phrases and clauses, and many conditional and parenthetical clauses, are subordinate in importance to the main clauses, and so must be given less prominence in reading."[99] Or two groups may be of equal importance and enforce each other. The antitheses describing the king's mixed emotions, defeated joy—auspicious and dropping eye—mirth in funeral—dirge in marriage—delight and dole, must be read as parallel rather than contrasting expressions; each one goes to demonstrate the speaker's warring passions. Attempting to read these groups as contrasting, rather than parallel, ideas will quickly turn the speech into a ludicrous and unintelligible mass of words.

Cause and effect relationships often appear obvious to the eye, but are quite difficult to express unless the speaker understands the relationship. The cause-effect relationship in a line such as the following is not very difficult to understand.

> The thane of Cawdor lives; why do you dress me
> In borrowed robes?

The grouping is set off by the semicolon; the second group is a question based on the result of the cause in the first group. In other words, "Because the Thane of Cawdor is still alive, I cannot be called by his title." The cause-effect relationship in Duncan's speech is not quite as apparent, yet is obviously the only relationship that will add to the meaning of the line:

> There's no art
> To find the mind's construction in the face.
> He was a gentleman on whom I built
> An absolute trust.

The inflection and stress *can* make it read, "It is easy to find the mind's construction in the face." While it is possible to break down the above into more than two groups, the two sentences are linked by cause and effect. In other words, "As there is no way to determine a man's way of thinking by looking at his face, I have mistakenly placed all my trust upon a traitor." In the following lines, also from *Macbeth,* we see the cause-effect relationship used with one cause and several effects.

> Yet do I fear thy nature;
> It is too full o' th' milk of human kindness
> To catch the nearest way. Thou wouldst be great,
> Art not without ambition, but without
> The illness should attend it. What thou woulds't highly,
> That woulds't thou holily; woulds't not play false,
> And yet woulds't wrongly win . . .

Because Macbeth has too much of the milk of human kindness, he (1) will not catch the nearest way, (2) does not have the illness that ambition should have, (3) would attempt to take "holily" what he wants highly, and (4) would not play false even though he would accept ill-gotten gains. At times the relationship will reverse itself and become effect to cause. Gina, in *The Wild Duck,* suggesting her own dislike of Old Werle, dampens Hedvig's happiness at the thought of her father at "Mr. Werle's big dinner party" with an effect to minor cause and then, after a short pause, to the prime cause: "You know, he's not really Mr. Werle's guest. It was the son invited him. [*after a pause*] We have nothing to do with that Mr. Werle."

Often too, words within groups are purposely left out by the playwright, generally to give a more natural flavor to the dialogue; such ellipses can cause difficulty even when they are obvious to the eye. Ibsen has Old Ekdal, for example, leave out pronouns and speak in short phrases: "Can't say that, sir. Get a shot now and then perhaps. Of course, not in the old way. For the woods you see—the woods, the woods —! (*Drinks*) Are the woods fine up there now?" Such a speech can cause difficulty for the inexperienced actor unless he mentally supplies the missing pronouns. Often too, the author will leave out connective words such as "therefore," "on the other hand," "hence," etc., and leave a space instead of supplying the word. The actor can maintain the proper groupings and achieve the proper rhythms if he will mentally supply the omitted word or words.

> What, sir, not yet at rest? The King's a-bed
> He hath been in unusual pleasure, and
> Sent forth great largess to your offices.
> This diamond he greets your wife withal,
> By the name of most kind hostess; and shut up
> in measureless content.

Paraphrased the line might read, "What sir, are you not yet at rest? The King has gone to bed. He has been feeling unusually good and he has sent wonderful gifts to your servants. With this diamond he greets your wife, calling her the kindest of hostesses, and he has gone to bed completely content." Within the Shakespearean language, the ellipses are:

> What, sir [are you] not at rest? The
> King's a-bed
> He hath been in unusual pleasure, and
> [he has] sent forth great largess to your offices.
> [with] This diamond he greets your wife withal,
> By the name of most kind hostess; and [he is now] shut up
> In measureless content.

Now let us return to the sentence word, the word that carries the principal meaning in the word group. These sentence words are the pivotal words of each group. One can often identify them by the simple process of thinking of the line as a telegram at ten dollars a word. It is surprising how many words one can do without at that price. The words left after all extras have been crossed out will be the pivotal words. Each group will build toward, or away from, the pivotal word, and it is these words that will usually take the emphasis. Once the word groupings have been settled upon and the pivotal words discovered, then the actor must decide how he is going to emphasize the important pivotal words. Any method that will make the pivotal words stand out from the rest of the words will serve the purpose, providing it also serves the rite in progress and the role being played. Loudness, sharpness, softness, longer duration, changing the pitch radically, a pause before the word, after the word, sliding into the word, attacking the word abruptly, any and all will emphasize the word. The easiest way, and hence the most overworked way, is to punch the word, that is, to give it a little more volume than the rest of the group. There is nothing wrong with such a method, providing it is used in conjunction with all the other possible methods. Always the method should correspond to the thought being expressed. "Meaning will be clear when the thought-carrying words stand out in a bright pattern against a background of less important words."[100] In general, when one is in doubt about what to emphasize above and beyond the meaning-carrying words, the rule to follow is to emphasize the new material. For example:.

MACBETH: If we should fail?
LADY MACBETH: We fail?

> But screw your courage to the sticking-place
> And we'll not fail . . .

The word "fail" is used three times. Macbeth almost certainly will stress the fail, for it is his biggest concern. If he were to say, "If *we* should fail," he would imply that someone else would not, if he stresses the *should,* he will be asking for an alternate plan, and if he emphasizes the *If,* then he will be suggesting that there is not much chance of failing. So the meaning-carrying word for Macbeth, the word the group builds to, is *fail.* Lady Macbeth can, since no one knows for sure what kind of punctuation Shakespeare meant to follow her "fail" (though the question mark or the exclamation mark is generally used) stress the same word, as Eva Le Gallienne used to do in the role, thus meaning, "If we fail, we fail, that's all there is to it." Or, one can stress the *we* and use the question mark meaning that such a course of events is highly unlikely. But regardless of what interpretation she gives the "We fail," her second *fail* must be subordinated to the new material, in this case the word *not.*

Also, words that are used for contrast or for comparison generally will need emphasis. The contrasts in the lines,

> Good things of day begin to droop and drowse,
> Whiles night's black agents to their preys do
> rouse.

are easily seen and vocalized, yet when the contrasts are separated even a little they become more difficult to recognize and are often overlooked. In Macbeth's famous and rather difficult speech contemplating the murder of Duncan, the contrasts are numerous and involved.

> If it were done when't is done, then't were well
> It were done quickly; if the assassination
> Could trammel up the consequence, and catch
> With his surcease success; that but this blow
> Might be the be-all and the end-all here,
> But here, upon this bank and shoal of time,
> We'd jump the life to come. But in these cases
> We still have judgement here, that we but teach
> Bloody instructions, which being taught, return
> To plague the inventor. This even-handed justice
> Commends th' ingredients of our poison'd chalice
> To our own lips . . .

The speech might be divided into two sections, the first six and a half lines setting up the wish, the last six and a half contrasting the actualities that Macbeth sees stemming from the deed. Such a speech, for any actor, will continue to yield meaning even after many playings. The different meanings of the word "done," for example, in the first two lines and the punctuation itself need thorough examination. In order that the actor see the necessity for emphasis, the director might do well to paraphrase the speech for him as he sees it. For example:

If the deed were completed when it was ended, then all would be well. If it were ended quickly, that is, if the murder could net up all the results within itself and be successful, all would be well. If the murderous blow would accomplish everything and end everything to do with it here on this earth, just on this plane of living, then we would take our chances in the next world. But, unfortunately, in these matters we still have the judgment to face on earth. All we really do is to teach others to follow our example and those students return to kill their teacher. This fact of judgment here, the judgment of those who have learned by our example, will end in our own murder.

Basically the speech is built in the two parts, which are contrasted with each other. That basic contrast must be vocalized if any of the more difficult meaning is to be clear to an audience. Notice that in the paraphrasing I have changed the punctuation, or at least, have ignored it. Hence, in the first three lines,

> If it were done when't is done, then't were well
> It were done quickly; if the assassination
> Could trammel up the consequence, and catch . . .

the meaning will be clearer and the speech will read aloud better if it is grouped (as it is in the Theatre Masterworks album *An Evening With William Shakespeare* directed by Margaret Webster). "If it were done when tis done, then 't were well. It were done quickly, if the assassination could trammel up the consequence, and catch, etc . . ."

However, because Elizabethan punctuation was aimed at "pointing" the speech for delivery rather than indicating the syntax of a sentence and because, in all probability, Shakespeare was not responsible for the punctuation that has come down to us, such groupings are a matter of personal preference for actor and director.

Certain words will almost never take emphasis. The most important of these is, I believe, the personal pronoun. For some reason the inexpert reader will feel impelled to jump heavily on the "I," "you," "him," "she," and so on. Generally such pronouns will not need emphasis because they fall within the large group of words which Parrish labels "implied." Any word whose meaning is strongly implied does not need the reinforcement of voice. In general, the personal pronoun will be so strongly implied that the true meaning of the sentence will be lost if that pronoun is stressed. One does not need to say "*I* am going to go for a walk" unless the meaning is that I am going, instead of, or in spite of, someone else. The same is true in the speech above, in the line "We'd jump the life to come." The "We" should not be stressed, and if it is, the meaning of the line will be lost.

Personal pronouns are not the only example of implied words, however. Any word whose meaning is implied in the context of the line will not need to be stressed. One would not emphasize the word "flew" in a sentence about a bird, but "flew" would probably need the emphasis if one was describing the first airplane flight at Kitty Hawk. Nor would one emphasize the word "sit" when describing a group of students in a classroom: "The students sit in a classroom." As sitting is the normal thing for students to do in such a location, the meaning is implied.

Another class of words that does not need to be given emphasis is what Parrish has called the "echo" words. These are words whose function it is to echo words or ideas that have already been established. Staying with Macbeth for an example, look at the opening lines of one of the most famous of all speeches from that play, the dagger speech from Act II, scene i:

> Is this a dagger which I see before me,
> The handle toward my hand? Come, let me clutch thee.
> I have thee not, and yet I see thee still.
> Art thou not, fatal vision, sensible
> To feeling as to sight? or art thou but
> A dagger of the mind, a false creation,
> Proceeding from the heat-oppressed brain?
> I see thee yet, in form as palpable
> As this which now I draw.
> Thou marshall'st me the way that I was going,
> And such an instrument I was to use.
> Mine eyes are made the fools o' th' other senses,
> Or else worth all the rest: . . .

In the first line, the movement of the voice is toward and

away from the word "dagger," which is the new material in the scene. The personal pronouns "I" and "me" are, as usual, implied, but are also echos of the times Macbeth has already used them. "Thee" is always the echo for "dagger." Notice the use of the word "see" and its echoes "sight" in the fifth line and "eyes" in the twelfth line. Even "vision" in the fourth line is an echo of "see" in line one, with "fatal" being the new material that needs the stress. While "sight" is a kind of echo of "see," it is also used in contrast with "feeling" in the same line

> A dagger of the mind, a false creation,
> Proceeding from the heat-oppressed brain?

and is contrasted with

> . . . in form as palpable
> As this which now I draw.

Simple echo and contrasting words are not difficult to see and to express, especially when they occur in the space of a few lines, but when, as is often the case, they occur pages, or even scenes and acts, apart they may easily escape attention. The playwright will repeat his ideas over and over again, using different words and different situations to make the same point. In such cases the repeating of words and ideas may not be used as echoes, but rather as repetition for emphasis. The director and the actor must make sure they understand not only *how* the poet has used his words and ideas, but *why* he has so used them.

Once the decision has been made as to what will receive the emphasis within the speech and what will not be emphasized, the actor must have techniques of making the emphasis meaningful and artistic. How the new material should be made to stand out from the echoes, the implied and the nonessential becomes the director's problem only when the actor cannot accomplish his task. Any technique will be satisfactory providing it brings the particular ideas to the surface, and providing it does not draw attention to itself.

Many young actors, perhaps to make sure they are "right," tend to stress every word, and hence end by stressing none at all. Another common fault to guard against is the punching of words; often "word punching" will be found within definite vocal patterns.

Once again, one of the most effective means of empha-. sizing words is by means of the pause. A pause before the important word or phrase, a pause after the word, as if in contemplation, or often a hesitation within a word will make that word stand out from the rest. Speaking the word more loudly is, of course, effective, but it soon draws attention to the technique. Lowering the voice, elongating the word, clipping it short, changing the voice quality—any and all are effective. Just as Hamlet suggests that the action and the word must be suited, so must the voice and the idea be suited. Any method of emphasis which fits within the rite in progress, and is "natural" to the actor using it, is a good method. "Meaning will be clear when the thought-carrying words stand out in a bright pattern against a background of less important words."[101] The director will do well to memorize Parrish's words of wisdom. Too many plays have been lost because the audience was not made conscious of the "bright pattern" of ideas and emotions.

In summary then, meaning is carried forward by word groups, not by individual words. Each group of words will have certain pivotal words upon which the principal meaning and/or emotion will rest. The sentence construction will usually, but not always, be such that the build within the sentence is to and away from those pivotal words. Words and groupings which are used as comparisons or contrasts with other words or groupings almost always need emphasis and special attention to show the intended connection. Generally speaking, new ideas, that is ideas which have not previously been introduced, will need to be emphasized, while ideas that have already been introduced will be subordinated. Without close examination, it is often difficult to know whether the playwright is repeating an idea for emphasis or whether he is using repetition as an echo of what has gone before.

Echo words, words and ideas that "echo" those already introduced, and *implied words,* words that carry their own meaning so strongly that no stress is needed, should not receive emphasis; they should be pushed into the background in order that the pivotal words, contrast and comparison words, and new material can receive the emphasis and hence stand out clearly and easily.

You cannot squander your accents recklessly! A stress misplaced distorts a word or lames a phrase, whereas it should be a help to it.

The accent is a pointing finger. It singles out the key word in a phrase or measure. In the word thus underscored we shall find the soul, the inner essence, the high point of the subtext.[102]

The Working Rehearsal

A method of breaking down the playwright's lines into word groups and of finding the words and ideas that need to receive emphasis is essential to the actor, and hence to the director, just as knowing the techniques of emphasizing the correct ideas and words, once they have been discovered, is essential to both. Yet the director is not required, or expected, to stop rehearsals and give his cast a short course in oral interpretation whenever difficulty is encountered. Such luxuries as teaching during the rehearsal are generally excluded by the time factor. Still, the young director needs to have some idea of how one goes about working with a cast during this difficult "interpretation" period of rehearsal.

The first fundamental to bear in mind, and one that is often the first to be forgotten, is that the rehearsal is for the actor. It is his time to discover, with the director's help and guidance, the author's intent. Once he has found that intent, the rehearsals become a search for the best way to convey that intent, along with all the poet's overtones, to the audience—to find "the truth of a situation and then to illuminate it so that everyone can see," as Montgomery Clift is quoted as saying about the art of acting.[103] Everything that is planned for and all that occurs during the rehearsal should further the actor's search. Finally, when the search for ways and means is concluded the remaining time must be spent in "setting" both the intent and the techniques of conveying it.

The director may find that the visual interpretation—the blocking—and the vocal interpretation—the line reading— go hand in hand. Many directors prefer to work on the two aspects of interpretation simultaneously and, of course, in the final analysis, it is impossible to separate them completely. Nonetheless, I prefer to rough block the entire show first and then go back and work out the line readings. Naturally the blocking changes and is expanded during the "interpretation" rehearsals but, as was pointed out in the discussion of blocking, the basic approach to the vocal interpretation will be set once the rough blocking is completed. If the director knows both his theory of stage movement and the play he is working on, very little of the original blocking will have to be adjusted or changed. However, he should never hesitate to change his blocking when it is evident that the movement is coming between the actor and the meaning or feeling of the line.

Actors of any experience will quickly see that in the original blocking they are being fitted into a pattern, and some may resent that. In such a case, the director must convince the actor that the pattern is only a preliminary one and can be changed if it is seen to be foreign to the intent. The director should encourage the actor to demonstrate the move or reading he feels to be correct, and convince him that he should never feel that the original move or reading is the only possible one. It is wise, I feel, to block first and "interpret" secondly because an actor needs something to "hang on to" in the early rehearsals. The simple fact of knowing where on the stage the line is to be read will often give an actor the confidence to try new and different vocal inflections. Though splitting the rough-blocking rehearsals and the vocal interpretation can be helpful in any group, I believe it is most helpful in the amateur theater and strongly recommend it to directors working with high school, college, or civic groups.

In order to get a glimpse at the problem of working with the actor, let us assume that we are in rehearsal for *The Wild Duck*. Interpretation work has just started on Act II, the show is rough blocked, the actors have their crosses written into the scripts, and all understand that any move or any picture can be changed if the need is discovered. The stage manager is checking all the moves while the director is sitting on the fore-part of the stage, close to the actors. All the concern is placed on finding the meaning, and then a reading that will convey that meaning. Emotional content is discussed, but no attempt is made at this early rehearsal to capture the character's true feeling. We are concerned only with the meaning and how the lines interlock within the scene and how they relate to the scenes that have gone before. In general, it is wiser if the director does not hold a script during these rehearsals; instead he should put all his energies into listening. Each line is read by the actor portraying the role, and each move is taken. The fundamental question is always, What is the character saying? (or doing), and, when necessary, What is the author saying? Obviously the director is fairly certain of what the lines mean or he could not have blocked the play even roughly, but strange and wonderful things can and do happen when one hears a good actor take a line to himself. All sorts of new and exciting avenues open up to the director, and he must often hold himself in check or he will be off and running down a blind alley that makes for a good line reading, but ruins the author's intent.

Remember, the play is only roughly blocked, that is, the general crosses have been blocked in, but the business has not been touched; only the composition, the basic outlines, of the designs is present. The rough blocking has been done with elementary emphasis, balance, stability, and sequence in mind. The picturizational quality of the movement has only been suggested. For our purposes we will take only the first dramatic action in the opening scene of the act.

ACT II

HIALMAR EKDAL'S *studio, a good-sized room, evidently in the top story of the building. On the right, a sloping roof of large panes of glass, half-covered by a blue curtain. In the right-hand corner, at the back, the entrance door; farther forward, on the same side, a door leading to the sitting room. Two doors on the opposite side, and between them an iron stove. At the back a wide double sliding door. The studio is plainly but comfortably fitted up and furnished. Between the doors on the right, standing out a little from the wall, a sofa with a table and some chairs; on the table a lighted lamp with a shade; beside the stove an old armchair. Photographic instruments and apparatus of different kinds lying about the room. Against the back wall, to the left of the double door, stands a bookcase containing a few books, boxes, and bottles of chemicals, instruments, tools, and other objects. Photographs and small articles, such as camel's-hair brushes, pencils, paper, and so forth, lie on the table.*

GINA EKDAL *sits on a chair by the table, sewing.*

HEDVIG *is sitting on the sofa, with her hands shading her eyes and her thumbs in her ears, reading a book.*

GINA: *(glances once or twice at Hedvig, as if with secret anxiety; then says)* Hedvig!

HEDVIG: *(does not hear)*

GINA: *(repeats more loudly)* Hedvig!

HEDVIG: *(takes away her hands and looks up)* Yes, Mother?

GINA: Hedvig dear, you mustn't sit reading any longer now.

HEDVIG: Oh, Mother, mayn't I read a little more? Just a little bit?

GINA: No, no, you must put away your book now. Father doesn't like it; he never reads hisself in the evening.

HEDVIG: *(shuts the book)* No, Father doesn't care much about reading.

GINA: *(puts aside her sewing and takes up a lead pencil and a little account book from the table)* Can you remember how much we paid for the butter today?

HEDVIG: It was one crown sixty-five.

GINA: That's right. (*puts it down*) It's terrible what a lot of butter we get through in this house. Then there was the smoked sausage, and the cheese—let me see (*writes*)—and the ham (*adds up*). Yes, that makes just—

HEDVIG: And then the beer.

GINA: Yes, to be sure (*writes*). How it do mount up! But we can't manage with no less.

HEDVIG: And then you and I didn't need anything hot for dinner, as Father was out.

GINA: No; that was so much to the good. And then I took eight crowns fifty for the photographs.

HEDVIG: Really! So much as that?

GINA: Exactly eight crowns fifty.

The rite is one of Waiting for Father; it will be repeated under quite different circumstances in Acts IV and V and the director will probably point this out to the cast.

Gina is introduced in her basic role of "mother" while Hedvig is playing her usual role with her mother, "daughter-companion." Both characters are completely unconscious of their roles. It is important to point out to Hedvig immediately that her role of "daughter-companion," which she usually plays with her mother, is quite different from her semiconscious role of "daddy's little girl," which she will drop into the moment she sees her father enter.

Though the scene is the opening of the second act, neither Gina nor Hedvig appeared in Act I, hence it is probable that this is the first interpretation rehearsal for either of the two women. The director will, unless he has worked with both actresses before, explain the purpose of the rehearsal and how it is to be conducted. Having done so, he will nod to Gina and the first line, "Hedvig!" is read. Because of the exclamation point after the line, the actress playing Gina reads the "Hedvig!" with anxiety that is far from secret. She has gone on to her second "Hedvig!" before she hears the director quietly suggest that she drop her voice considerably for this opening line and that she allow the glances which Ibsen suggests to convey the anxiety rather than the voice. The actress points out that as the eyes become very important in the later scenes, perhaps the thought needs pointing right away. The director agrees that the eyes do indeed become vitally important, but Ibsen has taken care to stress the early planting of the idea by the conversation alone, and the actress need not attempt to point what will, in two more lines, become quite apparent. Gina tries the line much more lightly in a more normal voice without hint of strain; she likes the effect and goes on to the next "Hedvig!" This time she is too subdued for the director's wishes. As the actress portraying Gina is a mother of a ten-year-old boy, the director reminds her of the hundreds of times she has had to speak her child's name more than once before she caught his attention. The director explains that in such a case there is often no real anger, just a little trace of irritation at not being "paid attention to," especially as the mild reprimand that she is going to administer is not for a first offense. Hedvig is an avid reader and Gina often must remind her not to strain her eyes. If the actress playing Gina is not a mother herself, she has at least been a daughter and can probably be made to recall something in her own childhood that would correspond to the situation in the play. This is not to imply that the consequence would have to be as serious as loss of her eyesight, but something at least that the child liked to do that the mother was continually warning her not to overdo. Such a recollection may take a bit of time, for when the actress does remember some incident

really knows why her mother is interrupting her reading, that in fact she has been unconsciously expecting it for quite some time, further, that she heard the first call but ignored it in order to finish the page and the sentence on the next page.

"So how does such a direction help the author's intent?" our student director asks, not without reason. Actually, it may not. The reason for the suggestion is twofold: such a reading will give the actress a reason for apparently not hearing the first interruption and secondly, it will help her to begin thinking in terms of a little girl who likes to read, growing up in a household where reading is not an accepted form of relaxation. The director then explains to the actress that the reading he is looking for is more as if the line were saying, "Yes, Mother, I heard you even though it may look as if I didn't." She tries this approach but it comes out bored and a little sarcastic, as though the actress was thinking "O.K., O.K., I heard you." The director explains that this is not the reading he is seeking and in fact, it is a reading that would be completely foreign to Hedvig Ekdal. Rather, he simply wants a reading which says, in effect, "Yes, Mother, I heard you, only this is so interesting I couldn't pull myself away right now." Hedvig feels, as the lines point out later in the scene with Gregers, that her parents make much too much of her weak eyes, and though she would seldom disobey them, she cannot help smiling at their groundless concern. The actress sees what the director is driving at and gives a satisfactory reading.

Gina's next line, "Hedvig dear, you mustn't sit reading any longer now," is read a little too sentimentally for the director's ear. The actress, taking her cue from the "dear" and anticipating the tragic death, again is pushing too hard and "reading into the lines." Again the director stops the actresses and discusses the relationship within the rite in progress. They are Waiting for Father; Gina is playing mother and Hedvig is playing daughter-companion. Gina knows perfectly well that Hedvig is a dutiful child and would not argue for the sake of arguing, thus she is simply stating a fact that she knows will be accepted. The irritation that was just noticeable in the mother's second "Hedvig!" has disappeared, and the line is read in the same manner as "time for bed now" is stated in thousands of homes. Though the actress sees what the director is after, she has difficulty with the proper inflection; the director suggests that she work on it later as long as she knows what is wanted. She gratefully agrees and the rehearsal continues. Hedvig's line, "Oh, Mother, mayn't I read a little more? Just a little bit," sounds too much like a complaint, rather than a request. The actress states that she was trying not to get sentimental and was attempting to give Hedvig a little backbone instead of the syrupy sweet little girl quality. The director agrees with her intent, but points out that while Hedvig does have backbone, she is not impertinent, nor is she impatient with her mother's lack of understanding. She simply would like to read a little more but knows she will not be allowed to do so. In order to establish the relationship that will hold for the entire play, the director here suggests that she take Ibsen's suggestion of shutting the book, which appears before her next line, as she is making her request to continue reading. The shutting of the book as she is asking to be allowed to read a little more will help get across the idea that Hedvig is a dutiful girl, but one who makes at least a token effort for her own way. The director explains that he would like to use the line to demonstrate that Hedvig loves reading and is not afraid to question her mother, but is sure enough of her mother's reactions to know that she will be adamant once she has made up her mind. The voice, the director explains, will be asking for more time, while the action will say that Hedvig accepts the authority of her parents.

Gina, listening closely to the discussion between Hedvig and the director sees the intended relationship and reads her next line, "No, no, you must put away your book now," with just the right amount of insistence but without any argumentative quality in her tone of voice. Before finishing the line, "Father doesn't like it; he never reads hisself in the evening," the actress interrupts herself and asks, "Now is she saying that because father never reads, that no one should read, or is it simply that Hedvig can't read any longer because father doesn't like it?" The director answers that he believes that Gina looks up to Hialmar even more than Hedvig does. Hedvig has grown up respecting the great and talented man, but Gina has moved from one circle of society to another by marrying Hialmar. She knows him for what he is, but she loves him a great deal. The fact that father doesn't like Hedvig reading in the evening is reason enough, but when the fact that father himself does not read in the evening is added, then certainly Hedvig will not want to do it. Gina goes back and reads the entire line, likes the effect, and waits for Hedvig's response. Hedvig, not knowing what to do with her line, "No, Father doesn't care much about reading," tries it as a straight matter-of-fact statement. The director stops her and asks how a move to put the book away would feel on that line. The actress is neutral and seeing the move executed, the director decides that the line tries a move to the small bookcase up left center. After

THE DIRECTOR

is too important a clue to Hialmar's character to have it thrown away on an upstage move. Still, some sort of move does seem to work for the line. He then suggests that the actress try a rise on the downstage side of her chair, on the line, and take the cross during Gina's next line. The feeling the director wants on the reading is a slightly puzzled one, as if it is one of the things that Hedvig has never been able to understand about her father. It is not, the director hastens to explain, that Hedvig looks down on her father for his lack of love for reading, but rather, that it is odd and that she can't understand his feeling. She is the one that must be wrong, but she cannot really accept that either. The actress tries the rise and the reading suggested and both seem to work. Now that she has changed a move, she will be out of position for all the rest of her rough blocking. The director suggests that she try the line and move over again to see if she can time the cross with the book to allow her to do a turn on her next line, "It was one crown sixty-five," and then to put the book away as Gina writes down the figure after her, "That's right." Now Hedvig can return to her original seat at the table on her line, "And then the beer."

With Hedvig's new move "in," the actresses are asked to go back to the original troublesome line and try the sequence through. Now the concentration will be on Gina's lines. Gina returns to her "No, no, you must put away your book now," etc . . . and all goes well for a couple of lines. When Gina reaches the question, "Can you remember how much we paid for the butter today?" she suggests that she might take her account book out a line earlier than Ibsen suggests in order to be ready to figure her expenses when the question comes up, and as the director is generally opposed to holding up lines for business, he agrees. He points out that the business on the earlier line "he never reads hisself in the evening" must not interfere with the attention on the line but will, if handled correctly, make the point less obviously character exposition, in short, will make the scene more relaxed and more natural. The actress, stressing the poverty of the family proceeds, makes too much of "It's terrible what a lot of butter we get through in this house. Then there was the smoked sausage, and the cheese—let me see *(writes)*—and the ham *(adds up)*. Yes, that makes just—" The director points out that Gina here is simply thinking aloud, her concentration, her action, if you will, is figuring the accounts, not voicing an opinion upon the high prices of food or the huge appetites of her family. Hedvig's line, "And then the beer," is now being read as she returns to the table and hence is being directed pretty much directly into the audience. Hedvig is reminded that her father loves his evening glass of beer and quite possibly she is the one who reminded Gina to buy it. Thus she might be thinking of her father's reaction when she suggests later that he have a glass of "beautiful fresh beer" and be smiling in happy anticipation. The next difficulty arises when Hedvig fails to see that her line "as Father was out" doesn't need emphasizing, because it is in reality an echo of Act I where we see Hialmar out in society. When this point is made, the director backtracks a bit to point out to her that her line concerning Hialmar's not reading is in contrast to his lines in Act I in which he attempts to give Gregers an impression of culture and learning. In the same manner the lines mentioning butter, smoked sausage, cheese, and the beer are compared with Gregers' lines in Act I concerning Hialmar's weight, "You have put on flesh and grown almost stout."

And so it goes all through the play, line by line, changing

moves, attempting different readings and roughing out a general vocal direction for the actors to follow. During the ensuing weeks, the readings may, and probably will, change, perhaps completely, as the actors become better acquainted with the characters they are portraying and as the director discovers more and more of the subtleties of the play. Each new inflection can open up new meanings and emotions and each new insight will add to the overall "rightness" of the drama.

When the actor cannot understand what the director is attempting, or when he will not understand either the director or the author's intent, then a different technique must be employed. Such cases can turn into long and involved discussions. Unless the point in question is vital to the overall interpretation of the play, it is wiser to ask the actor to lay the problem aside for a moment when you and he may have more time to think and discuss it in private, when the two of you will not be holding up the entire company. Finally, if a difference persists the director's best move is to ask the actor to show him what he has in mind—not to talk about it, but to try it in the scene. Then the director must either accept the idea or reject it firmly.

As has been suggested earlier, often when the actor is not getting the desired reading, the director can paraphrase the line, giving the rewritten line the same inflection he hopes to hear in the actor's reading. The important thing to ascertain is whether the reading is not being achieved because the actor is having technical difficulties in getting a particular inflection, or whether he is attempting to bring out another meaning in his reading. Tone copying, that is, paraphrasing and giving the desired inflections, should be used only to demonstrate to the actor what meaning or emotion the director is seeking. The director should point out that he does not care how the actor gets that meaning or emotion as long as that particular meaning is the one that comes across.

Another, and actually less honest, but sometimes very practical, method is for the director to question the line following the difficult line. Then, while discussing the following line, the director can read the troublesome one and hope that the actor will be sharp enough to pick up the desired reading. This method, while seemingly most obvious, is used by some directors with great success and much more often than one would believe possible. It is suggested only as a way out when an actor is so unsure of himself that he gets angry at paraphrasing and tone copying.

In actuality, however, I believe that in both the professional theater and in the amateur theater much too much time is wasted when the difficult lines are not read for the actor. True, I have repeatedly stated that the actor, too, is an interpretive artist and must be treated as such, but his purpose is to interpret the author's intent, and anything that helps him do his job should be welcomed rather than scorned. If the director makes it understood that he is reading a line not with the idea of the actor copying his inflection, but rather with the thought of showing the actor the meaning he wants to come across, then the actor has no cause to feel insulted. The director is justified in taking the quickest way to let the actor know what he wants, and often there is only *one* reading that will be acceptable to the director. It is childish, I believe, to beat around the bush when a simple line reading will solve the problem. The director should, however, remember in such cases to read the line to show the meaning, and in almost all cases to exaggerate that meaning in order that the actor can see what he is doing. Most directors are not nearly as skilled as actors as the people who are working for them. It is really quite a shock when a director sees or hears a really good actor mimic him exactly. Not only does it not do much for the play, it is extremely hard on the director's ego.

When dealing with actors who are sensitive about line reading, the director can generally find some way of using tone copying to make his point. Always the director should make sure that the actor knows he is free to use any means he wishes to get across the desired meaning.

Often when difficulties are met in interpretation between actor and director the fault lies in the different ways of looking at the line. The director may be attempting to solve some technical problem of balance or contrast, while the actor is lost in the complexities of the character's personality. In such a case an explanation of the technical problems will simplify the problem for all concerned. Actors, because they are so involved in techniques, even when they are not consciously aware of it, are quick to understand such problems.

When the actor is having difficulty finding the emotional quality of the scene, the improvisational technique is often surprisingly successful. The use of analogous scenes with a basis in the actor's life, rather than in the life of the character, will often be successful in laying bare the basic emotion and the vocal pattern needed in the play. For example, in Lorca's *House of Bernarda Alba,* there is a scene in which the old servant, Poncia, attempts to warn Bernarda of the approaching tragedy among her daughters. In such a scene, where the background and whole milieu of the play is foreign to the American actor, improvising a scene in which an old, nosy, but well-meaning, neighbor attempts to warn a young mother that her husband is being seen with the waitress from the coffee shop and that sooner or later some "friend" in the neighborhood is going to bring it up to her face, might do to give Poncia an idea of the kind of actions and inflections needed in the play.

Often, too, especially where the actors are not prone to use their imaginations, improvising offstage scenes can be most helpful. I recall a college production of *Heartbreak House*, in which the scenes between Ellie and Hector were giving difficulties. A rather extensive improvisation of the first meeting of the two gave Ellie the romantic idea of Hector she had failed to conjure up from her own imagination. The same sort of improvisation might prove very helpful in *Wild Duck*, if the walk that Gregers and Hialmar take at the end of Act III were to be played. Improvising scenes with characters who do not appear, but are frequently mentioned in the script, can often start a sluggish imagination moving in the right direction.

Another technique that is helpful is that of changing an element of the scene that is giving trouble; for instance the location, a park bench to a barroom, a living room to the vestibule of a church; or the situation itself, a board meeting to a Ladies Aid Society meeting, the planning of a murder to the planning of a practical joke; even changing the climate from hot to cold, or vice versa can sometimes provide the new element that will allow the actors to get hold of the true feeling of the scene. Using exactly the same situation but changing the time element to *now*, can also have amazing results.

So often when a scene is not going well the fault lies in the actor's understanding. He feels he is accomplishing the required ends, but his understanding of the ends is almost, but not quite, that of the director. In such a case, improvising the scene in the actor's words will often lay bare the difference and hence the difficulty. This exercise has the added advantage of reminding the actor how to listen to all the words, rather than for a particular cue word.

The director can learn a great deal that will help him in later rehearsals if he watches very closely as the actors grope toward a better understanding of their characters. Important and revealing business can be developed simply by noting the actor's early instinctive pantomime. Often only the barest suggestion of that pantomime will be present, but when, in a later stage of rehearsal, the actor is reminded of what he started to do before he really knew what he was trying to do, he will be able to fill out and complete the instinctive urge he felt in the earlier rehearsal.

Difficult scenes (and any scene can be a difficult scene no matter how easy it seemed at an earlier stage) can sometimes be helped back on the right road by stressing the rhythm for the actors. Pounding the rhythm on the edge of the stage for a speech or for a scene will often help. Setting scenes to the right music will sometimes bring the glimmer of understanding to the actor's eye.

The director must be careful not to ask for too much too soon from his actors but, on the other hand, he should not allow one actor to slow down the entire company. The ideal is, of course, to bring the entire cast to the various stages of preparation at the same time, but this is much easier said than done. Actors have even more individual differences, if such a thing is possible, than do "normal" folk, and their methods of arriving at performance level will cover the range of possibilities. Forcing an actor, before he is ready to perform, can block his creative instinct completely, but waiting until dress rehearsal, or worse still, opening night, to discover whether or not a particular idea is going to work is generally disastrous, and always, too hard on the nerves.

The rehearsal period is, or should be, the most exciting and rewarding time for both the actor and the director. Both parties must enjoy rehearsal, and it is primarily up to the director to see that the right atmosphere is set. Further, rehearsals are an experimentation time for all concerned, including the author, when the play is untried; and a laboratory so filled with fermenting experiments is an exciting, but at the same time, rather dangerous place. The wrong move, especially by the director, can cause the experiments to fizzle out in a puddle on the floor, or blow up in his face.

Because of all the experiments in progress, rehearsals should generally be closed. Any actor is apt to feel embarrassed when he tries something that does not work, or when he is trying to change a vague feeling or idea into concrete action. He knows that people not closely acquainted with the actor's work think that acting is easy and that the most difficult part is memorizing the lines. He will look bad in rehearsal if he is judged from a performance viewpoint, and he knows it. Because of the purposeful fumbling that the actor must go through, friends and outsiders should not be allowed to "sit in" at rehearsals. The director should remember that if he is planning on inviting a colleague, the cast should be made aware of the fact before the visit takes place. Time after time I have had actors come to me, when there was no door man to keep the curious outside, and ask in a low whisper who that person at the back of the house was and could they ask him to leave. Any outsider in the house can limit and inhibit an actor, often much more than

Part V
THE DIRECTOR
IN PRODUCTION

Casting

There must, in the various tasks performed by the director, be one which is neither the most difficult nor the most important. That particular task, however, does not spring readily to mind. If casting the play does not fall under one of the above headings, then it will in all probability fall under the other. While directors may disagree about the relative importance or difficulty of casting, few will argue about its tediousness. Granted, the first audition held for a new show, or in a new place, will carry more than a little excitement for the director, but lucky indeed is that director if the excitement lasts out the audition time. The simple truth is that unless the director can call upon actors who have worked successfully for him in past productions, he is faced with hours and hours of listening time. True, every now and then an exciting talent will come along that will make any director sit up and take notice, but unfortunately the average actor, in any situation, is just that—average, and always it is the above average actor for whom the director searches. No matter what system of auditions is preferred by the director, in the final analysis, the director's decision will be based upon a guess. Hopefully the guess is an educated one, but in any event, it is a guess of the actor's potential. A great deal depends upon the "rightness" of that guess; thus it behooves the director to narrow the guessing field as much as is possible. He must bear in mind, however, that regardless of the precautions he takes, any role assigned on the basis of the auditions alone, that is to say, any casting completed without knowing how that actor will respond to that director is, to say the least, highly speculative. One method of narrowing the guesswork, to a degree at least, is to make sure that the entire company understands that no casting is final until at least the end of the first week. Such a precaution not only protects the director, it also protects the actor from embarrassment and failure. Even such a precaution, however, will only eliminate part of the guesswork, for until the experience arrives, no one knows how he will act under the strain of rehearsals and the tension of the opening night.

It is because of the guesswork involved that every college department, as well as every little theater group, is usually accused of being a closed shop by those who do not get roles. Always there is a clique around the director who are "in" and "are the only ones who have any chance at all." Though some directors would deny it, there is always a grain of truth in such accusations, that is, if the director knows his job, and if he truly cares about the finished product. Certainly, other things being equal, the director will tend to choose from those he *knows* can produce for him. Part of the job of any college department is to improve the work of its students and, if a senior with several plays under his belt cannot out-act the first-year student fresh from high school, then either the freshman is extremely talented, or the department had better look to its directors and see what is happening. No one expects the basketball, or the football, or the debate coach to field a new team each time they play a game, or even each season, yet some people seem to think that in order for everyone to have a chance the audience should be exposed to the inexpertness of beginners.

The same guesswork in casting is responsible for each professional director having actors that appear for him time after time, much to the annoyance of the nonworking members of Equity. A director of any experience knows that he can be, and often is, wrong on his guess about the potential of an actor. He further knows that even when he is sure of the talent, some other factor completely outside his control may interfere with the actor's performance.

The great actor who brings about nervous breakdowns for the other members of the cast and sends the director to a rest home may occasionally be worth the sacrifice, but not very often. The college "star" who knows more than the director and gives the entire program a bad name by cutting all his morning classes because he "slept late" is not the actor to consider often. (Of course, if he is really outstanding and you are doing *King Lear* or *Peer Gynt*—well— then—maybe—.)

The presence of a great amount of guesswork should not, however, tempt the director always to take the easy way out and use only those whom he has used in the past, for any theater, whether it be college, civic, or Broadway, lives on new blood, and without new blood and new faces, no organization can grow or even stay alive. All phases of theater involve, for even the most exacting director, some degree of compromise, and casting, especially in the amateur theater, involves a considerable amount of compromise. Where, when, and how the director meets and makes these compromises will, in the long run, be decided by his personal philosophy of life and art.

Casting is, I believe, more important in the professional theater than in the amateur. It is, in the professional theater,

very often *the* most important aspect of the production. A
star may well make or break the show. The right name, or
combination of names, may make the show successful
whether it is artistically acceptable or not. Secondly, casting
is more important in the professional theater than in the
amateur because in the professional theater the assumption
is always that the perfect person is available for the role if
(1) the management can find him, and (2) if they can meet
his price once he has been found. Always too, the right type
is available—the director need never worry about making
the twenty-year-old look like a forty-year-old. "Oh, yes,"
says the student, "but what the director seeks is someone
who can act like a forty-year-old and maybe the twenty-year-
old actor can do it better than can the person who is really
forty." Maybe, but not often, and in the long run, not only
will the forty-year-old look more like a forty-year-old, he or
she will be a much better actor than will the twenty-year-old.
The director who does not use the forty-year-old because he
does not believe in typecasting will be able to boast that he
does not typecast, but I fear that is all he will be able to
boast.

Finally, casting is more important in the professional
theater than in the amateur because when good people, that
is, actors who know their art and profession, are signed to
play, the director can often get by without knowing his
profession. A playwright, for example, who does not know
the principles of staging can often hide his ignorance as a
director behind the knowledge of his cast and stage manager; such cases are not unusual in the theater.

Casting itself assumes less importance in the amateur
theater simply because it must. The director's choice is
limited and often is not decided by the question "Who is
best able to play this role," but rather by the question "Who

has the best chance of getting away with it?" Almost always
the director must use those people who show up for the
auditions; seldom does he have a file of actors to call in to
read. In any case, the number that want to be in the
production will far exceed those who have talent and ability.
In direct contrast to the professional theater, the director
here takes it as a matter of course that he will have more to
do than simply direct the play; he assumes, and always
rightly so, that he will have to spend a great deal of
coaching time with his actors, and that he will, beside
directing the play and coaching, teach many of his casts the
basics of acting as well. The director in the amateur theater
considers himself fortunate if he finds a full cast of imaginative, flexible, enthusiastic, and energetic people. Indeed any
director who is so fortunate can well let experience, know-
how, and even talent, go by the boards (although he had
better make sure that his most important roles are not
completely lacking in the last commodity). It is for some
combination of the attributes of imagination, enthusiasm,
energy, flexibility, and talent that the wise director searches.

The director must bear in mind that while the open
audition can be extremely trying for him, such an audition
is much more trying for the actors involved. To request, or
to require, that another human being reveal himself to you
is, regardless of the method, asking a great deal. Yet this, in
essence, is what the director is asking of those who wish to
be considered for a role. To request or require an artist to
produce for you on demand without preparation is, in most
cases, asking the impossible. Yet many directors appear to
demand this very impossibility. Faced with such requirements, even the most experienced will quail. Few of us
search for situations in which our hopes for the immediate
future are left to the decision of others, and all of us seek to

avoid situations in which we are apt to be declared incompetent. Yet the audition is just such a situation. In the professional theater when one reaches an elevated stature, auditions can become a pleasant meeting over coffee or cocktails where actor, producer, and director talk over the pros and cons of the particular actor doing a role. In most situations, amateur or professional, the actor is placed in the position of saying "This is the best I have, please buy." Often, especially in the amateur theater, that would-be actor is silently saying "Please tell me I am good enough to be in your play." All too often, when that actor sees his name is not included in the cast list, he decides that he was not "good enough." Indeed, such may well be the case; maybe he wasn't good enough and perhaps he never will be. The director, then, must remember that while a particlar auditioner may be only number thirty-nine to him, it is chance number one for the actor auditioning, and while it may be tedious for the director, it is nerve shattering and earth quaking for the actor. When two such different and separate attitudes toward a single event are in evidence—the boredom of the director, forced to sit through hour after hour of run-of-the-mill or worse auditions, and the nervousness of the actor to whom the audition is the "big break"—then both will profit by careful examination of their roles and their purposes in this infamous rite of the theater. The director must know the exact purpose of the particular audition: for what qualities he is searching; when it is advisable to allow the actor extra time, and when his time should be kept or cut to the minimum; how to make sure the audition machinery is as efficient as conditions will allow; and when to make compromises.

The purpose of the audition may be to survey the talent available, to eliminate those who cannot be used, to find certain types, to choose those who will be invited back for a final reading, or to cast a particular part or parts. The quality the director is seeking may be as broad as imagination or as specific as a physical type. The director may decide that by giving an actor an extra few minutes he can eliminate him from his thinking, or that he can save both the actor and himself time at a future audition by awarding him a role then and there (this may be dangerous, but at times it is necessary). The time element involved in any audition is vital, but the director must remember that the purpose is never that of adhering to a prearranged schedule, rather the schedule is arranged in order to help. When it is seen to hinder, then it must be disregarded temporarily.

The actor too must know what he is trying to do and, ideally, what the director is looking for. The actor's reason for appearing, regardless of the kind of audition, is to make a favorable impression on the director. His purpose is to so impress the director that when later, in the quiet of his office, he is attempting to make sense out of his hurried notes, the actor's face, voice, name, talent, etc. keep popping into his mind, until the director is automatically thinking that the actor must be used. At an open audition the actor's job, then, is to make an impression that will assure his being called back for another reading. The actor should know that after hours of listening to scenes, or readings, any director is apt to sink into a lethargy from which only the most obvious burst of talent can shake him. The tediousness of auditions, for the director, inclines me to agree with a technique suggested by Robert Porterfield, of the famed Barter Theater, while talking to an acting class of young college students. Porterfield, in stressing the importance of making an impression on the director, recounted his own early experience in the professional theater. He told how, after waiting in great fear for several hours for his name to be called, he eventually lost that fear out of sheer boredom, and when his turn came to enter the inner sanctum and audition for the director, he simply did not care in the least about the outcome, or about much else either. In response to the director's query did he sing, Porterfield smiled and shook his head; dance? "Not much"; well then, the director wanted to know, did he act? "A little," Porterfield replied, but he was, he went on to say, "the best hog caller in the state of Virginia," and he then proceeded to give the assembled judges an example of his homey art. Although the director was not in the market for hog callers, he did remember the voice and the face. When later a need for replacements developed, the hog-calling boy from Virginia was foremost in the director's mind. Thus, Porterfield told the class, he got his first job in the theater. In much the same vein, I recall an extremely talented actress who preferred to audition with scenes from Hamlet, with herself in the role of the melancholy Dane. The director who did not remember the "kook" who did such a fine job with Hamlet was the exception rather than the rule. Such auditions are memorable and often successful not only because they are different and will arouse a sleepy director, but also because they demonstrate the imaginative and dramatic flare, the theatrical verve that every play needs.

The type of audition used to find the best actors will depend somewhat upon the type of play to be produced. Regardless of the type of play, eventually the audition will involve reading from the script, and then the actor should be given the chance to show himself at his best, not, as is often the case, at his worst, with a cold reading. It is true that some directors believe they can "peg" a good actor by a cold reading, but I doubt it, unless a great deal of time is spent with the actor at that reading. Because of the inability of many good actors to sight read, the script should be made available to the actors before the audition. One can argue that making the actor find his own script is a good sign, as does Marian Gallaway,[104] but in the press of daily tasks there seems to be little point in making things more difficult for the would-be actor. True, one can learn a bit about the interest of the actor who has taken the trouble to find the script, but generally one can learn as much by talking with him for a few minutes.

Even when the scripts are made available for the actors before the audition, and perhaps *especially when* they are made available, the director will be wise to prepare a short summary of the play and short, broad sketches of each of the characters to be cast. Not only will the material give the actors something to do while they are waiting their turn, it will also give the actor a sense of security and something concrete to hang onto when his turn arrives. Actors who have read the script for themselves are very apt to have formed mistaken impressions (that is, mistaken as far as the director's particular production is concerned) about the play and the characters. They may well have overlooked interesting possibilities in some of the characters and hence, in a short reading, hurt their audition by their reading of the script. Armed with a director's summary of the play and short, suggestive character sketches, they will have a chance to put what they know about the play together with what the director is looking for in the play and hence have a much better chance of giving a good account of themselves.

No matter what type of audition is planned, the me-chanics will work more smoothly if some sort of form is used to record the necessary information about each actor. Such a form should include name, address and phone; physical characteristics, race, height, weight, age, hair color, and anything else the director may wish to know in that line; past experience, including the roles played, where played, and who directed; availability for rehearsal (this is especially important, of course, in the amateur theater, and a class schedule in college circles will often be helpful). In the professional theater a blank should be provided for the agent's name, but in most cases the professional actor will carry his picture with a résumé and all necessary information. A sample form might be as follows:

AUDITION INFORMATION

Date _____   Show—*The Wild Duck*

Name _____ Phone (Home)_____ (Work)_____

Sex _____ Race _____ Age _____ Weight _____ Height _____

Color of Hair _____   Class _____

EXPERIENCE:

PLAY   ROLE   DIRECTOR   PLACE

Range of theater interest:

Sound _____ Scenery construction _____ Lights _____

Props _____ Costumes _____ Publicity _____ Painting _____

Usher _____ Acting _____ Dance _____

Other theatrical interest _____

Do not write below this line

A great deal of time may be saved if the director is able to provide the auditioning group with a proposed rehearsal schedule. Such a procedure may well eliminate those who will find it impossible to accept a role and thus provide more time to work with those who are available.

In almost any situation the number of persons wishing to be considered will necessitate a series of auditions rather than a single audition. The first of such a series should have as its purpose the elimination of those who are not usable. This first audition will be most helpful to the director if each person is given an equal amount of time to present a short scene. The length of the audition need not be long. I am reminded of one famous actress who found that she had to conduct auditions for a scholarship named after her. She was appalled to find that she was expected to listen to literally hundreds of applicants. She quickly decided that each applicant should be asked to prepare a one-minute scene. When asked if one minute of acting was a fair test she replied that if they were qualified, one minute would be more than enough, and if they were not, one hour would not be of any help to them. When the audition is to serve as an elimination round, the short prepared scene is, I believe, by far the best. Even when the actor has the "wrong" view of the character and the play, even when he is choosing a scene from some play in which he has been "wrongly" directed, the director should be able to spot whether there is enough potential to warrant a further reading.

The final audition should always be with proposed members of the cast reading together from the script to be produced. The director will then be able to think in terms of the necessary unity and contrasts called for in the script.

Types of Auditions

The *open audition* (with publicity notices which state simply that auditions will be held for a forthcoming play, or for a coming season, as the case may be, at such and such a time, each prepared audition limited to three minutes) will be effective in allowing the director to form an overall impression of the talent available in order that he may begin the process of elimination. It is usually wise to allow more than one day for such auditions, for it is impossible to predict what sort of response the publicity will get. I can recall a director of a children's theater project being stunned by the hundreds of children he found waiting for him at the announced time. In a like manner I was once late for an announced open audition in New York because I could not make my way through the waiting crowd of actors blocking traffic. After auditioning for some eight hours, without a lunch break, I was told I must vacate the hall, and I can vividly recall the anger and hate in the air as I walked out of the building through the crowd of still-waiting actors. Such difficulties can be avoided by setting up a schedule, either beforehand, or even as the actors appear for the audition. The simple process of having a person meet the entering actors and assigning them a time to appear will save both time and nervous systems. Even so, the director should not take a chance on losing the services of a good actor because he is trying to maintain a schedule. At best, any open audition will run considerably behind schedule, but if the director is to get an overall picture and give a specified minimum amount of time to each actor, the difficulties and the drawbacks of the open audition can be endured by both actor and director.

The open audition can be held with either a reading from the script or, as I believe is the better plan, the three-minute prepared scene. The prepared open audition is difficult to inaugurate in a college or civic theater situation, for new-comers and inexperienced freshmen, for example, will have no idea of how to go about preparing such a scene. But once the audition has become a part of the theater tradition, it will prove most helpful to the director for, in the long run, the prepared open audition is the best method of separating the wheat from the chaff.

Once the open audition has been held and the director is aware of the amount of interest and has some idea of the level of talent available, the field must be narrowed still further. The *personal interview* becomes an excellent possibility as the next step. In such an interview the director can talk with the actor in private and often discover the depth of his interest as well as his potential. One director, who must hold many auditions throughout a season, likes to ask the candidate in such an interview such questions as, "Who is your favorite actor of the present?" "of the past?" "What is your favorite play?" and finally, "If you could be any person you wished, who would you choose?" The first question tells him whether or not the candidate is familiar with the present-day theater and what his idea of good acting encompasses. The second will show whether or not the candidate is familiar with the history of the theater. The third will give some idea of the actor's familiarity with the literature of the theater, and the last question will give the director more than an inkling of just how satisfied the actor is with his own adjustment to life. Such questions, asked in a casual manner, can help to "break the ice" between actor and director and, at the same time, be most revealing to the director.

After a short conversation the director can, in the personal interview, ask each actor to read for him from the play. The director will have some idea of what the actor can do from the three-minute audition and he will be able to suggest a particular character for the actor to read. In any such case, the director should also ask the actor what role he would like to read and take the time to hear him read it, even though the director may feel, on the basis of the prepared audition, that the actor is not suited to that role. Whether or not the actor has had an opportunity to read the play, and as I suggested that opportunity should, if possible, be made available to him, the director should not expect a finished or even a smooth reading. He should ask the actor to read first, without discussion, and then, regardless of how close the actor comes to what the director has in mind, the director should suggest a reading quite different from what he has just listened to. In such a manner the director can find out how flexible and how open to suggestion the actor is, a vital factor from the directorial viewpoint. I generally prefer to read with the actor in such interviews; not only does it do away with the third party, but by changing the readings of the cue lines, I can often determine how sensitive the actor's ear is.

The *final audition* should be held, if possible, on the stage with other members or possible members of the cast present. The readings should be from the play and conducted by the director from the house. The director can concern himself with ensemble casting and at the same time test voices. In this final audition the director should also make suggestions and may, if he so desires, see the actors in motion. As always, he is looking for a combination of natural talent, imagination, enthusiasm, energy, and flexibility, as well as a group that seems to fit the overall intent of the author.

The musical, the opera, the dance drama, or any play calling for special talents will obviously have to have auditions that will discover the necessary talent. Always, in the musical audition, the actors should sing something with which they are completely familiar. The ability to read music will be helpful but it is not at all a necessity. When dancing becomes a factor the director may want to look at some prepared bit, then both he and the choreographer test the actor with the kind of movement they are planning to use in the play. The actor-dancer who possesses a fine classical ballet technique may not be much help if the show is a 1930 musical and the choreographer is planning on a tap dancing approach. Pantomimes can often tell the director a great deal about movement as well as the degree of imagination. A simple request that the auditioner skip in a circle around the stage will also be helpful in letting the director see how the actor moves.

Often when there are a considerable number of people interested in auditioning, the director is tempted to double-cast the production. Such a procedure is, I believe, a criminal waste of time for all concerned. If the director is to have two equally good casts then he must double the rehearsal time, for one actor will not be able to take the same movement as another, nor will the feeling of a scene be the same even if, heaven forbid, the movement and the inflection are the same. Rather than double-cast, the director should do two plays and save himself boredom and dissatisfaction. Double-casting is not fair to the cast nor to the audience. It is a waste of time and talent, and thus should be avoided. This is not to suggest that a system of understudies cannot be used, but understudies' rehearsals are not practical until the play opens and seldom, outside of the professional theater, is a run long enough to merit their use. If the director feels he needs extra insurance concerning a particular part or parts, he might be wise to try the "standby" system, often used in the professional theater, whereby an actor will be asked to familiarize himself with another's role in case he should have to go into rehearsal for a sudden replacement. I have never found any such system necessary in the amateur theater, and though I have had a few close calls and have had occasions when minor parts had to be shifted quickly, I have never had to cancel nor postpone an opening because a major role could not go on.

When the final casting is completed, the director still has that first week of rehearsals before he makes any role final. Though this procedure may seem hard on the actors it is necessary, for try as he may, the director cannot eliminate the guesswork involved in attempting to "size up" another individual. Even with the added insurance of one week, still the director is going to find, all too often on opening night, that once more he has guessed wrong. He will improve with experience, but try as he will, he will often be "playing a hunch" and hunches are never a sure thing. Once the casting is completed, the director can only work hard to prove to himself that he was right in his selection. Without that kind of work, he may be sure that he will be wrong.

Casting in the Civic Theater

As in most other aspects of theater, casting in the civic theater is a problem unto itself. Though the idea of using a casting committee in either the college or the professional theater is, in my opinion, absurd, such a procedure in a community theater has much to recommend it. In fact, a casting committee in a civic theater is often an excellent idea for at least two reasons. First, the choice is generally (though not always) considerably more limited and the spread of talent not nearly as wide as one is apt to find in either of the other theater situations. As the choice is more limited and the differences to be found in amount and kind of talent smaller, the results of the casting process are not nearly as significant. Secondly, if there is one vital principle in civic theater, it is the principle of participation, hence a casting committee involves more people and therefore a wider cross-section of the community. The person to person involvement can be extended by changing the members, or at least some of the members, of the casting committee for each production. Perhaps the ideal arrangement is to have both a casting committee and a talent committee. The talent committee's job is to get a big turnout for the casting committee to audition. The director must be careful to make sure that the committee really does do the casting and is not simply a rubber stamp for his choice. Certainly he should be available for consultation and may even veto a choice if it appears that the committee has made a drastic mistake, but his function in such a situation should be one of adviser. As is suggested above, in no other situation would I recommend a casting committee, but in the civic theater the procedure has much to offer and should be explored thoroughly.

The procedure of casting used by the committee will not differ markedly from the procedures used in any other theater. There is, however, one possible exception; while open auditions are not recommended in either the collegiate or professional theater, they may help to draw people and stimulate interest in the community theater. Timid but interested would-be actors may appear just to listen and through their listening come to the conclusion that they can do as well as or better than the readers. Here again, the key word is participation and if allowing any and all to listen to the readings aids in participation, then it aids in the theater's growth and should be used.

Rehearsals

Just how much planning should be done before the director walks into the first rehearsal is a matter which finds little agreement among those who work in the theater. Some authorities maintain that the director should prepare a complete prompt book with each move, each sound and light cue, and each idea for interpretation included. Others feel that the director should read the play through a certain number of times, each time with a different aspect of the production in mind. I would suggest that the best method is to read the script through to catch the feeling of the play and then proceed with the complete rite-role analysis. Before rehearsals start the director needs to get inside the play. If he knows his business and has some experience he can trust his and the actors' reactions to the line during rehearsals. He must, however, thoroughly understand the play and the author's intent. Whether or not the play should be pre-blocked is a matter for the individual director to decide. Under no conditions do I believe that pre-blocking can be final; it must always be open to suggestion and change.

Prerehearsal Planning

I believe the director should see the actor move on the stage and should hear him read the author's lines after he has become familiar with the script before any blocking or any final interpretation is set. The director's prerehearsal responsibility, then, is to become completely familiar with the play and to know thoroughly the author's intent. To say that the director must know the play is not to say that he must know how it is going to be played, for it is one of the most exciting and interesting aspects of theater that the same idea can be played, and understood by the audience, in a variety of ways. *Any* way is the correct way *if* the author's fundamental intent is retained without distortion and *if* the playing is "natural" for the actors within the context of the drama.

Preparation of a complete prompt book, as prescribed by some authorities, seems to be an academic, and often sterile, device. Why, then, do I suggest the rite-role breakdown? Because such a breakdown is only a method of getting to the intent; it is only a theatrical way of seeing the script as live theater. It will suggest possible staging, but it will not block or interpret the play.

Certainly every director should have had the experience of making a prompt book either before, during, or after the production, if only for the experience of seeing the tremendous amount of detail necessary in any production. Beyond the student stage, however, the prompt book should become the responsibility of the stage manager and be put together during the rehearsal period. In any case, if a prompt book is prepared before rehearsals begin, and in some instances it might make the director feel more secure, its function should be to aid the memory of the director, not be used as a blueprint for the staging.

Beyond the director's analysis of the script, his prerehearsal planning will be concerned primarily with the physical side of the production, such as the set design, the costumes, rehearsal space, and ample rehearsal personnel (for example, in a musical each director needs a rehearsal pianist and a stage manager). The special effects and the lighting mood should be discussed with the proper personnel. The prop list, which will be changed considerably during rehearsal, should be drawn up and the search begun for any hard-to-find properties. Furniture must be found and approved by the director. Perhaps most important of all, all deadlines, for costumes, set, props, lights, everything that is to be used in the play, should be determined and adhered to. It is vital, however, that in the mountain of details that quickly forms, the director does not forget his original reaction to the play and to the characters.

In the final analysis, the amount of prerehearsal planning and the sort of planning that is used depends primarily on the director himself. If he prefers to work from detailed plans, and if he finds such plans helpful, then certainly he should use them. If, on the other hand, he works better by trusting his instincts and memory, then detailed plans will only confuse and get in the way. The prime factor is the director's analysis, but even in this aspect the director must remember that the actor's view from inside the play may reveal as much or more than did the director's initial analysis.

Experiment and Exploration

Rehearsals are, as I have repeatedly stated, a time of experiment and exploration for both actor and director, thus any rehearsal schedule is a guide, an estimate that the director makes, based on past experience of how long each division of the play will take to work out, and perfect.

Broadly speaking, any rehearsal period might be broken up into three stages: becoming acquainted with the script and finding the best way for the particular cast to translate the written words into action; working that action until it becomes an integral part of the actors and automatic to the stage crew; and finally running the play through for tempo, rhythm, and that quality Stanislavski has called the "unbroken line." The actors must find the line their character follows through the play and then have time to follow that line in rehearsal. The dress rehearsals are the final segment of the third stage.

Each director will have his own view concerning the amount of time spent on each stage of the rehearsal. One, if not *the* most important, thing to remember is that actors, especially amateurs, require a considerable amount of "running time." By running time, I mean playing time without interruption from the director. Though it is a difficult thing to learn and to remember, it is a fact that hundreds of small details that might take hours and hours of valuable rehearsal time will work themselves out in the run-through. So much can be accomplished by the actors themselves when they know exactly what they have to do and how much time they have to do it in. The director who schedules a run-through a week, of whatever work is done, will not only know where he is and what has been accomplished, he will know what he *must* work on if he is to be ready on opening night.

Furthermore, the director must remember that in acting, as in most other fields of endeavor, it is wiser to work on one thing at a time. To discuss the deep Freudian motivations of the character, when the actor is trying to remember what cross he is supposed to be taking, or the exact word order in the line, may make the director feel he is being helpful, but it will seldom benefit the production. It is extremely difficult for the beginning director to sit quietly when he has just had an inspiration, or when he knows the actor is thinking wrongly, but the director who continually interrupts the actor's concentration and confuses him with more or different ideas is asking for trouble. A quick nod and a word with the actor at the rehearsal's end will usually accomplish more. The director must remember to give the actor a chance to work out his own problems and not be too quick to interrupt what may be only an experiment or, more probably, concentration on some other phase of the acting problem.

How much time should be planned for the rehearsal and how many rehearsals should be held will also find a great variety of opinions. The estimate will range from twenty to forty-five or even, in the Moscow Art Theater, over a hundred. Actually, the number of rehearsals will depend upon several factors: the length of the show, the amount of time available before the announced opening, the kind of show being produced and, most of all, the method and the speed of the director. Any summer stock director has developed a system of rehearsing a play (granted, not in any depth) in order to have it ready in one week's time for opening night. Often the stock director has simply compressed his usual system; he has not left out any of the stages, he has simply not developed any one of the stages. A six-week method of rehearsal becomes a six-day method in stock. Obviously, only the high points are touched, but the system remains intact.

Amateurs need longer periods of rehearsal than do professionals, not because it takes them longer to learn lines or movement (though it often does take them longer to associate movement with line), but because they have seldom developed the technique of discovering and making a character their own in a short time. The amateur needs time to absorb the play, to let it seep into his life almost through a process of osmosis, where the professional can dive in head first and live there all his waking hours. The professional can, if necessity demands, compare the play and/or the role to something he has done in the past, and thus, rather than start from scratch, he can take the fundamentals from an earlier experience. I am not suggesting that such a practice is a healthy one for the actor, but as any summer stock director knows, a show a week calls for quick techniques rather than fully developed artistic character studies. Because of the lack of technique and the necessity of living a life other than that of an actor the amateur also needs more uninterrupted run-throughs than does the professional to get the feel of the play.

The time spent in rehearsal in the professional theater is seldom left to the director's whim. It is decided either by Actor's Equity or by the producer's bankroll; hence the remarks which follow are aimed primarily at planning the amateur rehearsal schedule.

I prefer to open a play in the middle or at the end of the fifth week of rehearsal. However, if the play is extremely difficult, or if I am in a situation in which I do not know the work of any of the actors, I will sometimes add a week to the schedule. In general, though, I find six weeks a little too long.

The key factor in drawing up the schedule is, of course, the date of the opening. Thus I find it easiest to work backward from that date, rather than forward to it. If, for example, the play is to open on a Wednesday, then the dress rehearsals will have to start not later than the previous Sunday. The technical rehearsal preceeding the first dress will then fall on the Friday or Saturday (or both) depending upon the complications of the show and the experience of the crew. Such a schedule would call for uninterrupted run-throughs, act by act, to begin one week prior to the first dress and to continue every night until the first technical rehearsal. This would require all the acts to be blocked and interpreted a minimum of a week before the first dress or ten days before opening. With the opening planned for the middle of the fifth week, three unscheduled weeks remain, or for all practical purposes, a week for each act. Thus the final schedule will allow a week for each act, a week for the play as a whole, and three full dress rehearsals. If, as is often the case, the director finds he can rehearse only five nights a week, he will have four nights to work and one night each week for a run-through to see what he has accomplished.

Sample Rehearsal Schedule

Personally, I do not find it helpful, however, to break the rehearsals into an act per week. Rather, I prefer to work from top to bottom on each stage of rehearsal. As soon as an act is blocked, I will run it, but only once, then on to the next act, and so on until the entire play is blocked. As quickly as the last act is blocked and run, I return to the top and walk through the entire play before starting on the next stage. If one rehearsal period is figured to block and run an act, such a schedule should work. Rather than spend a week on each act, one week will be spent primarily on blocking, one on interpretation, and one on strengthening characters and business. But in each stage, the play is considered as a whole. With the first reading out of the way—held the week preceeding the start of daily rehearsals, perhaps in my home or on stage—the schedule would appear as follows:

FIRST WEEK

Monday—Block and walk through Act I
Tuesday—Block and walk through Act II
Wednesday—Block and walk through Act III
Thursday—Walk through entire play for blocking only
Friday—Walk through entire play for blocking only

The repeat on Thursday and Friday is suggested because, especially in the early blocking rehearsals and in the first interpretation rehearsals, it is almost impossible to judge the amount of time that will be needed. The goal of the first week's rehearsal in the above schedule is to complete the rough blocking of the play by the end of the first week. In that time the entire play will have been touched at least three times and possibly four. If the week goes perfectly, the interpretation rehearsals can start on Friday, but as things seldom do go perfectly and as the first complete walk-through for blocking can become a real tangled mess, especially if the actors are not used to writing down their directions, it is wise to leave a little leeway and plan for some hitch in the proceedings. Almost assuredly, if the blocking is completed by Wednesday night, the complete walk-through can be accomplished by the end of the re-hearsal on Friday. If two days are spent in getting the actors familiar with their positions on stage, no harm is done; if only one is needed, fine, the director goes into the second week one day ahead of the game. He can be sure the day will be needed before opening comes around.

With the stage manager checking the movement of each actor, and the director sitting on the front of the stage listening to the readings line by line, the work on interpretation begins.

Monday—Act I	run it if time permits
Tuesday—Act II	run it if time permits
Wednesday—Act III	run it if time permits
Thursday—Run entire play	
Friday—Run entire play	

Again the extra time is allowed on Thursday and Friday, and for the same reason it is allowed in the blocking rehearsals. During the early interpretation rehearsals, the director can be virtually certain that things will go very slowly, but as the actors see where the characters are heading and what the director is attempting to do, the pace will pick up considerably. It should be noted that the run-throughs in the first and second week are not without interruption; the stage manager is continually checking movement and the director will correct any glaring misreadings. The actors too must feel free to question their memory or their scripts whenever they feel unsure.

After two weeks of rehearsal the entire play has been covered a minimum of five times, excluding the initial reading. The goal of the third week is to make sure the actors know exactly what they are saying and doing. The character problems will be explored and the business set. All props should be added during this week of rehearsals in order that the actors and the director may have ample time to add business that the props suggest. The concentration, however, is on character depth.

Monday—Act I	props used
Tuesday—Act II	props used
Wednesday—Act III	props used
Thursday—Acts III, II, I	
Friday—Acts I, II, III	

By the end of this third and all-important week of rehearsals the actor should know exactly where he is going. He should be line perfect by the week's end and be able to concentrate on smoothness, pace, and believability. The reversal of the act order on Thursday is to make sure the actors and the director have a chance to play and study Act III while they are still fresh, and it also points out any lack of understanding of the continuity of the play. The actor who truly sees the connection between events in Act I and events in Act III will not be troubled by the shift; the actor who has not bothered to think about the connection will not only be revealed for special attention from the director, he will be forced to attempt to make the connections in his own mind.

FOURTH WEEK

During this week an extra rehearsal is added. I have placed it on Sunday, but Saturday will serve as well. The extra rehearsal is needed to provide time for a completely uninterrupted run-through, act by act. The director will give notes at the end of each act, but the principal reason for the run-through is so that the director can see just where the most glaring weaknesses are in each act and can rough out the detailed work needed during the week.

In this week the rehearsals are split, the first half given over to detailed work on an act, the last half used for running the other two acts. The play is covered each night. During the running acts, notes are given at the conclusion of each act.

Sunday—A complete run-through with no stops or interruptions for any reason whatsoever.

Monday—First half: detailed work on Act I
Second half: run II and III (notes at the end of each act)

Tuesday—First half: detailed work on Act II
Second half: run I and III (notes at the end of each act)

Wednesday—First half: detailed work, Act III
Second half: run I and II (notes at end of each act)

Thursday—Complete run-through with notes at the end of each act. Any difficulties should be re-run on stage at the act's conclusion. The curtain call should be set and run no later than this rehearsal.

Friday—Technical rehearsal or same as Thursday, depending on the complications of the script and the experience of the crew.

Saturday—Technical rehearsal.

The technical rehearsal presents quite different problems and will probably be under the guidance of the technical director, but the final responsibility is still that of the director and he should run the rehearsal from the house. The actors should not be expected to produce at this rehearsal, only to repeat the cue lines in the same tempo as they will be during the actual performance. Each cue, sound, light, curtain, scene change, special effect, difficult costume change, anything and everything which depends upon the backstage crew participation should be run until it is right. The procedure can be to go through the entire play and then go back at the end of each act and pick up the cues that didn't work, or it can be to jump from cue to cue. The technical director, the director, and the stage manager should decide beforehand exactly how this long and tiring, but vitally important, rehearsal is to be handled.

FIFTH WEEK

The first rehearsal with full makeup and costume will often need much more time to get started than the preceding rehearsals. The actors should be given time to experiment with their makeup and to complain about their costumes. For this reason it is often wise to schedule this first full dress on a Sunday afternoon, and warn the cast that dinner may be very late that night.

> Sunday—Full-dress rehearsal. Show to be run by acts but without any interruptions whatsoever. Notes at the end of each act. Makeup should be carefully checked from all parts of the house.
> Monday—Full dress: a good time to invite a few friends in to see their reaction. This rehearsal should be conducted as if it were an actual performance with notes at the end of the performance.
> Tuesday—Same as Monday.
> Wednesday—Opening.

From the Sunday preceding the first full dress, the cast should be warned that no interruptions will be tolerated. Only the director can stop the performance, and he will be wise not to do so unless it is absolutely necessary. The cast must learn to "cover" mistakes, and no mishap, including the failure of the lights or the set falling, is a reason for the actor to break character. A stage pause; when an actor forgets a line or goes blank, is the responsibility of everyone on the stage; all should be familiar enough with the script and with the scene to cover for any other actor who has momentary difficulty. At the full-dress rehearsals, especially on the two preceding the opening, the cast should respond as if there were an audience in the house. No member of the cast should appear in the auditorium, no noise should be heard from backstage. Simulating the actual performance is highly important for amateurs and helpful for any group.

When and how notes should be given will depend again upon the director's method of working. Some directors prefer to give their notes through the stage manager, some prefer to hand each actor a written note, others prefer to assemble the entire cast and give all the notes aloud. I prefer the last method, for often everyone can learn from the notes, and any suggested changes are automatically known to all. Often if the note is of a personal nature and might embarrass the actor to have it read in public, the director can call him over after the rehearsal is concluded and give him the note in private. In general however, it is the way the note is given that will make the difference, and the director must remember that almost always the actor is begging for help.

The director should plan to have someone with him at all the run-throughs in order that he need not take his eyes from the stage to write a note. If the stage manager is available so much the better; if not, then perhaps an assistant should be assigned to that task.

The invited audience should be forewarned that the entertainment is not a performance but a rehearsal. The actors should be made aware of any audience at least several days before that particular rehearsal takes place.

The rehearsal schedule outlined above is merely one way of attacking the problems of readying a play. Some directors, the late Robert L. Gordon, for example, preferred to rework each French scene (that portion of a play not interrupted by the entrance or exit of a major character) until it was completely set in every detail. Many directors work perfecting each act before passing on to the next and such a method has much to recommend it. The danger lies, I believe, in having an uneven production with the first act overrehearsed and the final scene barely touched.

The rehearsal atmosphere can make or break the play; the actors and the director create the atmosphere, but it is the director himself who is primarily responsible. The mechanics of the rehearsal also have a great deal to do with the atmosphere and the failure to start on time will quickly demoralize the most enthusiastic cast. Sitting around waiting for one or two members of the cast to appear, or waiting while the director finishes a conversation with someone, means that valuable time is being wasted. The actor or the director who keeps the company waiting for him is not only inconsiderate and impolite, he is a threat to the success of the production. All rehearsals should begin promptly. Lateness should not be tolerated. The second lateness should result automatically in the loss of the role. The director who trains his stage manager to be ready, watch in hand as the hands of the clock reach the agreed-upon time, will find that in a very short time the entire cast will take great pride in the fact that to be late is a crime. In general, the best plan is to keep the starting time the same, and then insist that all the actors are there waiting for their entrance when it comes up. To insist that the entire cast be in the hall when the rehearsal starts is not, I believe, necessary. The important thing is that they make their entrances and are there for notes at the end of the act. The actors must be warned, of course, that they must get the stage manager's permission to leave the hall once the rehearsal starts and that he must know where they are at all times in case the director finds it advisable to skip around within the act.

The director must also take great pains not to allow interruptions during the rehearsal period. Only vital and immediate problems should be allowed to intrude upon the rehearsal time. For example, if a phone is available within the rehearsal room, the cast should not be allowed to receive calls or to call out on it during the rehearsal. All messages are given directly to the stage manager and he does not forward them until the break.

Both actors and director need frequent breaks during the rehearsal. A five-minute break each hour, or a ten-minute break every two hours will prove helpful to everyone. The time of the break should be strictly adhered to; if a five-minute break is called it should not run to ten and fifteen minutes. The cast needs to know how much they can accomplish, where they can go within the break time.

The director needs to remember that he too needs a break from the rehearsal. His concentration is more continuous than any of the actors' and unless he does have a chance to rest occasionally, his efficiency and his powers of observation will lessen considerably. Hence it is a wise policy to remind the cast that the break is not a time for questions about the show. The director who spends the entire break working with an actor in trouble has not profited by the break, and neither has the actor.

During rehearsals actors are concentrating, naturally on their own roles, and tend to forget that the play continues when they leave stage. For that reason they will often take their exit and continue their offstage cross directly to the director's seat in order to ask him about the scene just played. The director must establish at the first rehearsal that his attention must remain on the stage and that actors are not to question him while his concentration is with the players rehearsing.

The length of the rehearsal period will vary with the show and the amount of time available for the rehearsals before opening but, in general, a three-hour stretch or, at most, a four-hour period is about the limit for most casts. In the professional theater the hours of rehearsals are controlled rather strictly by Actors' Equity, but even so, as an actor can rehearse up to eight hours a day with, I hasten to add, an hour for lunch and dinner, a carefully worked out schedule can keep a director and stage manager going almost around the clock. The director cannot produce continually any more than the actor can, so the length of the rehearsal is as important to him as it is to the cast. In a college or civic theater situation a rehearsal that begins at 7:00 should break by 10:30, or by 11:00 at the latest. Of course, dress rehearsals will often run longer, but a cast that opens a show completely exhausted after an all-night dress rehearsal will not give a very good account of itself.

As a general rule, it is wise for the director to make himself available to the cast, both before and immediately after the rehearsal. His enthusiasm, or lack of same, will be communicated directly to the cast, and he must not appear to simply be working the rehearsal into his spare time. Often too, the director can solve problems by inviting an actor who is in difficulty for a quick cup of coffee after rehearsal where, away from the stage itself, character problems may be talked over in a relaxed manner.

The matter of setting a deadline for learning lines is worth commenting upon. When the question arises, as it generally will in an amateur situation, the wisest policy is to state that there is no such deadline. The lines cannot be committed to memory until after the interpretation rehearsals, and the director must be firm about this, but should be memorized as quickly as possible once the actor knows what the director wants from the line. Professionals can be expected to go their own way without the director making any comment; if they prefer to learn their lines immediately and then work on the reading, fine, most can do this. Noel Coward, for example, is said to request that his actors appear at the first rehearsal with the lines memorized. With amateurs such a policy would be foolhardy. If the director assumes that the actor will learn his lines as quickly as possible, the actor will generally live up to expectations. When the lazy actor is encountered, as he will often be, a warning may be given that after a certain date no books will be allowed on stage. When the recalcitrant actor is forced to go through the evening taking prompts continually, and holding up the rest of the cast, he will, in all probability, show up the next night in much better shape. At such rehearsals, when sufficient time has been given for line learning, one should be merciless, and no matter how long the rehearsal takes, even if the stage manager has to throw the actor every line, let the actors fight it out. Almost always, one such rehearsal is sufficient.

Many actors hesitate to lay down their scripts because holding the book gives them a feeling of confidence, and without something in their hands, they feel naked and unprotected. When a schedule is built around the idea suggested above and the entire play is covered, time after time the actor invariably knows more of the lines than he thinks he does. At any rate, suggesting to the actor that he give it a try without the script before he feels he can make the attempt will show both the actor and the director where he is weakest. The learning of lines should not be allowed to interfere with the process of readying the play. Frequently reminding the actors that the lines are about one fifth of their problem will put the memorization process in its proper perspective.

The Prompter

The actor rehearsing without a script in hand brings up the subject of the prompter. This position, so often slighted in the theater, is vital to a smooth running rehearsal. Prompting takes intelligence and sensitivity. A good prompter, one who knows when to speak and when to wait and let the actor fight it out for himself, can speed the memorization time immensely. He can keep a rehearsal moving if he knows when each actor needs help and when he needs to struggle. Whether or not a prompter should be used during the performance is up to the individual director (I always use one for at least the first week of a run), but a good prompter should always be found for the rehearsal period. If the director will spend just a little time with the prompter before the line-learning process begins, he will save both time and nervous energy in the long run.

The Curtain Call

Sometime during the last ten days of rehearsal—I prefer the rehearsal preceding the technical—the curtain call must be set. In the amateur theater the cast often has to be made aware of the importance of the call, and of the fact that it must be rehearsed until it is technically perfect. The curtain call is not, as some actors and directors seem to believe, a chance for the cast to see if their friends are in the house; rather, it is an integral part of the audience's evening in the theater. The call is the final impression that the audience carries away with them, and a sloppy call can often severely damage an otherwise fine impression.

If more than one call is to be taken, the director should devise a method of building the call to some sort of climax. Either the principals are given separate calls or a walk-on call is used, opening on a bare stage and having the minor characters enter singly or in pairs, depending upon the size of the cast. While some college and civic theater directors seem to believe that any call except a full company call will sow the seeds of division in the organization, I am not of that feeling. If, however, the director feels strongly about single or group calls, then the full company call should be carefully planned and should probably be limited to one curtain.

Trick calls can add tremendously, providing the show will take them, and providing the calls are truly clever. Perhaps one of the most important aspects of the call, and the one most often overlooked in the amateur theater, is that of speed. An audience will be impressed with the number of calls they see. If they see six calls take place before their eyes they will be that much more impressed with the play they have just witnessed, and the fact that the six calls took place in the space of time generally given to one need not be pointed out in the program notes. A cast rehearsed to clear quickly at the final curtain, and to get into position quickly for the curtain call, will often be able to take five or six calls in the same amount of time an unrehearsed and unthinking cast will be fortunate enough to get one. Though the calls must not seem hurried from out front, the offstage movement must be made on the double, often at a run.

Always the call should be in keeping with the show. I recall watching a rather moving college performance of Miller's *All My Sons* and feeling the shocked reaction in the house when Joe, who had just committed suicide, came out for his single call full of life and with a gigantic, happy smile on his face. The spell was broken and only a young college kid stood before the house saying by his very good feeling, "Fooled you, didn't I?" Without feeling guilty about deliberately misleading the audience, for in one respect that is what theater is all about, the director must bear in mind what the audience expects and wants to see. If Joe had taken his call slowly, as if he were tired out from the effort of the show, if the smile had been a humble rather than a triumphant one, the audience would have accepted the actor as an actor rather than as someone who had just pulled the wool over their eyes. The call for any tragedy should be stately and, for the leads, the feeling should be that they have given their all for the experience the audience has just enjoyed.

Often, a curtain call for a farce can be continuation of the show or, in the case of a mystery or melodrama, a comment on the type of show itself. Regardless of the type of call used, it must be well rehearsed and quickly executed. There is no excuse for the director allowing the audience to sit and applaud loud and long. Either the calls should be taken quickly or the house lights should come up announcing to all that the evening is over.

How many calls should be taken will depend upon the amount of the applause, but if the director does not have full confidence in the judgment of the stage manager, a particular number of calls should be set, well below that which can be normally expected, and that number should be adhered to. Few things are more embarrassing to the audience, as well as to the cast, than to have the curtain open again just as the feeble applause is dying away—the cast smiles apologetically, the audience feels that they have let the actors down and turn in the aisles to start applauding again just as the curtain closes. Such gruesome experiences can be avoided by simply stressing that there will be one, two, or three calls, and no more, even if the house is going mad with enthusiasm. If the stage manager understands that he can kill the scattered applause simply by calling for the house lights, a great deal of embarrassment can be avoided for all. In any event, the cast must be informed and re-hearsed to hold their curtain-call position until the stage manager releases them.

The Musical

Rehearsing the musical and the review present some particular problems, but those problems are primarily in-volved with scheduling. When a musical is going into rehearsal, the director is often faced with an extremely tight schedule, for book, music, and dance must receive sufficient rehearsal and stage time. In the professional theater, the music and dance will often begin their rehearsals consider-ably before the book is touched. If sufficient prerehearsal planning is accomplished, such a system can work very well, but if, as often happens, the musical director is heading in one direction, while the choreographer is going in another, and the director in still another, only confusion results. I have made the mistake of thinking that the musical director and I saw eye to eye and then finding that the staging that led into the number could not possibly work with the musical interpretation that the performer had committed to memory. Since that costly and unfortunate experience, I have made it a point to be present at all the early musical rehearsals. When time allows, I believe the best method is to work a musical much like a straight show, that is, from beginning to end, cutting around the staging problems presented by the songs and dances until the book is blocked and the character direction is set. Musical rehearsals held during this period are centered solely on learning the notes, for the interpretation must be in the hands of the director. The choreographer, too, must work closely with the director and the style of dancing must be agreed upon before any dance rehearsals take place.

The musical production on any level can turn into an ugly hassle between the various directors unless the lines of authority are clearly drawn and understood from the very beginning. Obviously, the final authority must rest with one of the directors and that director should be the stage director. The final interpretation must be a joint affair, for the musical director will probably be in the pit, and the performances themselves under his baton, but nonetheless, in case of differences of opinion, only the director can decide.

Three rehearsal halls should be available for the musical and the distance between them should not be greater than a couple of minutes walk. The schedule must be worked out in great detail, for never will there be enough time for the dancers to sit around and wait for their numbers to come up, or for the second leads to waste time standing idly in the wings. Once there is agreement and understanding among the three directors, all three aspects should be working at the same time. Each director needs a piano and a rehearsal pianist at his disposal, as well as a stage manager to assist him.

Whether or not the director is staging the musical numbers, and if possible he should be, one of his prime concerns in any dramatic offering that includes music must be getting into, and out of, the musical numbers easily and quickly.

In any sort of stage directing, the author's intent is the prime factor, and the musical is no exception. Assuming that it is a well-written musical the composer and the book author are not at odds in their intent, and if such is the case, the director's task is easier insofar as discovering that intent.

The music will tell the director the kind of movement the play will take and often the style the acting must follow. All theater, as has been pointed out, implies a degree of exaggeration, and the exaggeration inherent in the musical in most cases is greater than that in the straight play. Even though the musical must be "believable," it is the necessity of being believable within the framework laid down by the playwright that concerns the director. The fact that the characters may, at any time, break into song or dance requires that the entire structure of the stage form be exaggerated to a greater extent than in the straight play. The acting style cannot be as "naturalistic" as in the modern middle-class tragedy. The style of acting will actually come much closer to the old melodrama than to anything else. Even so, it must be consistent and believable within the framework of the musical comedy.

In order to assure the necessary flow, a musical comedy needs even more uninterrupted run-throughs than the straight play. The musical also needs more dress rehearsals, for costume changes can often be complicated and difficult.

The Review

The review, musical or otherwise, also has its own built-in rehearsal problems but they are not, I believe, as great as those of the full-fledged musical. In the review, by the nature of the material, it is a fairly simple matter to break up the rehearsals into small segments. Here again, a considerable number of run-throughs are a necessity, for the pacing of a review is second only to the material itself. The principal problems facing the director of the review are twofold, programming and developing quickly recognizable types. The arrangement of the material, for pace and variety, is vital and extremely difficult. The acting problems are most often concerned with finding the general type that will be quickly recognizable by the audience, for most of the sketches are one-liners followed by a blackout. Even songs will depend upon a quick impression. The director who spends much time on the subtleties of characters will be wasting his and the actors' rehearsal time.

The Stage Manager

Backstage organization should be complete and running before the first technical rehearsal takes place. The entire crew should have seen at least one run-through before they disappear backstage. The stage manager, and probably one assistant, should have been on the job at the first rehearsal and the stage manager, himself, from the earliest planning stages. He should be present at the auditions and, if necessary, read with the actors. The entire playing space and the backstage area is the domain of the stage manager and the director should treat it as such. It is there that the stage manager will need authority during the dress rehearsals and the performances and it is never too soon to start building that authority in the eyes of the actors. On the professional stage, of course, the director's contract usually ends with the in-town opening and the stage manager acts in his place from then on. In the amateur theater the stage manager remains the director's most important aid, but he should be completely in charge backstage from the first dress to the strike.

Often, the stage manager can perform a valuable function by acting as a liaison between the technical director and the director. With all his duties, the stage manager must be prepared to spend fully as much time on the play as the leading actor. He will have to be in on the building, and in the civic theater setup, often have to act as the technical director. Above all, the stage manager must be thoroughly familiar with the show. Because he works jointly with the technical director and the director, the stage manager should be a common choice, but once again the director's decision must be final for no director can function at near capacity when he does not trust or get along with his stage manager.

One of the stage manager's assistants will be placed in charge of props, another, sound and special effects, and still another, lights. Each scene shift, each sound or light cue should be called by the stage manager or, if no communication is possible between stage left and stage right, the stage manager must have an assistant on the far side of the stage to call any necessary cues.

He should not be expected to have any particular duties, rather he should troubleshoot and be ready to cover any emergency that may develop.

The number of persons backstage will be agreed upon among the director, the stage manager, and the technical director. In this case, if the stage manager knows his job, he should be the final authority. In no case should visitors be allowed backstage during the running of a show. In most houses visitors are required to leave the backstage area at the half hour.

The director in the amateur theater should spend some time with the stage manager before the work begins on a given production in order that both parties are sure of the duties and responsibilities of the stage manager. If, as will often be the case, the stage manager is new to his job, considerable time should be spent familiarizing himself with this important job.

Performance

Once the rehearsals and the last actor-director conference have been completed, the director is ready for that most frightening of all nights, the opening. His conduct backstage before the opening can have a tremendous effect on the cast. Of course, he will be nervous, and so will the entire cast, but the director must not be *openly* worried. A cast is quick to pick up the director's mood and thus a good director may have to call upon his own acting ability to show a confidence he does not feel. During the dress rehearsals the actors should have gotten into the habit (I am speaking of the amateur theater but many a professional has found that it is a habit he never loses) of touching each piece of costume and each personal prop. It is all too easy in the excitement of opening night, or in the hurry before any performance, to think one sees everything necessary when, in reality, the coat or vest or muff has been moved during the day. If the actor takes pains to have a checklist and to make sure that he actually touches everything he uses in the show, the chance of show-spoiling mistakes will be considerably lessened.

Whether or not the director makes a short speech to the cast before curtain depends upon his own personality and his relationship with the cast. I find it helpful.

During the performance itself the director's place is out front, not backstage in the way of actors and crew alike. The cast may expect to see him backstage between acts, and there is no reason why he should not go back. If he does elect to visit backstage between acts, he must be careful to appear confident, even if the preceding act has not gone well. Regardless of what *has* happened, it is the next act on which the actors should be concentrating, not the fluffs that occurred in the past act.

In the amateur theater every effort should be made to keep the cast up after the excitement of the opening. One method of doing this is to give notes after every performance and all during rehearsal to stress the continuous good performance, rather than simply a good show opening night. The actors should be concerned with improving their performance each night, and if they automatically assume that the director will be giving notes after each performance, they will be thinking in terms of improvement rather than resting upon their hard work during rehearsals and the praise of their friends after the opening.

The director, too, must be thinking in terms of improvement during the run. He should not be afraid to change something when he sees that he has been wrong in either his interpretation or his staging. The performance is the time when the director checks his own work and he must be flexible and critical enough to see where he has been wrong if the play is not "going over." He can learn from each performance if he will watch the play, watch the audience, and listen to comments as the audience leaves at the end of the evening. Very often, when the house is filled with an audience instead of a few invited friends, things which were only a little irksome during the rehearsals become glaring faults that must be corrected. When the director is even suspicious that a better way might be found, he should search until either he finds it, or the show closes. Brush-up rehearsals should be expected by the cast if the run is to be any length.

The view, which I have found often in the amateur theater, that once the dress rehearsals start no changes can be made, misses one of the most interesting and instructive times in the production of a play. To be objective about one's work is always difficult, but one of the beautiful things about the art of the theater is that it is possible to redo, after it has been done. In the amateur theater especially, the cast, the director, and all concerned should be aiming at that perfect performance that is always just out of reach. Until a show closes it is never too late to improve. In the professional theater with weeks and weeks of out-of-town tryouts, or previews, the actors and director have a chance to test their work. In the amateur theater, there may only be three or four nights, but each night should be an improvement over the preceding performance. The familiar second-night letdown need not occur if neither actor nor director is satisfied with anything less than perfection.

Opening-night performances and opening-night reactions

are exciting but are not to be regarded as final in any sense of the word. The cast is generally tired after a week of rather intensive rehearsal and they are almost always, in the amateur theater, playing only on their nerves. They are much too "high" to do much more than let the conditioned response set up in the rehearsal period take over. No matter how the performance goes, the director is apt to feel that it did not go as well as it might have. Often, when he reads the reviews the next day, he gets so angry at the ignorance of the writer that he forgets his own dissatisfaction with the play and simply transfers that dissatisfaction, with a little extra added for good measure, to the "critic."

Luckily, in the amateur theater, the review seldom means much from a box-office point of view, and even less from an artistic viewpoint. This country is not, even in the large cities, overly populated with intelligent, knowledgeable critics, and if the large city papers are deficient (and they are), the smaller city and college newspapers are even more so. The cast should be forewarned about the possible reviews and told not to take them seriously either way. Usually the review will be composed by the young man or woman who believes that the critic's job is to find fault, or by some gushing young thing who loves everything about the live theater. Neither is at all helpful to the director. If, however, the director is fortunate enough to have a real critic writing the reviews, that is, one who has some background in theater, is acquainted with good literature, and can put together a sentence that makes sense, then the piece should be studied in detail and if changes are called for, they should be accomplished. In any case, the director often must either cheer up his battered cast, or bring them down from the skies before they go on stage for their second performance.

References

1. E. K. Chambers, *The Medieval Stage* (Oxford, 1903), II, 80–81.

2. Lee Simonson, *The Stage Is Set* (New York, 1932), pp. 293–294.

3. Constantin Stanislavski, *My Life In Art,* trans. J. J. Robbins (New York, 1948), pp. 199–200.

4. *Ibid.,* p. 201.

5. *Ibid.,* p.199.

6. Edward Gordon Craig, *On the Art of the Theatre* (New York, 1957), p. 99.

7. *Ibid.,* pp. 100–101.

8. *Ibid.,* pp. 171–172.

9. *Ibid.,* pp. 104–105.

10. Some of these books are: *The Seagull, Produced by Constantin Stanislavski* (New York: Theatre Arts Books, 1952); *Othello, Produced by Constantin Stanislavski* (New York: Theatre Arts Books, 1948); V. Stevens (ed.), *Stanislavski Directs* (New York: Funk & Wagnalls, 1954); N. M. Gorchakov, *K. Stanislavsky 1863–1963* (Moscow: Progress Press, 1963).

11. Craig, p. ix.

12. Stanislavski describes how the Meiningen Players were able to stage much of the creative work of the great poets by the use of direction technique, without much real acting talent. See *My Life In Art,* p. 198. Several writers have, on the other hand, pointed out the mistakes Stanislavski made in adding sound to cover the pauses he could not understand in his first Chekov play *The Seagull.*

13. Otto Baensch, "Art and Feeling," in *Reflections on Art,* ed. Susanne K. Langer (New York, 1958), pp. 26–27.

14. *Ibid.,* p. 30.

15. Wilder has a brief discussion of this multiple artistry in his

article "Some Thoughts on Playwriting," in *The Intent of the Artist,* ed. Augusto Centeno (Princeton, 1941), pp. 85, 89–90. Some of Shaw's thoughts on the subject can be found in his article "The Art of Rehearsal," in *Directing the Play,* ed. Toby Cole and Helen K. Chinoy (New York, 1953), pp. 142–147.

16. Augusto Centeno, *The Intent of the Artist* (Princeton, 1941), p. 8.

17. *Ibid.,* pp. 9–10.

18. *Ibid.,* pp. 8–9.

19. Allardyce Nicoll, *The Theory of the Drama* (New York, 1925), p. 9.

20. Aristotle, "On Poetics," in *The Works of Aristotle. Great Books of the Western World* (Chicago, 1952), II, 684–685.

21. *Ibid.,* pp. 686–687.

22. *Ibid.,* p. 684.

23. Stark Young, *The Theater* (New York, 1954), p. 37.

24. The reader is referred to Young's discussion which points out that the argument often used to discredit the importance of plot, namely that there are only some thirty-six plots in all, is not valid since it was situations and not plots that Gozzi was speaking of. ". . . while the number of situations may be so limited, the plots to be woven around them are innumerable." Young, *The Theater,* p. 37.

25. *Ibid.,* p. 48.

26. Nicoll, p. 68.

27. Dante Alighieri, "Epistle to Can Grande," extracted from *A Translation of Dante's Eleven Letters* by C. S. Latham (Boston, 1892), as found in *European Theories of Drama,* ed. Barrett H. Clark (New York, 1947), p. 47.

28. Young, p. 40.

29. Nicoll, p. 87.

30. *Ibid.,* p. 124.

31. *Ibid.,* pp. 87–88.

32. *Ibid.,* p. 88.

33. John E. Dietrich, *Play Direction* (New York, 1953), pp. 71–90.

34. Such literary critics as T. S. Eliot, Eric Bentley, and Francis Fergusson have expressed much the same idea.

35. Francis Fergusson, *The Idea of a Theater* (Garden City, 1953), p. 125.

36. Henry Fielding, *The History of Tom Jones* (New York, 1950), p. 759.

37. It would appear possible at least that when the playwrights were bitten by the bug of "realism," the acting schools chose not realism, whatever that is, but informality to be reflected in the artistic mirror. Hence the scratching, the sloppy diction, and the ungraceful stance associated with the "dirty tee-shirt" school of the 1950s and at least the first half of the '60s.

38. David W. Thompson, "Interpretative Reading as Symbolic Action," in *The Quarterly Journal of Speech*, XLII, No. 4 (December 1956), p. 394.

39. It is remarkable how well established the rite of Taking a Drink on stage appears to be. I have watched many young actors go through almost exactly the same pattern in rehearsal without thinking about it at all. Such stereotyped ceremonies are a good example of what Stanislavski describes as "established clichés" which "have become traditional, and are passed down from generation to generation; as for instance spreading your hands over your heart to express love, or opening your mouth wide to give the idea of death." Constantin Stanislavski, *An Actor Prepares*, trans. Elizabeth Reynolds Hapgood (New York, 1936), p. 23.

40. T. S. Eliot, *Selected Essays* (New York, 1950), pp. 27–29.

41. Eric Bentley, ed., *The Play, A Critical Anthology* (New York, 1951), p. 142.

42. Eliot, p. 28.

43. The Playboy Clubs of 1965–68 are full of such semiconscious role-players.

44. August Strindberg, *The Father*, trans. Elizabeth Sprigge, *Six Plays of Strindberg* (Garden City, 1955), p. 56.

45. *Ibid.*, p. 68.

46. Brian W. Downs, *A Study of Six Plays by Ibsen* (Cambridge, 1948), p. 151.

47. Olaf Paulsen.

48. Henrik Ibsen, *Letters of Henrik Ibsen*, trans. Laurvik & Morrison (New York, 1905), p. 384.

49. "Who is this they follow? And with such maimed rites?" *Hamlet:* V, i.

50. "I can think of few scenes that give better scope for comedy-acting of the finest kind than the conversation between husband and wife when Hialmar's vision of a dignified separation fights with

his desire to remain at home drinking Gina's excellent coffee and living on the money she earns by doing his photographic work." Storm Jameson, *Modern Drama in Europe* (New York, 1920), p. 106.

51. Hermann J. Viegand, *The Modern Ibsen* (New York, 1925), p. 145.

52. Barrett H. Clark and George Freedley, eds., *A History of Modern Drama* (New York, 1947), p. 15.

53. Viegand, p. 165.

54. A. E. Zuker, *Ibsen, The Master Builder* (New York, 1929), p. 191.

55. Martin Lamm, *Modern Drama,* trans. Karin Elliot (Oxford, 1952), p. 125.

56. Jameson, p. 105.

57. Viegand, p. 143.

58. Professor Alrik Gustafson in lecture, University of Minnesota, 1956.

59. Zuker, p. 193.

60. Stanislavski, *An Actor Prepares,* p. 22.

61. Centeno, p. 96.

62. Alexander Dean has labeled most of the techniques described herein and in my opinion no one has come up with better labels, so I borrow freely throughout this section. Alexander Dean, *Fundamentals of Play Direction* (New York, 1956).

63. George II, Duke of Saxe-Meiningen, "Pictorial Motion," in *Directors on Directing,* ed. Toby Cole and Helen K. Chinoy (New York, 1953), pp. 81–82.

64. See note 62.

65. Stanislavski, *An Actor Prepares,* p. 33.

66. *Ibid.,* p. 37.

67. Dean labels these symmetrical, asymmetrical, and aesthetic.

68. I must admit that my productions seem to fall pretty much to the pattern he suggested.

69. I once received a manuscript so designated, apparently in all seriousness, as I could no more decide what the would-be playwright had written than could he.

70. Stanislavski, *An Actor Prepares,* pp. 34–35.

71. Young, p. 69.

72. As Joseph Conrad phrases it in *Lord Jim,* "The truth dis-

closed in a moment of illusion." Joseph Conrad, *Lord Jim* (New York, 1900), p. 209.

73. "The primary function of all magical acts, I am suggesting, is to generate in the agent or agents certain emotions that are considered necessary or useful for the work of living; their secondary function is to generate in others, friends or enemies of the agent, emotions useful or detrimental to the lives of these others." R. G. Collingwood, *The Principles of Art* (New York, 1958), pp. 66–67.

74. Collingwood, p. 78.

75. Edwin Duerr, *The Length and Depth of Acting* (New York, 1962), p. 49.

76. Arthur B. Keith, *The Sanskrit Drama* (Oxford, 1924), p. 363.

77. Centeno, p. 12.

78. Plato, *Ion,* in *Great Dialogues of Plato,* trans. W. H. D. Rouse (New York, 1956), p. 18.

79. *Ion,* p. 20.

80. Aristotle, *Rhetoric* III, vol. 9, p. 653.

81. William James, *The Principles of Psychology. Great Books of the Western World* (Chicago, 1952), vol. 53, p. 743.

82. Duerr, p. 481.

83. Stanislavski, *An Actor Prepares,* p. 28.

84. Duerr, p. 19.

85. Stanislavski, *An Actor Prepares,* p. 210.

86. Duerr cites Morris on p. 379: "Clara Morris, *Life on the Stage* (New York, 1902), pp. 326–329, reprinted in Nagler, Sources, pp. 562–563."

87. Stark Young, "Acting," in *The Flower in the Drama* (New York, 1955), p. 11.

88. Stanislavski, *An Actor Prepares,* pp. 201–202.

89. Plato, *Great Dialogues,* p. 18.

90. See note 80.

91. Stanislavski, *My Life in Art,* p. 276.

92. Duerr, p. 31.

93. Aristotle, *Rhetoric,* p. 654.

94. Constantin Stanislavski, *Building a Character,* trans. Elizabeth Reynolds Hapgood (New York, 1949), p. 113.

95. John Ruskin, "Education Means Knowing Words," in *Sesame and Lillies, I,* as found in *Reading Aloud,* Wayland Maxfield Parrish (New York, 1953), p. 48.

96. Stanislavski, *Building a Character*, p. 123.

97. *Ibid.*, pp. 104–142.

98. Parrish, p. 30.

99. *Ibid.*, p. 31.

100. *Ibid.*, p. 37.

101. *Ibid.*, p. 37.

102. Stanislavski, *Building a Character*, p. 143.

103. Arthur Knight, "S R Goes to the Movies," in *Saturday Review* (April 12, 1958), p. 44.

104. Marian Gallaway, *The Director in the Theater* (New York, 1963), p. 232.

Appendix

RITE-ROLE ANALYSIS OF THE WILD DUCK

THE WILD DUCK

Rites

ACT I
1. Preparing the Room
2. The After-Dinner Drink

ACT II
1. Waiting
2. Homecoming
3. Family Conference
4. Entertaining Guest
5. Leave-taking
6. Retiring for the Night

ACT III
1. Working
2. Entertaining Guest
3. Luncheon Party (maimed)
4. Father-Son Conference
5. Leave-taking

ACT IV
1. Business
2. Waiting
3. Family Conference
   (maimed)
4. Informal Call
5. Formal Call
6. Informal Call
7. Comforting Child

ACT V
1. Waiting
2. Diagnosis
3. Persuasion
4. Musing
5. Homecoming (maimed)
6. Forgiveness (maimed)
7. Laying Out the Body
   (maimed)

THE WILD DUCK

Rites and Dramatic Actions

Act I—Werle's Home

SCENE	CHARACTERS	RITES AND DRAMATIC ACTIONS
		Preparing the Room
I	Pettersen, Jensen	gossiping about employer
II	Pettersen, Jensen, Waiter	announcing unwanted visitor
III	Pett., Jen., O. Ekdal	asking favor
IV	Pett., Jen.	gossiping about visitor
		The After-Dinner Drink
V	Pett., Jen., Mrs. Sorby, Gregers, Hialmar, Werle, others	giving instructions
VI	Gregers, Hialmar, Werle, others, Flabby Gentleman, Thin-haired Gentleman, Third Gentleman	pleasant conversation
VII	Gregers, Hialmar, Werle, others	commenting on thirteenth guest
VIII	Gregers, Hialmar	reassuring old friend describing melancholy existence explaining wife and marriage being suspicious of father's actions
IX	Gregers, Hialmar, Mrs. S., Werle	looking after loved one
X	Gregers, Hialmar, Mrs. S., Werle, F. Gent., T-h. G., Short-sighted Gent., Pett., Jen., others	clever conversation

SCENE	CHARACTERS	RITES AND DRAMATIC ACTIONS
XI	Same as X and O. Ekdal, Graberg	making embarrassed exit
XII	Same as X	denying father instructing servants defending self idle conversation announcing departure dramatizing self bidding farewell
XIII	Gregers, Mrs. S., Werle, Pett., others	checking up on servants
XIV	Gregers, Mrs. S., Werle, Pett., F. Gent., others	invitation to perform
XV	Gregers, Werle	accusing father defending self accusing father discussing mother offering son proposition explaining proposition being suspicious of father revealing plans to son accusing father
XVI	Werle	contemptuously commenting on son

Act II—Hialmar's Studio

Waiting

SCENE	CHARACTERS	RITES AND DRAMATIC ACTIONS
I	Gina, Hedvig	figuring daily budget discussing father
II	Gina, Hedvig, Old Ekdal	coming home
III	Gina, Hedvig	discussing grandfather discussing father
IV	Gina, Hedvig, Old Ekdal	making transparent excuses
V	Gina, Hedvig	discussing grandfather

SCENE	CHARACTERS	RITES AND DRAMATIC ACTIONS
		Homecoming
VI	Gina, Hedvig, Hialmar, O. Ekdal	greeting father discussing grandfather
VII	Gina, Hedvig, Hialmar	discussing triumph changing costumes coaxing father and attempting to hide bitter disappointment discussing important improvements
		Family Conference
VIII	Gina, Hedvig, Hialmar	discussing grandfather reminding husband of work reprimanding wife coddling father sentimental reconciliation giving concert
		Entertaining Guest
IX	Gina, Hedvig, Hialmar, Gregers	welcoming old friend meeting the family
X	Gina, Hialmar, Gregers	discussing daughter
XI	Gina, Hialmar, Gregers, Hedvig	serving beer coddling father
XII	Gina, Hialmar, Gregers	discussing daughter questioning closely
XIII	Gina, Hialmar, Gregers, O. Ekdal	introducing grandfather
XIV	Gina, Hialmar, Gregers, O. Ekdal, Hedvig	eating and discussing the good-old days hinting at wonderful surprise unveiling surprise discussing the wild duck renting a room degrading self

SCENE	CHARACTERS	RITES AND DRAMATIC ACTIONS
		Leave-taking
		bidding farewell
		Retiring for the Night
XV	Gina, Hedvig, O. Ekdal	discussing guest
XVI	Gina, Hedvig, O. Ekdal, Hialmar	eating and playing great man eating and putting grandfather to bed

Act III—Hialmar's Studio

Working

I	Hialmar	retouching photo
II	Hialmar, Gina	discussing new roomer informing wife of luncheon guests
III	Hialmar, Gina, O. Ekdal	mistakenly interrupting
IV	Hialmar, Gina	reminding husband of work
V	Hialmar	toiling at task
VI	Hialmar, O. Ekdal	attempting to interrupt son
VII	Hialmar, O. Ekdal (off)	attempting to interrupt father
VIII	Hialmar, O. Ekdal	convincing each other to stop work
IX	Hialmar, Gina	discussing grandfather and business
X	Hialmar, O. Ekdal	toiling at task
XI	Hialmar, Hedvig	turning work over to daughter
XII	Hedvig	working
XIII	Hedvig, Hialmar	interrupting daughter

Entertaining Guest

XIV	Hedvig, Gregers	tidying up pumping child

SCENE	CHARACTERS	RITES AND DRAMATIC ACTIONS
XV	Hedvig, Gregers, Gina	setting the table pumping wife
XVI	Hedvig, Gregers, Gina, Hialmar	greeting host discussing wild duck
XVII	Gregers, Hialmar	bragging to friend dramatizing the past avoiding embarrassing questions attempting to enlighten friend

Luncheon Party (M)

SCENE	CHARACTERS	RITES AND DRAMATIC ACTIONS
XVIII	Gregers, Hialmar, Relling, Molvik, Gina, Hedvig	introducing the new roomer furthering the life-illusion
XIX	Gregers, Hialmar, Relling, Molvik, O. Ekdal	exhibiting trophy
XX	Gregers, Hialmar, Relling, Gina, Hedvig	furthering the life-illusion playing the loving father attempting to present the claim of the ideal
XXI	Gregers, Hialmar, Relling, Gina, Hedvig, Werle	looking for son

Father-Son Conference

SCENE	CHARACTERS	RITES AND DRAMATIC ACTIONS
XXII	Gregers, Werle	attempting to understand son making veiled threats

Leave-taking

SCENE	CHARACTERS	RITES AND DRAMATIC ACTIONS
XXIII	Gregers, Hialmar, Relling, Gina, Hedvig	refusing to remain
XXIV	Relling, Gina, Hedvig	discussing the departed guest
XXV	Gina, Hedvig	wondering

SCENE	CHARACTERS	RITES AND DRAMATIC ACTIONS

Act IV—Hialmar's Studio

Business

| I | Gina, customers (off) | promising delivery |

Waiting

| II | Gina, Hedvig | discussing father |

Family Conference (M)

| III | Gina, Hedvig, Hialmar | playing cold and distant father |
| IV | Gina, Hialmar | settling accounts |

Informal Call

| V | Gina, Hialmar, Gregers | making follow-up call advising friend |
| VI | Gina, Hialmar, Gregers, Relling | advising the advisor discussing the child |

Formal Call

| VII | Gina, Hialmar, Gregers, Relling, Mrs. S. | announcing forthcoming marriage |
| VIII | Gina, Hialmar, Gregers, Mrs. S. | discussing old love discussing the groom-to-be refusing help |

Informal Call

| IX | Gina, Hialmar, Gregers | discussing the claim of the ideal |
| X | Gina, Hialmar, Gregers, Hedvig | coaxing father displaying gift adding up the evidence making dramatic exit |

Comforting Child

| XI | Gina, Gregers, Hedvig | going after husband |

SCENE	CHARACTERS	RITES AND DRAMATIC ACTIONS
XII	Gregers, Hedvig	persuading child to make sacrifice
XIII	Gregers, Hedvig, Gina	reporting on missing father
XIV	Hedvig, Gina	philosophizing

Act V—Hialmar's Studio

Waiting

I	Gina, Hedvig	reporting on missing father
II	Gina, Hedvig, O. Ekdal	taking morning walk
III	Gina, Hedvig	discussing grandfather
IV	Gina, Hedvig, Gregers	seeking news
V	Gina, Hedvig, Gregers, Relling	reporting father's whereabouts

Diagnosis

VI	Gregers, Relling	discussing mutual friend explaining illness explaining treatment

Persuasion

VII	Gregers, Hedvig	advising child reminding child of duty

Musing

VIII	Hedvig	wandering
IX	Hedvig, O. Ekdal	questioning grandfather
X	Hedvig	looking at gun
XI	Hedvig, Gina	interrupting child

Homecoming (M)

XII	Gina, Hialmar	announcing intentions
XIII	Gina, Hialmar	denying child

Scene	Characters	Rites and Dramatic Actions
XIV	Gina, Hialmar	preparing to leave home forever
XV	Hedvig	preparing to make sacrifice
XVI	Hialmar, Gina	eating and packing repairing gift
XVII	Hialmar, Gina, Gregers	explaining to friend making decision and giving orders
XVIII	Hialmar, Gregers	seeking advice blaming the doctor blaming the child playing martyr
XIX	Hialmar, Gregers, Gina	hearing shot joyfully explaining sacrifice
		Forgiveness (M)
XX	Hialmar, Gregers, Gina	forgiving one and all
XXI	Hialmar, Gregers, Gina, O. Ekdal	becoming alarmed and confused discovering the sacrifice summoning the doctor
XXII	Hialmar, Gregers, Gina, Hedvig	carrying in the child
		Laying Out the Body (M)
XXIII	Hialmar, Gregers, Gina, Hedvig, O. Ekdal, Relling, Molvik	examining the body
XXIV	Hialmar, Gregers, Gina, Hedvig, Relling, Molvik,	pronouncing death blaming God removing the body
XXV	Gregers, Relling	declaring suicide blaming the reformer announcing destiny

THE WILD DUCK

Rites and Roles

Act I

RITE	CHARACTER	ROLE
Preparing the Room		
	Pettersen	butler
	Jensen	servant
	Waiter	servant
	Old Ekdal	meek old man
The After-Dinner Drink		
	Pettersen	butler
	Jensen	servant
	Mrs. Sorby	hostess
		benefactor
		hostess
	Gregers	old friend
		overstrained son
		old friend
		sympathetic friend
		guilty son
		suspicious son
		helpful old friend
		suspicious son
		shocked friend
		suspicious son
	Hialmar	uncomfortable guest
		melancholy martyr
		shy guest
		embarrassed son
		martyr
	Werle	congenial host
		dejected father
		congenial host
		angry employer

RITE	CHARACTER	ROLE
	Old Ekdal	meek old man
	Graberg	clerk
	Others	congenial guests
	Gregers	suspicious son
		overstrained son
		bitter son
		man with a mission
	Werle	impatient father
		confident man
		angry man
		disappointed father
		contemptuous man

Act II

Waiting		
	Gina	mother
		kind daughter-in-law
		daughter-in-law
	Hedvig	daughter
		mother's helper
		granddaughter
		daddy's little girl
	Old Ekdal	happy old man
		nature lover
		sly grandpa
Homecoming		
	Gina	surprised wife
		proud wife
	Hedvig	daddy's little girl
		disappointed daughter
	Old Ekdal	proud father
	Hialmar	man of the house
		man of the world
		dutiful son
		witty man of the world
		handsome Bohemian
		irritated father
		man of affairs

RITE	CHARACTER	ROLE
Family Conference		
	Gina	good wife
		business partner
		loving wife
	Hedvig	daddy's little girl
	Hialmar	reprimanding husband
		martyr
		dear kind father
		musician
		contented husband and father
Entertaining Guests		
	Gina	woman of the house
		casual hostess
		apprehensive wife and mother
		proud mother
		apprehensive wife
		practical wife
		unenthusiastic landlady
	Hedvig	helpful daughter
	Hialmar	old friend
		proud father
		sorrowful father
		poor but willing host
		hungry host
		embarrassed man of the world
		proud man
		landlord
		confused man
	Old Ekdal	tipsy old man
		contented old man
		proud sportsman
		contented old man
	Gregers	old friend
		suspicious son
		meddling reformer
		self-abasing son
		philosopher

RITE	CHARACTER	ROLE
Leave-taking		
	Gina	uneasy wife
	Hialmar	old friend
	Hedvig	puzzled little girl
	Old Ekdal	tipsy old man
	Gregers	old friend
Retiring for the Night		
	Gina	uneasy wife
		practical wife
	Hedvig	puzzled little girl
		mother's helper
	Hialmar	man of destiny
		dutiful son
	Old Ekdal	drunken old man

Act III

Working		
	Hialmar	breadwinner
		superior husband
		man of affairs
		abused breadwinner
		busy worker
		dutiful son
		harried father
		proud inventor
		hard worker
		carpenter
	Gina	irritated landlady
		irritated wife
		practical wife
	Old Ekdal	old father
		irritated father
		busy worker
		carpenter

RITE	CHARACTER	ROLE
	Hedvig	daddy's little girl
		daddy's helper
		busy worker
Entertaining Guest		
	Hedvig	busy worker
		hostess
		loving daughter
		dreamer
		proud owner
		puzzled little girl
	Gregers	friend of the family
		inquisitive friend
		meddler
		suspicious son
		helpful philosopher
		reformer
	Gina	busy housewife
		careful wife
		irritated wife
	Hialmar	embarrassed host
		chagrined sportsman
		man of the world
		dutiful son
		strong hero
		melancholy son
		inventor
		puzzled man
		irritated man
Luncheon Party (M)		
	Gregers	guest
		reformer
		suspicious son
	Hialmar	host
		hungry host
		hurt son
		dutiful son

RITE	CHARACTER	ROLE
		hard-working man of the house
		contented husband
		loving father
		upset host
		host
	Relling	guest
		psychiatrist
		irritated psychiatrist
	Molvik	guest
		proud daemonic
		ill guest
	Gina	servant
	Hedvig	servant
	Old Ekdal	successful hunter
	Werle	indignant father
Father-Son Conference		
	Gregers	defiant son
		bitter son
	Werle	distressed father
		dejected father
		disappointed father
Leave-taking		
	Gregers	impatient reformer
	Hialmar	reliable old friend
	Relling	concerned psychiatrist
	Gina	concerned wife
	Hedvig	confused little girl

Act IV

Business		
	Gina	businesswoman
Waiting		
	Gina	practical wife and mother
	Hedvig	perturbed daughter

RITE	CHARACTER	ROLE

Family Conference

Gina
- practical wife
- truthful wife
- unhappy wife

Hedvig
- happy daughter
- frightened little girl
- confused little girl
- concerned little girl

Hialmar
- hurt but resolute husband
- angry man
- soft-hearted father
- noble man
- loving father
- businessman
- interrogator
- betrayed husband
- stern accuser
- misunderstood man

Informal Call

Gina
- sorrowful wife
- practical woman
- tearful wife

Hialmar
- martyr
- irritated martyr
- melancholy martyr
- heartbroken father
- self-sacrificing father

Gregers
- disappointed reformer
- conscientious reformer

Relling
- angry psychiatrist
- persuader
- family doctor

Formal Call

Gina
- old friend
- concerned mother
- proud wife

Hialmar
- righteous man
- noble man of honor

RITE	CHARACTER	ROLE
	Gregers	dutiful stepson
		threatening stepson
		apprehensive friend
		meddling reformer
	Mrs. Sorby	old friend
		bride-to-be
		ex-lover
		straightforward woman
		old friend
	Relling	rejected lover
		spiteful ex-lover
		hurt ex-lover
Informal Call		
	Gina	practical wife
		frightened wife
		practical mother
		practical wife
		anxious wife
		angry mother
		frightened wife
	Hialmar	noble breadwinner
		puzzled man of honor
		philosopher
		curious father
		bewildered man
		stunned father
		righteous man
		wronged husband
		bewildered man
		distraught husband
	Hedvig	daddy's little girl
		puzzled child
		hurt little girl
		frightened little girl
	Gregers	self-satisfied reformer
		confused reformer
		meddler
		proud reformer
		confused reformer

RITE	CHARACTER	ROLE
Comforting Child		
	Gina	upset mother
		practical mother
		philosopher
	Hedvig	frightened little girl
		miserable little girl
		little girl
		resolute daughter
		frightened, hurt little girl
	Gregers	uneasy man
		meddling reformer
		comforter

Act V

Waiting		
	Gina	concerned housewife
		thoughtful daughter-in-law
		concerned wife
		relieved wife
		practical housewife
	Hedvig	worried daughter
		worried granddaughter
		rebuking little girl
		practical daughter
	Old Ekdal	hurt old father
	Gregers	concerned friend
		puzzled reformer
	Relling	messenger
Diagnosis		
	Gregers	didactic reformer
		astonished friend
		loyal old friend
		indignant old friend
		resolute reformer
	Relling	realist
		would-be teacher
		psychiatrist
		kind friend

RITE	CHARACTER	ROLE
Persuasion		
	Gregers	rebuking friend
		meddler
	Hedvig	sensible child
Musing		
	Hedvig	thoughtful child
	Old Ekdal	irritated father
		sportsman
	Gina	busy mother
Homecoming		
	Gina	practical wife
		reprimanding wife
		concerned wife
		practical housewife
	Hialmar	befuddled man
		disowning father
		angry man
		wronged husband
		irritated man
		martyr
		exhausted martyr
		irritated martyr
		hungry martyr
		relenting husband
		cautious martyr
		melancholy martyr
		irritated man
		accuser
		martyr
		wronged father
		melancholy martyr
	Hedvig	joyful daughter
		deeply hurt daughter
		martyr
	Gregers	surprised reformer
		determined reformer
		joyful reformer

RITE	CHARACTER	ROLE
Forgiveness (M)		
	Hialmar	tender loving father
		forgiving husband and father
		astonished man
		excited man
		frightened father
		distracted father
	Gregers	joyful reformer
		stunned man
	Gina	joyful wife
		frightened mother
		distraught mother
	Old Ekdal	resentful father
		melancholy philosopher
Laying Out the Body (M)		
	Hialmar	anxious father
		unbelieving father
		hopeful father
		melodramatic father
		ennobled father
	Gina	anxious mother
		heartbroken mother
		practical mother
	Relling	family doctor
		man of science
		cynical doctor
		prophet
		realistic philosopher
	Gregers	astonished man
		terrified man
		hopeful reformer
		indignant friend
		disillusioned reformer
	Molvik	family friend
		minister of God
		ashamed sot
	Old Ekdal	melancholy philosopher

THE WILD DUCK

Roles

HIALMAR

Act I

The After-Dinner Drink

uncomfortable guest
melancholy martyr
shy guest
embarrassed son
martyr

Act II

Homecoming

man of the house
man of the world
dutiful son
witty man of the world
handsome Bohemian
irritated father
man of affairs

Family Conference

reprimanding husband
martyr
dear kind father
musician
contented husband and father

Entertaining Guest

old friend
proud father
sorrowful father
poor but willing host
hungry host
embarrassed man of the world
proud man
landlord
confused man

Leave-taking

old friend

Retiring for the Night

man of destiny
dutiful son

Act III

Working

breadwinner
superior husband
man of affairs
abused breadwinner
busy worker
dutiful son
harried father
proud inventor
hard worker
carpenter

Entertaining Guest

embarrassed host
chagrined sportsman
man of the world
dutiful son
strong hero
melancholy son
inventor
puzzled man
irritated man

Luncheon Party (M)

host
hungry host
hurt son

dutiful son
hard-working man of the house
contented husband
loving father
upset host
host

Leave-taking

reliable old friend

Act IV

Family Conference

hurt but resolute husband
angry man
soft-hearted father
noble man
loving father
businessman
interrogator
betrayed husband
stern accuser
misunderstood man

Informal Call

martyr
irritated martyr
melancholy martyr
heartbroken father
self-sacrificing father

Formal Call

righteous man
noble man of honor

Informal Call

noble breadwinner
puzzled man of honor
philosopher
curious father
bewildered man
stunned father

righteous man
wronged husband
bewildered man
distraught husband

Act V

Homecoming

befuddled man
disowning father
angry man
wronged husband
irritated man
martyr
exhausted martyr
irritated martyr
hungry martyr
relenting husband
cautious martyr
melancholy martyr
irritated man
accuser
martyr
wronged father
wronged husband
melancholy martyr

Forgiveness (M)

tender loving father
forgiving husband and father
astonished man
excited man
frightened father
distracted father

Laying Out the Body (M)

anxious father
unbelieving father
hopeful father
melodramatic father
ennobled father

Roles

GREGERS

Act I

The After Dinner Drink

old friend
overstrained son
old friend
sympathetic friend
guilty son
suspicious son
helpful old friend
suspicious son
shocked friend
suspicious son

Interrogation

overstrained son
bitter son
man with a mission

Act II

Entertaining Guest

old friend
suspicious son
meddling reformer
self-abasing son
philosopher

Leave-taking

old friend

Act III

Entertaining Guest

friend of the family
inquisitive friend
meddler
suspicious son
helpful philosopher
reformer

Luncheon Party (M)

guest
reformer
suspicious son

Father-Son Conference

defiant son
bitter son

Leave-taking

impatient reformer

Act IV

Informal Call

disappointed reformer
conscientious reformer

Formal Call

dutiful stepson
threatening stepson
apprehensive friend
meddling reformer

Informal Call

self-satisfied reformer
confused reformer
meddler
proud reformer
confused reformer

Comforting Child

uneasy man
meddling reformer
comforter

Act V

Waiting

concerned friend
puzzled reformer

Diagnosis

didactic reformer
astonished friend
loyal old friend
indignant old friend
resolute reformer

Persuasion

rebuking friend
meddler

Homecoming

surprised reformer

determined reformer
joyful reformer

Forgiveness (M)

joyful reformer
stunned man

Laying Out the Body (M)

astonished man
terrified man
hopeful reformer
indignant friend
disillusioned reformer

Roles

GINA

Act I

Act II

Waiting

mother
kind daughter-in-law
daughter-in-law

Homecoming

surprised wife
proud wife

Family Conference

good wife
business partner
loving wife

Entertaining Guest

woman of the house
casual hostess
apprenhensive wife and mother
proud mother
apprehensive wife
practical wife
unenthusiastic landlady

Leave-taking

uneasy wife

Retiring for the Night

uneasy wife
practical wife

Act III

Working

irritated landlady
irritated wife
practical wife

Entertaining Guest

busy housewife
careful wife
irritated wife

Luncheon Party (M)

servant

Leave-taking

concerned wife

Act IV

Business

businesswoman

Waiting

practical wife and mother

Family Conference

practical wife
truthful wife
unhappy wife

Informal Call

sorrowful wife
practical wife
tearful wife

Formal Call

old friend
concerned mother
proud wife

Informal Call

practical wife
frightened wife
practical mother
practical wife
anxious wife
angry mother
frightened wife

Comforting Child

upset mother

practical mother
philosopher

Act V

Waiting

concerned housewife
thoughtful daughter-in-law
concerned wife
relieved wife
practical housewife

Musing

busy mother

Homecoming (M)

practical wife
reprimanding wife
concerned wife
practical housewife

Forgiveness (M)

joyful wife
frightened mother
distraught mother

Laying Out the Body (M)

anxious mother
heartbroken mother
practical mother

Roles

HEDVIG

Act I

Act II

Waiting

daughter
mother's helper
granddaughter
daddy's little girl

Homecoming

daddy's little girl
disappointed daughter

Family Conference

daddy's little girl

Entertaining Guest

helpful daughter

Leave-taking

puzzled little girl

Retiring for the Night

puzzled little girl
mother's helper

Act III

Working

daddy's little girl
daddy's helper
busy worker

Entertaining Guest

busy worker
hostess
loving daughter
dreamer
proud owner
puzzled little girl

Luncheon Party (M)

servant

Leave-taking

confused little girl

Act IV

Waiting

perturbed daughter

Family Conference (M)

happy daughter
frightened little girl
confused little girl
concerned little girl

Informal Call

daddy's little girl
puzzled child
hurt little girl
frightened little girl

Comforting Child

frightened child
miserable child
little girl
resolute daughter
frightened hurt little girl

Act V

Waiting

worried daughter
worried granddaughter
rebuking little girl
practical daughter

Persuasion

sensible child

Musing

thoughtful child

Homecoming (M)

joyful daughter
deeply hurt daughter
martyr

Roles

RELLING

Act I

Act II

Act III
Luncheon Party (M)

guest
psychiatrist
irritated psychiatrist

Leave-taking

concerned psychiatrist

Act IV

Informal Call

angry psychiatrist
persuader
family doctor

Formal Call

rejected lover
spiteful ex-lover
hurt ex-lover

Act V

Waiting

messenger

Diagnosis

realist

would-be teacher
psychiatrist
kind friend

Laying Out the Body (M)

family doctor
man of science
cynical doctor
prophet
realistic philosopher

Roles

OLD EKDAL

Act I

Preparing the Room

meek old man

The After-Dinner Drink

meek old man

Act II

Waiting

happy old man
nature lover
sly grandpa

Homecoming

proud father

Entertaining Guest

tipsy old man
contented old man
proud sportsman
contented old man

Leave-taking

tipsy old man

Retiring for the Night

drunken old man

Act III

Working

old father
irritated father
busy worker
carpenter

Luncheon Party (M)

successful hunter

Act IV

Act V

Waiting

hurt old father

Musing

irritated father
sportsman

Forgiveness (M)

resentful father
melancholy philosopher

Laying Out the Body (M)

melancholy philosopher

Roles

WERLE

Act I

The After-Dinner Drink

congenial host
dejected father
congenial host
angry employer
impatient father
confident man
angry man
disappointed father
contemptous man

Act II

Act III

Luncheon Party (M)

indignant father

Father-Son Conference

distressed father
dejected father
disappointed father

Act IV

Act V

Roles

MRS. SORBY

Act I

The After-Dinner Drink
hostess
benefactor
hostess

Act II

Act III

Act IV

Formal Call
old friend
bride-to-be
ex-lover
straightforward woman
old friend

Act V

Roles

Molvik

Act I

Act II

Act III
Luncheon Party (M)
guest
proud daemonic
ill guest

Act IV

Act V

Laying Out the Body (M)

family friend
minister of God
ashamed sot

A Selected Bibliography

BOOKS

Aristotle. *The Works of Aristotle. Great Books of the Western World*, Vol. II. Chicago: Encyclopaedia Britannica, Inc., 1952.

Bentley, Eric. (ed.). *The Play, A Critical Anthology*. New York: Prentice-Hall, 1951.

Centeno, Augusto. (ed.). *The Intent of the Artist*. New Jersey: Princeton University Press, 1941.

Chambers, E. K. *The Medieval Stage*, Vol. II. Oxford: Oxford University Press, 1903.

Clark, Barrett H. (ed.). *European Theories of Drama*. New York: Crown Publishers, 1947.

———— and George Freedley (eds.). *A History of Modern Drama*. New York: D. Appleton-Century Co., 1947.

Cole, Toby, and Helen K. Chinoy, (eds.). *Directors on Directing*. New York: Bobbs-Merrill Co., 1953.

Collingwood, R. G. *The Principles of Art*. New York: Oxford University Press, 1958.

Conrad, Joseph. *Lord Jim*. New York: Doubleday & Co., 1965.

Craig, Edward Gordon. *On the Art of the Theatre*. New York: Theatre Arts Books, 1957.

Dean, Alexander. *Fundamentals of Play Directing*. New York: Rinehart & Co., 1956.

Dietrich, John E. *Play Direction*. New York: Prentice-Hall, 1953.

Downs, Brian W. *A Study of Six Plays by Ibsen*. Cambridge: Cambridge University Press, 1948.

Duerr, Edwin. *The Length and Depth of Acting*. New York: Holt, Rinehart & Winston, 1962.

Eliot, T. S. *Selected Essays*. New York: Harcourt, Brace & Co., 1950.

Fergusson, Francis. *The Idea of a Theater.* Garden City, N.Y.: Doubleday & Co., 1954.

Fielding, Henry. *The History of Tom Jones.* New York: Random House, 1950.

Gallaway, Marian. *The Director in the Theater.* New York: Macmillan, 1963.

Ibsen, Henrik. *Letters of Henrik Ibsen.* Translated by J. N. Laurvik & Mary Morrison. New York: Fox, Duffield & Co., 1905.

James, William. *The Principles of Psychology. Great Books of the Western World,* Vol. 53. Chicago: Encyclopaedia Britannica, Inc., 1952.

Jameson, Storm. *Modern Drama in Europe.* New York: Harcourt, Brace & Co., 1920.

Keith, Arthur B. *The Sanskrit Drama.* Oxford: Oxford University Press, 1924.

Lamm, Martin. *Modern Drama.* Translated by Karin Elliot. Oxford: Philosophical Library, 1952.

Langer, Susanne K., ed. *Reflections on Art: A Source Book of Writings by Artists, Critics & Philosophers.* Baltimore: The Johns Hopkins Press, 1958.

Nicoll, Allardyce. *The Theory of the Drama.* New York: Thomas Y. Crowell Co., 1925.

Parrish, Wayland Maxfield. *Reading Aloud.* New York: Ronald Press Co., 1953.

Plato. *Great Dialogues of Plato.* Translated by W. H. D. Rouse. New York: New American Library of World Literature, 1956.

Simonson, Lee. *The Stage Is Set.* New York: Harcourt, Brace & Co., 1932.

Stanislavski, Constantin. *An Actor Prepares.* Translated by Elizabeth Reynolds Hapgood. New York: Theatre Arts Books, 1945.

Stanislavski, Constantin. *Building a Character.* Translated by Elizabeth Reynolds Hapgood. New York: Theatre Arts Books, 1949.

Stanislavski, Constantin. *My Life in Art.* Translated by J. J. Robbins. New York: Theatre Arts Books, 1948.

Strindberg, August. *Six Plays of Strindberg.* Translated by Elizabeth Sprigge. Garden City, N.Y.: Doubleday & Co., 1955.

Weigand, Hermann J. *The Modern Ibsen.* New York: Henry Holt & Co., 1925.

Young, Stark. *The Flower in Drama.* New York: Charles Scribner's Sons, 1955.

Young, Stark. *The Theater.* New York: Hill & Wang, 1954.

Zucker, A. E. *Ibsen, The Master Builder.* New York: Henry Holt
& Co., 1929.

Articles and Periodicals

Knight, Arthur. "S R Goes to the Movies," in *Saturday Review*
(April 12, 1958), p. 44.
Thompson, David. "Interpretative Reading as Symbolic Action," in
The Quarterly Journal of Speech. Vol. XLII (December 1956),
No. 4. 389–397.

Index

Acting
  as magic, 192, 193
  as symbolic action, 191, 203,
    204, 231
  believable, 58, 59, 76, 165,
    191, 200, 212, 213, 237, 301,
    314
  defined, 231
  editions, 158, 159
  "Method," 201, 202, 207–213,
    214
  presentational, 58, 200
  realistic, 211, 213
  representational, 58, 200
  technique, 49, 124, 203, 204,
    208, 210, 213, 220, 234, 251,
    252, 254, 266, 268, 297, 314
    (in musicals)
  theories, 198
Actions, 54, 55, 61, 91, 92, 128,
    129, 165, 166, 170, 179, 207,
    209, 211, 213, 265, 269, 271
Actor, 185–229
  as artist, 11, 13, 164, 187, 188,
    189, 194, 195, 196, 208, 221,
    267
  as interpreter, 189, 192, 199,
    209
  blocking the, 129
  concentration of, 230

Actor (*cont.*)
  emotional, 198, 199, 200
  feeling of, 123, 124, 129, 174,
    195, 256, 269
  goal of, 191
  justification of, 164, 165, 212,
    213
  motivation of, 165, 212, 213
  responsibility of, 125, 177,
    209, 304
  technical, 198, 199, 200, 201,
    202, 203 (defined), 203–
    207, 214
Actors
  "in character," 24, 125, 160,
    161, 163, 165, 172, 173, 175,
    206, 207, 208, 226, 297, 301,
    303, 304, 315 (in reviews)
  types, 186, 202, 226, 228, 278,
    281
Actor's Equity, 4, 187, 220, 221,
    277, 297, 307
Actual line, 135, 140, 155, 157
Adaptation, 210, 211
Aeschylus, 192
Albee, Edward, 87
All My Sons, 311
Amateur theater, *see* Theater
Anderson, Sherwood, 29

An Actor Prepares, 14, 124, 142, 164, 201, 202, 208, 210, 228, 229, 230, 231, 295

An Enemy of the People, 84, 85, 86, 88

An Essay of Dramatick Poesie, 200

Archer, William, 76

Aristotle, 40, 41, 42, 43, 44, 45, 50, 52, 54, 57, 77, 80, 81, 82, 83, 193, 199, 200, 213, 232, 233

Auditions, 275–292; 280, 281 (types of); 284 (form); 279, 281, 286, 287, 291, 292 (open—); 285, 286 (first —); 285, 288 (final—); 287, 288 (personal interview); 289 (special—)

"Aurora's Wedding," 161

Author's intent, 5, 7, 14, 17, 18, 19, 20, 21, 24, 26, 34, 54, 55, 56, 72, 73, 126, 127, 130, 142, 151, 158, 159, 164, 165, 178, 201, 207, 209, 211, 213, 214, 219, 229, 232, 237, 238, 243, 254, 255, 256, 260, 261, 266, 267, 288, 292, 293, 314

Baensch, Otto, 27

Balance, 126, 145–150, 155, 157, 165, 177, 178, 179, 212, 256

Ballet, 161, 175, 289

Barter Theater, 281

Bartók, Béla, 5

"beat," 54

Beethoven, Ludvig van, 5

Bentley, Eric, 64

Bharata, 200

Blocking, 3, 16, 17, 20, 55, 123, 125, 126, 127–182, 181 (pre-blocking), 231, 254, 255, 256, 292 (pre-blocking), 298, 299

Body position, 137, 138, 139, 142, 155, 167, 168, 171, 177

Box office, 44, 48

Brecht, Bertolt, 132

Building a Character, 202, 236, 237, 242, 253

Candida, 68

Casting, 38, 47, 52, 55, 275–292; 275, 276, 277 (as guesswork); 288 (ensemble); 289 (double—); 290, 291, 292 (—in civic theater); 290, 291 (—committee)

Catharsis, 44, 192

Cause and effect relationships, 243, 244

Centeno, Augusto, 29, 30, 31, 33

Center of attention, 130, 131, 144, 157, 163, 166

Chaplin, Charlie, 156

Character, 41, 44, 46, 51 (in melodrama and farce), 77, 81, 82, 160, 180, 213, 234, 240

Characterization, 29

Children's theater, 32, 286

Choreography, 131, 132, 151, 175, 178, 289, 312, 313

Chronegk, Ludwig, 9, 10, 11

Cicero, 200

Civic theater, *see* Theater

Cleander, 192

Clift, Montgomery, 254

Climax, 175

Comedy, 48, 49, 50 (described), 51, 52, 83, 86, 111, 160, 161, 162, 163, 173, 179, 180, 204, 210, 211

Commedia dell' arte, 13, 46

Composition, 178

Conscious role-player, 63, 64, 65, 66, 67, 68 (defined), 70, 72, 88, 98, 99, 101, 102, 107, 109, 110, 119, 186, 232, 242

Contrast (emphasis), 135, 141

Copeau, Jacques, 189

Corpenning, Charlotte, 152

Covert actions, 235

Coward, Noel, 49, 151, 173, 308

Craig, Edward Gordon, 11, 12, 13, 14

Creditors, The, 174

Crime and Punishment, 31

Criticism, 38, 40, 41, 42, 53, 54, 80, 83, 85, 188, 200, 214, 320

Critics, 28, 38, 40, 44, 45, 52, 53, 85, 86, 88, 190, 200, 201, 217, 320

Curtain call, 302, 309, 310 (trick calls), 311, 312

Cyrano de Bergerac, 63, 110, 147

Daly, Augustin, 45, 59, 212, 213

Dante Alighieri, 50

Dean, Alexander, 52, 56, 140, 144, 150

Death of a Salesman, 66, 68, 174

Dialogue, 42, 45, 46, 61, 127, 143, 151, 152, 153, 154, 155, 156, 164, 170, 171, 174, 178

Diction, 42, 45, 46, 76, 77, 81, 82, 127, 199

Diderot, Dénis, 201

Dietrich, John E., 61

Directing technique, 3, 20, 50, 123–182, 187, 188, 266, 269, 270

Direction, principles of, 125, 126, 127–182

Director-actor relationship, 23, 24, 34, 55, 72, 73, 126, 185, 186, 187, 189, 190, 211, 215, 220, 221, 222, 224, 227, 232, 254, 255, 260, 266, 304

Director

as a mirror, 6, 124, 125

as artist, 5, 6, 7, 25, 32, 33, 126, 127, 130, 143, 151, 153, 188, 277

as final authority, 4, 5, 7, 12, 19, 186, 190, 302, 313, 316

as interpreter, 4, 12, 29, 37, 151, 188

despotic, 4, 5, 10, 11, 12, 15, 17, 188, 189

technical, 302, 303, 316, 317

musical, 312, 313

permissive, 15, 16, 188

responsible to: actor, 23, 220; audience, 7, 18, 20, 21, 186; board of directors, 4; producer, 4, 186; school administration, 4

responsibility of, 4, 5, 7, 18, 19, 20, 21, 23, 48, 125, 130, 144, 151, 174, 186, 188, 189, 220–222, 272, 293 (pre-rehearsal), 305

Doll's House, A, 66, 74, 75, 76, 84, 86
Dostoiévsky, Fiódor Mikháylovitch, 196
Dramatic action, 60, 61 (defined), 62, 63, 70, 72, 73, 89 (defined), 91, 93, 152, 153, 256
Dryden, John, 200
Duerr, Edwin, 208, 210

Echo words, 250, 251, 253, 265
Educational theater, *see* Theater
Eliot, T. S., 63, 64, 66, 67, 87
Elizabethan theater, *see* Theater
Ellipse, 244, 245
Emphasis, pointing, 124, 126, 130, 131–145, 155, 157, 164, 166, 168, 169, 172, 176, 177, 178, 256
Entrances, 3, 168, 170, 171, 172, 179
Etherege, Sir George, 174
Euripides, 198
Exits, 168, 169, 170

Farce, 38, 48, 50, 51 (defined), 52, 83, 150, 159, 160, 161, 162, 163, 173, 179, 210, 211, 311
Father, The, 67
Fergusson, Francis, 56
Fielding, Henry, 58
Focus, 131; 133, 134 (visual linè); 135 (actual line); 140, 143
Fokine, Michel, 5
Form, 27, 28, 33, 43, 45, 49, 76, 129, 132, 150, 151, 178, 179, 180, 211, 213, 214, 215, 314

French scene, 92, 305
French theater, *see* Theater
Fry, Christopher, 174
Fundamentals of Play Direction, 52, 56, 140, 144, 150

Gallaway, Marian, 283
Garcia Lorca, Federico, 268
Garrick, David, 58
German theater, *see* Theater
Gesture, 164, 171, 176
Getting Gertie's Garter, 38
Ghosts, 61, 62, 63, 65, 68, 69, 73, 75, 76, 84, 86
Gildon, Charles, 201
Given circumstances, 210, 211, 212, 232
Goals, 54, 91, 213 _____
Goethe, Johann Wolfgang von, 201
Good theater, 45, 46, 52, 86, 219
Gordon, Robert L., 305
Graduation Ball, 161
Graham, Martha, 5
Greek theater, *see* Theater
Griffith, D. W., 156
Group theater, *see* Theater

Hamlet, 46, 56, 58, 59, 110, 147, 148, 200, 239, 240, 241, 242, 243, 282
Hay Fever, 151
Heartbreak House, 269
Hedda Gabler, 65
Hegel, Georg Wilhelm Friedrich, 5
Height, 140, 141
Helpmann, Robert, 131
High school theater, *see* Theater
Hindu theater, *see* Theater

Hitchcock, Alfred, 224
Holding attention, 157, 163, 166
Holmes, Justice Oliver Wendell, 236
House of Bernarda Alba, 268

Ibsen, Henrik, 47, 61–120, 126, 147, 148, 210, 211, 244, 245, 255, 257–265, 269, 277
Idea of a Theater, The, 56
Implied meaning, 249, 250, 253
Improvisation, 46, 56, 268, 269, 270
Indian Captive, The, 152
Intent of the Artist, The, 29, 30, 31
Interpretation, 52, 55, 119, 160, 162, 163, 169, 178, 229–267, 299, 300 (rehearsal)
Ion, 198, 199, 230
Ionesco, Eugene, 69, 87

James-Lange theory, 206
Jameson, Storm, 86
Japanese theater, *see* Theater
Jones, Robert Edmond, 191
Joyce, James, 87

King Lear, 31, 47, 48, 179, 277
King, Philip, 45
Kipling, Rudyard, 172
Kiss and Tell, 50
Klee, Paul, 5
Kronek, Ludwig, *see* Chronegk

Lady's Not For Burning, The, 174
Lahr, Bert, 159
League of Youth, The, 76, 104
Le Gallienne, Eva, 247

Length and Depth of Acting, The, 208
Lerner, Alan Jay, and Loewe, Frederick, 68
Lescaze, William, 29
Les Précieuses Ridicules, 200
Levels, 141, 169
Life of Mr. Thomas Betterton, The, 201
L' Impromptue de Versailles, 200
Lines
    effect on emotions, 136, 137, 150, 179
    learning, 308, 309
Line readings, 162, 209, 222, 231, 235, 254, 256, 258–268
Little Women, 47

Macbeth, 31, 243, 244, 245, 246, 247, 248, 249, 250, 251
Magic if, 210, 211
Maimed rites, 93
Man of Mode, The, 174
Massine, Leonide, 5
Melodrama, 45, 48, 50, 51, 52, 59, 83, 93, 103, 111, 156, 213, 311, 314
Melody, 42, 77, 82
Merchant of Venice, 168, 169
Meyerhold, Vsevolod, 174
Michelangelo Buonarroti, 5
Miller, Arthur, 66, 68, 174, 311
Miss Julie, 69
Modern dance, 5
Modern Ibsen, The, 96
Molière (Jean Baptiste Poquelin), 200
Morris, Clara, 212, 213
Moscow Art Theater, 225, 296

Mother Courage, 132
Motivational unit, 54, 56, 61
Movement, justification for, 164, 165
Movement, quality of, 160, 161, 162, 165, 167 (negative quality), 167 (positive quality), 167 (strong and weak), 173, 178
Mozart, Wolfgang Amadeus, 5
Mr. Roberts, 47
Musical comedy, 131, 132, 175, 289 (casting), 294; 312, 313, 314 (rehearsing); 314 (acting in), 314
My Fair Lady, 68
My Three Angels, 161

Naturalism, 56, 233, 234, 314
Nātya-śāstra, 200
Negative, weak, 168, 169
Nicoll, Allardyce, 40, 46, 51
Nietzsche, Friedrich Wilhelm, 5
Nonrealistic drama, 210, 211, 212
No theater, *see* Theater
Noverre, Jean Georges, 5

Objectives, 54, 56, 210
Oedipus the King, 43
On the Art of the Theatre, 12, 13, 14
Opera, 289
Oriental theater, *see* Theater
Original scripts, 38, 48, 159
Overt actions, 235

Pantomime, 152, 212, 231, 270, 289

Parrish, Wayland Maxfield, 235, 237, 242, 243, 246, 249, 250, 252
Peer Gynt, 47, 68, 86, 88, 104, 110, 147, 148, 277
Peripety, 43, 45, 80
Peter Pan, 48, 162
Picasso, Pablo, 5
Picturization, 54, 124, 131, 150–156, 157, 165, 177, 178, 179, 256
Pitch, 232, 242, 246
Plato, 193, 198, 199, 208, 230, 236
Play analysis, 52, 54, 55, 60, 64, 73, 74, 75, 86, 119, 130, 153, 292, 293, 294
Playboy of the Western World, The, 68
Play
  defined, 45
  selection, 37, 38, 39, 40, 41, 42, 43, 44, 46, 47, 48, 52, 75, 219
Playing area, 150
Plot, 41, 42, 43, 44, 52, 55, 60, 73, 77, 80, 81, 152, 169, 180, 213
Poetics, 40, 41, 42, 43, 44
Pointing, emphasis, 74, 124, 126, 130, 131, 132, 136, 137, 143, 157, 166, 167, 169, 171, 204, 259
Porterfield, Robert, 281, 282
Positive, strong, 168, 169
Producer, 4, 7, 16, 17, 19, 38, 186, 199, 280, 297
Professional theater, *see* Theater
Prompt book, 292, 293
Prompter, 139, 309

Protagonist, 49

Psychic communication, 229, 230, 231

Punctuation, 238, 247, 248, 249

Pygmalion, 68

Quintilian, 200

Raisonneur, 101

Reading Aloud, 235, 237, 242, 243, 246, 249, 250, 252

Realism, 58, 63, 72, 85, 174, 201, 210, 212, 213, 234

Rehearsal, 32, 33, 47, 120, 137, 159, 162, 165, 168, 181, 182, 187, 196, 208, 209, 223, 226, 227, 231, 253–272, 285 (—schedule), 292–316, 298 (technical), 298–303 (schedule), 300 (interpretation), 302 (technical), 307 (length of), 312, 313 (musical), 315 (technical)

Rehearsals, dress, 271, 295, 298, 303, 304, 307, 316, 317, 319

Réjane, 214

Repetition, emphasis, 135, 251 (word), 253 (word)

Restoration theater, *see* Theater

Review, 315

Rhetoric, 199, 200, 232

Rhinoceros, 69

Rhythm, 27, 28, 44, 55, 200, 232, 245, 270, 295

Riccoboni(s), 201

Rites, 46, 54, 56, 57, 59, 60 (defined), 61, 62, 63, 64, 65, 70, 72, 73, 74, 75, 86, 89 (defined), 90, 91, 92, 93,

Rites *(cont.)*
94, 95, 96, 97, 98, 99, 105, 106, 107, 108, 109, 110, 111, 113, 116, 118, 119, 120, 152, 153, 154, 155, 156, 191, 210, 211, 232, 237, 246, 252, 258, 262, 280, 292, 293

Robbins, Jerome, 131

Roles, 46, 54, 56, 57, 63, 64, 65, 67, 68, 69, 70, 71, 72, 73, 74, 75, 86, 87, 88, 89, 90, 92, 93, 94, 95; (—in *Wild Duck*), 97–101 (Relling), 101–104 (Old Ekdal), 104–111 (Hialmar), 111–113 (Gregers), 113–115 (Gina), 115–117 (Hedvig), 117–118 (Werle), 119 (Mrs. Sorby), 119–120 (master role); 124, 191, 210, 211, 232, 234, 237, 246, 258, 262, 280, 292, 293

Roman theater, 193, 200

Rosmersholm, 68, 70, 71, 72, 76

Rostand, Edmond, 63, 64, 67, 110, 147

Ruskin, John, 236, 237

Russell, Bertrand, 5

Sainte-Albine, Pierre Rémond de, 201

Salvini, Tomasso, 232, 233

Saxe-Meiningen, George II, Duke of, 9, 11, 139

Scene, 54, 63, 91, 92, 96, 153, 154, 175, 213, 256

Scribe, Augustin Eugène, 101

Seami, Motokiyo, 200

See How They Run, 45

Semiconscious role-player, 66, 67, 70, defined: 74, 258

Sentence word, 237, 238, 246

Sequence, 126, 148, 155, 165, 177, 256

Sessions, Roger, 29

Shakespeare, 31, 46, 56, 63, 65, 67, 110, 147, 148, 159, 168, 169, 173, 179, 180, 181, 200, 239, 240, 241, 242, 243, 244, 245, 246, 247, 248, 249, 250, 251, 277, 282

Shapes, effect on emotions, 136, 137 (effect on emotion and —of a play), 150

Shaw, George Bernard, 29, 30, 49, 68, 69, 159, 178, 269

Single role-player, 69 (defined), 70

"slice of life" theater, 233

Socrates, 5

Space, 140

Spectacle, 42, 51, 77, 82

Stability, 148, 155, 165, 177, 256

Stage area, 138, 139, 148, 150 (tonal qualities), 175

Stage conventions, 57, 58, 59, 63, 128, 180, 205, 231, 234

Stage manager, 3, 9, 12, 58, 186, 209, 256, 278, 293, 294, 300, 303, 304, 306, 307, 308, 312, 314, 315, 316, 317

Stage movement, 17, 123, 132, 137, 149, 151, 158–178; 160, 207 (character movement) ; 160, 162, 163 (story telling movement); 160, 164, 165 (technical movement) ; 181, 255

Stage terms, 177

Standby, 290

Stanislavski, Constantin, 9, 10, 11, 14, 54, 58, 61, 124, 142, 164, 201, 202, 206, 208, 210, 228, 229, 230, 231, 236, 237, 242, 253, 295

Strasberg, Lee, 201

Stress, 244, 250, 251, 252, 253, 259

Strindberg, August, 67, 68, 69, 174

Style, 45, 49, 52, 59, 173 (defined), 174, 178, 200, 210, 215, 234, 314

Symbols, 73, 81, 82, 85, 86, 87, 128, 236 (vocal)

Synge, John Millington, 68

Television, 24, 38, 219, 235

Tempo, 28, 55, 170, 179, 242, 295

Theater

  Amateur: 4, 13, 18, 22, 32, 38, 39, 47, 49, 138, 141, 142, 162, 170, 172, 173, 176, 181, 187, 202, 209, 215–222, 224–229, 255, 267, 269, 276–280, 284, 287, 290–292, 295–297, 304, 307–311, 316–320

  Children's: 32, 286

  Civic: 4, 13, 33, 39, 187, 215, 217, 225–229, 255, 276, 277, 287, 290–292, 307, 310, 316

  Educational: 4, 13, 18, 32, 33, 39, 75, 76, 77, 125, 126, 149, 181, 187, 202, 215–222, 225, 226, 255, 269, 276, 277, 284, 287, 290, 307, 310, 311, 320

  Elizabethan: 56

  French: 8, 68, 101, 146, 200

  German: 201

Theater (*cont.*)
  Greek: 8, 43, 146, 192, 198–200, 210, 233, 235
  Group: 201, 208
  High school: 18, 32, 39, 219, 255, 276
  Hindu: 57, 193, 200
  Japanese: 193, 200
  No: 200
  Oriental: 58, 200
  Professional: 4, 13, 15–18, 32, 33, 37, 125, 126, 169, 171, 173, 176, 179, 187, 192, 202, 208, 209, 215–222, 224–226, 267, 277–281, 284, 286, 289, 290, 296, 297, 307, 308, 312, 316, 317, 319
  Restoration: 59
  Roman: 193, 200
  "slice of life": 233
Theater of the Absurd, 23
Théâtre Libre, 225
Theatrical truth, 45
Theme, 42, 45, 50, 55, 63
Theory of the Drama, The, 40
Thespius, 192
Thompson, David, 55, 60
Thought, 41, 42, 77, 81, 209, 240
Tom Jones, The History of, 58, 59
Tone-copying, 207, 222, 266, 267, 268
Tragedy, 31, 41, 42, 43, 46, 47, 48, 49, 50 (described), 51, 52, 72, 75, 80, 83, 86, 111, 115, 118, 136, 150, 160, 161, 162, 163, 173, 211, 311
Tragicomedy, 160
Twelfth Night, 65, 179, 180, 181
Type casting, 278

Unbroken line, 295
Unconscious role-player, 65, 66, 67, 68, 69, 72, 88, 99, 101, 102, 107, 112, 113, 116, 119, 232, 258
Understudies, 289
Under the Gaslight, 45, 59, 213
Unit, 54, 56, 61
Unity, 131, 188, 285

Vakhtangov, Eugene, 208
Van Gogh, Vincent, 5
Variety, 142, 168
Vaudeville, 56
Visual line, 133, 134, 135, 136, 140
Vocal interpretation, 231

Wagner, Wilhelm Richard, 5
Webster, Margaret, 249
Weigand, Hermann J., 96
West Side Story, 132
Wild Duck, The, 65, 69, 76–120, 210, 211, 244, 245, 255, 257–265, 269
Wilder, Thornton, 29
Williams, Tennessee, 68
Wizard of Oz, The, 132
Word contrast, 247, 248, 251, 253, 265
Word emphasis, 246, 247, 247 (new material), 248, 249, 251, 251 (new material), 252, 253 (new material), 254, 259
Word groupings, 237, 238, 239, 241, 242, 243, 244, 245, 246, 247, 248, 249, 252
Word pointing, 249

Young, Stark, 44, 45, 50, 190, 191, 214